CHINA'S GILDED AGE

Why has China grown so fast for so long despite vast corruption? In *China's Gilded Age*, Yuen Yuen Ang argues that not all types of corruption hurt growth, nor do they cause the same kind of harm. Ang unbundles corruption into four varieties: petty theft, grand theft, speed money, and access money. While the first three types impede growth, access money – elite exchanges of power and profit – cuts both ways: it stimulates investment and growth but produces serious risks for the economy and political system. Since market opening, corruption in China has evolved toward access money. Using a range of data sources, the author explains the evolution of Chinese corruption, how it differs from the West and other developing countries, and how Xi's anti-corruption campaign could affect growth and governance. In this formidable yet accessible book, Ang challenges one-dimensional measures of corruption. By unbundling the problem and adopting a comparative-historical lens, she reveals that the rise of capitalism was not accompanied by the eradication of corruption, but rather by its evolution from thuggery and theft to access money. In doing so, she changes the way we think about corruption and capitalism, not only in China but around the world.

Yuen Yuen Ang is Associate Professor of Political Science at the University of Michigan. Her book *How China Escaped the Poverty Trap* (2016) received the Peter Katzenstein Book Prize in Political Economy and the Viviana Zelizer Book Award in Economic Sociology. She has been named an Andrew Carnegie Fellow for "high-caliber scholarship [on] some of the most pressing issues of our times." In addition, she has received grants, fellowships, and an essay prize from the American Council of Learned Societies, Andrew W. Mellon Foundation, Chiang Ching Kuo Foundation, and Gates Foundation. Her commentaries and interviews have appeared on the BBC and CGTN, and in *Foreign Affairs*, *The New York Times*, *Project Syndicate*, *The Wall Street Journal*, and media outlets around the world.

CHINA'S GILDED AGE

The Paradox of Economic Boom and Vast Corruption

Yuen Yuen Ang

University of Michigan, Ann Arbor

CAMBRIDGE
UNIVERSITY PRESS

CAMBRIDGE
UNIVERSITY PRESS

University Printing House, Cambridge CB2 8BS, United Kingdom

One Liberty Plaza, 20th Floor, New York, NY 10006, USA

477 Williamstown Road, Port Melbourne, VIC 3207, Australia

314-321, 3rd Floor, Plot 3, Splendor Forum, Jasola District Centre, New Delhi - 110025, India

103 Penang Road, #05-06/07, Visioncrest Commercial, Singapore 238467

Cambridge University Press is part of the University of Cambridge.

It furthers the University's mission by disseminating knowledge in the pursuit of education, learning and research at the highest international levels of excellence.

www.cambridge.org
Information on this title: www.cambridge.org/9781108745956
DOI: 10.1017/9781108778350

First published 2020
First paperback edition 2021

A catalogue record for this publication is available from the British Library

ISBN 978-1-108-47860-1 Hardback
ISBN 978-1-108-74595-6 Paperback

To mentors, friends, and acquaintances in need

Contents

List of Figures . . . . *page* viii

List of Tables xi

Acknowledgments xiii

1 Introduction: China's Gilded Age 1

2 Unbundling Corruption across Countries 23

3 Unbundling Corruption over Time 52

4 Profit-Sharing, Chinese Style 85

5 Corrupt and Competent 119

6 All the King's Men 153

7 Rethinking Nine Big Questions 180

Appendix 213

References 232

Index 249

Figures

1.1 Corruption and GDP per capita. *page* 3

1.2 China as a "gigantic outlier" *vis-à-vis* the United States. 4

1.3 Unbundling corruption into four types. 9

2.1 Total and unbundled UCI scores in one visual. 33

2.2 UCI scores and ranks by country. 33

2.3 Comparing the UCI and CPI ranks. 34

2.4 Comparing the UCI and overall perception scores. 36

2.5 China vs. Russia's UCI scores. 39

2.6 China vs. India's UCI scores. 41

2.7 China vs. the United States' UCI scores. 44

2.8 UCI scores and income levels are negatively correlated. 47

2.9 All rich countries are low in speed money but not in access money. . 48

3.1 Banner in Shenzhen, showing Deng Xiaoping and the words
      "Stick firmly to the Party's fundamental path for 100 years." 58

3.2 President Bill Clinton listens as Chinese Premier Zhu Rongji
      makes a statement on the South Lawn of the White House
      in 1999. 60

3.3 Land proceeds financed an infrastructure boom in the 2000s,
      including high-speed rail, as seen here in Hangzhou. 63

3.4 Chinese President Xi Jinping and other top leaders. On the
      far right is Wang Qishan. 66

3.5 Corruption cases involved larger sums over time. 70

3.6 Corruption with exchange exploded but corruption with theft
      shrank. 72

3.7 Bribery rose while embezzlement and misuse of funds declined. . . . 73

3.8 Bribery took up a growing share of corruption over time. 74

3.9 Comparison of bribery and embezzlement trends by monetary value. 74

3.10 Comparison of bribery and embezzlement by rank of officials involved. 75

3.11 Media mentions of transactional corruption, by year and term, 1988–2012. 79

3.12 Media mentions of non-transactional corruption, by year and term, 1988–2012. 81

4.1 Zouping, one of the 136 counties in Shandong province where I did research. 99

4.2 Fringe components made up 76 percent of compensation. 100

4.3 Fringe compensation varied far more widely than formal wages. . . . 101

4.4 Growth of fringe compensation outpaced formal wages. 103

4.5 Total bureaucratic income exceeded average urban wages. 103

4.6 Increasing agency collections was more rewarding in the short term. 108

4.7 Expanding the tax base was more rewarding in the long term. 108

5.1 Media coverage of Bo Xilai before and after his fall. 122

5.2 Media coverage of Ji Jianye before and after his fall. 124

5.3 Bo Xilai is surrounded by reporters when arriving at the 11th National People's Congress in Beijing in 2010. 125

5.4 Chongqing's economy surpassed the national average under Bo. . . 128

5.5 During Bo's tenure, Chongqing saw a rapid construction boom. . . . 129

5.6 Chongqing's economic boom was heavily driven by investment. . . . 131

5.7 Chongqing's debt-to-GDP ratio kept rising. 132

5.8 In this screenshot, Ji Jianye stands trial at a court for taking bribes. . 136

5.9 Ji Jianye strategically branded Yangzhou as a blend of ancient city and modern civilization. 138

6.1 An anti-corruption exhibition in Zhejiang, featuring videos of Xi Jinping, artwork, and posters. 155

6.2 Poster on the "eight-point regulations," including restrictions against gambling, Internet surfing, banqueting, and drinking at work. 158

6.3 Wave-like hazard rate of fall among city Party secretaries. 166

6.4 Effects of patron's fall on city leaders' likelihood of fall. 172

6.5 Falls of national and local officials since 2013. 174

6.6 Screenshot from the website of the Chinese central government, warning against "lazy governance." 178

7.1 Comparing corruption in China's and America's Gilded Ages. 187

7.2 Corruption reports in China from 1990 to 2016. 189

A1.1 Updated replication of the WSJ's scatterplot on corruption and growth rate. 216

Tables

1.1 Analogously to drugs, different types of corruption harm
in different ways . . . . *page* 12

2.1 Unbundling four corruption categories into sub-categories 28

2.2 Advantages of the UCI over standard perception measures 31

2.3 China vs. Russia on speed money 40

2.4 China vs. India on speed money and access money 42

2.5 China vs. the United States on access money 45

3.1 Official statistics capture only two of four corruption categories
in my theory 71

4.1 Three layers of China's bureaucracy 89

4.2 Linkages between revenue sources and compensation 105

5.1 Top 10 words describing Bo Xilai before and after his fall 122

5.2 Top 10 words describing Ji Jianye before and after his fall 124

5.3 Milestones in Bo Xilai's career path 126

5.4 Bo's deliverables across five areas of social welfare 130

5.5 Milestones in Ji Jianye's career path 137

6.1 High turnover rate among city Party secretaries 167

6.2 Geographic distribution of falls by region and province 168

6.3 Determinants of downfall among city Party secretaries 171

7.1 China and the United States at equivalent levels of income 185

A2.1 UCI scores and ranking for 15 countries 218

A3.1 Bribery by small vs. large cases and low vs. high rank 220

A3.2 Embezzlement by small vs. large cases and low vs. high rank 220

A4.1 Deconstruction of budgets 223

A4.2 Breakdown of compensation and associated line items 223

A4.3 Descriptive statistics of independent and dependent variables 223

LIST OF TABLES

A5.1 Corrupt, competent, both, or neither? 226

A6.1 Definition and sources of variables 229

A6.2 Descriptive statistics 229

Acknowledgments

Producing a book is like producing a film. For every hour of action on a film, thousands of hours of footage were produced and discarded. Not one but many sponsors and individuals work behind the scenes to create a brief sequence of shots. It is the same way with a book, even though it may appear still on paper.

All production requires, first and foremost, financial support. For this, I thank a private foundation that wishes to remain anonymous, whose generous funding enabled my research and valuable time off for writing. I also thank the Chiang Ching Kuo Foundation for a supplemental grant, as well as the University of Michigan's Lieberthal–Rogel Center for Chinese Studies and the Office of Research for their generous research and subvention grants.

One of the greatest joys of writing this book has been working with a talented team of professionals and research assistants: Nathan Baylis, Amy Cesal, Siddharth Chaudhari, Peixu Fang, Michael Thompson, Jiang Zhentao, and Simeng Zeng. Jane Menton skilfully assisted with this project over the course of its evolution and offered helpful comments on my drafts.

Data collection, whether qualitative or quantitative, requires the generosity of many people. This book draws on fieldwork and interviews I've conducted in China over the years. Again, I wish to thank my research hosts and assistants, who welcomed me into their country and helped me learn about it, as well as the hundreds of bureaucrats and businesspeople who shared their memories and experience. Their stories form the "footage" with which I made this "film."

For the Unbundled Corruption Index (UCI), which appears in Chapter 1, I thank all the expert respondents from around the world who took time from their busy schedule to complete the survey. Several colleagues offered comments early on that helped improve the survey design, including Omolade Adunbi, John Ciociari, Rick Hall, Linda Lim, Ann Lin, Erin McDonnell, and Anne Pitcher, among others. Getting busy people to respond is perhaps the biggest challenge in conducting expert surveys. Thus I extend my sincere appreciation to Linda Lim, Global Integrity (especially Alan Hudson and Johannes Tonn), Ross Business School, and the Wallace Program for connecting me with respondents.

Next, I want to thank many colleagues for feedback at various stages of writing. I thank Anna Grzymala-Busse, Ho-Fung Hung, Diana Kim, and Dan Slater for their formative comments at a book workshop at the Social Science Historical Association just as the book was taking shape. The Center for Global Development, based in Washington, DC, graciously hosted a subsequent book workshop, where I benefited from comments from Masood Ahmed, Charles Kenny, Amanda Glassman, Scott Guggenheim, Scott Morris, Michael Moses, Vijaya Ramachandran, William Savedoff, and Michael Woolcock.

Atul Kohli kindly invited me to present an early chapter from this book some years ago at the Princeton State Building Workshop in New Delhi. His comments propelled me to temporarily set aside that project for a larger book on economic and institutional coevolution, which became *How China Escaped the Poverty Trap*, and to return to the problem of corruption now, through a comparative-historical lens. Michael Woolcock carefully read the manuscript and offered constructive feedback; in particular, his combination of expertise as a social scientist and development practitioner pushed me to speak to both theoretical and practical concerns. Conversations with Scott Guggenheim and Mark Pyman yielded valuable insights on fighting corruption in the most difficult settings. Alan Hudson lent much needed encouragement for pressing ahead with the task of "unbundling corruption." Comments from Alice Evans and Duncan Green, both excellent writers, not only improved the substance of my arguments but taught me how to write better. Jean Oi, Mark Pyman, Andrew Walder, Michael Walton, and Yifan Wei provided timely feedback on my final draft.

Over the years, I also benefited from valuable suggestions from Pranab Bardhan, Daniel Berkowitz, Pamela Brandwein, Yongshun Cai, Allen Hicken, Pauline Jones, James Kung, Xiaojun Li, Kenneth Lieberthal,

Melanie Manion, Jim Morrow, Jia Nan, Elizabeth Perry, Yumin Sheng, Matthew Stephenson, Mark Tessler, Daniel Treisman, Andrew Wedeman, Martin Williams, Mariah Zeisberg, the editors and reviewers at Cambridge and Oxford University Presses, and participants at various events: the University of Southern California's China Conference on Institutions and Markets, organized by Jia Nan and T. J. Wong, along with discussant Peter Lorentzen; the University of Chicago's East Asia Workshop, particularly John Padgett; Princeton University's State-Building Workshops, organized by Miguel Centeno, Atul Kohli, and Deborah Yashar; and the Governance Workshop at Stanford University's Center on Democracy, Development and the Rule of Law, organized by Francis Fukuyama. I thank two anonymous grant reviewers at the private foundation who funded my research for their useful, encouraging feedback; they saved this book from being hijacked by Reviewer 3's demands, which, if imposed, would ensure that the book could not be published or would become eminently worthless.

At Cambridge University Press, it is an extraordinary privilege to work with Robert Dreesen. I thank him for his trust, which gave me precious space to create and even be quirky. I also thank the production team at the Press, including Steven Holt, Robert Judkins, and Erika Walsh.

My special gratitude goes to Pamela Brandwein, Nancy Burns, Nicholas Howson, Pauline Jones, Peter Katzenstein, Michael Woolcock, and Mariah Zeisberg, for wisdom and lifeboats, and as always, to my family, especially my husband Chia-Yu Tang, who is my first and still toughest teacher on thinking outside the box. Along the way, many others have lent a kind word, a lesson, a helping hand, and guidance. To these individuals and the readers of my first book, whose support allowed me to keep writing, I thank you.

Years ago, I attended a talk by playwright David Henry Hwang, who said, "The reward of creation lies in the process itself." At the time, I couldn't appreciate his statement, but now I do.

CHAPTER 1

Introduction: China's Gilded Age

A mass of facts tells us that if corruption becomes increasingly serious, it will inevitably doom the party and the state. We must be vigilant. In recent years, there have been cases of grave violations of disciplinary rules and laws within the party that have been extremely malign in nature and utterly destructive politically, shocking people to the core.

President Xi Jinping, 19 November 2012

In 2012, the Chinese Communist Party (CCP) faced its biggest political scandal in a generation: Bo Xilai, one of the Party's most senior leaders, was arrested on charges of graft and abuse of power. When Xi Jinping was named China's paramount leader later that year, he warned that corruption would "doom the Party and the nation,"[1] and, soon afterward, launched the most vigorous anti-corruption crackdown in the Party's history. Decades before Xi, China observers had pointed to the country's serious corruption problem.[2]

According to conventional wisdom, corruption hurts economic growth.[3] Cross-national regressions show a strong correlation between corruption and poverty. For development agencies and many academics, eradicating corruption is a prerequisite for economic development.[4] In

---

[1] Edward Wong, "New Communist Party Chief in China Denounces Corruption in Speech," *The New York Times*, 19 November 2012.

[2] Lu (2000); Manion (2004); Sun (2004); Wedeman (2012); Pei (2006; 2016).

[3] Mauro (1995); Mo (2001); Svensson (2005); Treisman (2007). As Treisman sums up in a review article, "The correlation between economic development and perceived corruption is extremely robust. It survives the inclusion of a variety of controls ... and it can be found in each region of the world" (Treisman 2007, 225).

[4] James Wolfensohn, Address to the Board of Governors at the Annual Meetings of the World Bank and the International Monetary Fund, 1 October 1996; International

recent years, corruption has stoked popular discontent and led to the toppling of authoritarian regimes, including those in Egypt and Tunisia.[5]

China, however, presents a paradox. Since opening markets in 1978, China has achieved "the fastest sustained expansion by a major economy in history," according to the World Bank.[6] Why has China's economy grown so fast for so long despite vast corruption?

This book shows that, in fact, China is not as exceptional as we think it is – the closest parallel is the United States in the late nineteenth century, a period characterized by both feverish growth and glaring inequality, conniving plutocrats and corrupt politicians. What we have witnessed since 1978 is China's Gilded Age in the making. The assumption that all corruption hampers growth is over-simplistic. To explain China, we must fundamentally revise our beliefs about the relationship between corruption and capitalism.

WHAT MAKES CHINA AN OUTLIER?

The most widely used indicator of corruption is the Corruption Perception Index (CPI), which Transparency International (TI) releases every year. According to the CPI, in 2012, the year Xi declared corruption an existential threat to the Party, China was ranked 80th out of 174 countries, with a score of 39 out of 100 (where 100 is cleanest).[7] Other countries in this category include El Salvador, Malawi, Jamaica, Serbia, and Sri Lanka – all of which have far weaker economies. This cursory comparison has led many commentators to cast China as a "gigantic outlier."[8]

Monetary Fund (2016); OECD (2016). See also Mauro (1995); Rose-Ackerman (1997); Kaufmann *et al.* (1999); Bhargava (2005).

[5] "Once Feared Egypt Official Gets 12 Years and Fine," *The New York Times*, 5 May 2011; "Corruption Enrages Tunisians," *The New York Times*, 4 June 2017.

[6] Website of the World Bank, "The World Bank in China," www.worldbank.org/en/coun try/china/overview (accessed 19 November 2019).

[7] Another cross-national perception-based measure of corruption is the World Bank's Worldwide Governance Indicator's Corruption Control Index. Since its release in 1996, China has always ranked below the 50th percentile.

[8] As Huang of the Brookings Institution writes, "Corruption retards economic growth. But China is the outlier." Likewise, the economist Mauro states that "its breakneck economic growth combined with perceptions of widespread corruption" makes China "a gigantic outlier," while Rothstein calls it a "profound outlier." See Yukon Huang, "The Truth about Chinese Corruption," *Diplomat*, 29 May 2015; Paolo Mauro, "Curbing Chinese Corruption," *China–US Focus*, 30 September 2015.

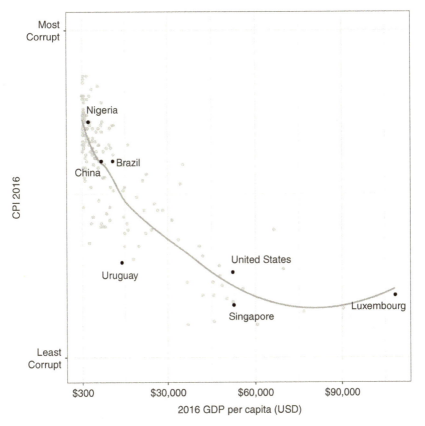

Figure 1.1 Corruption and GDP per capita.

China *is* a "gigantic outlier" – but not in the ways most analysts assume. In fact, at China's level of GDP per capita, it is not unusual to have moderately high corruption,[9] as Figure 1.1 shows.[10] Nor is China an outlier when corruption levels are plotted against GDP growth rates (see the Appendix).[11] Corrupt countries tend to be poor, and poor countries usually have higher growth rates than rich countries.[12]

---

[9] Plotting corruption scores against GDP per capita is a standard way of assessing the relationship between corruption and economic development (Svensson 2005; Treisman 2007; Kenny 2017). Figure 1.1 is a partial replication and update of a scatterplot in Svensson (2005).

[10] CPI scores are from Transparency International and GDP figures are from World Bank Development Indicators. This figure includes 155 countries.

[11] Tom Orlik, "Eight Questions: Andrew Wedeman, China's Corruption Paradox," *The Wall Street Journal*, 26 March 2012.

[12] This pattern is known in economics as "convergence" (Oded 1996).

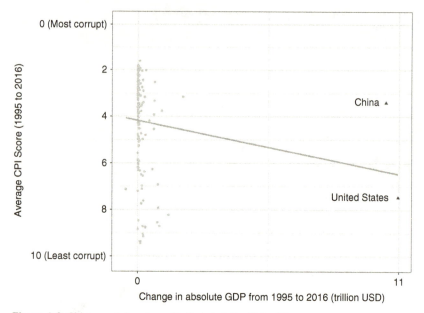

Figure 1.2 China as a "gigantic outlier" *vis-à-vis* the United States.

What's truly extraordinary about China is that no similarly corrupt country has come anywhere close to reaching its scale of economic expansion. As Figure 1.2 shows, only two countries in the world achieved nearly 11 trillion US dollars in absolute GDP growth from 1995 to 2016: China and the United States. The popular image of the Chinese anomaly reflects the stark difference between the two superpowers: the United States is rated as one of the world's cleanest countries, whereas China is corrupt. Equally remarkable is China's rare distinction of sustaining four decades of rapid growth, whereas other developing countries typically lurch back and forth.[13] This implies that Chinese growth was not a temporary fluke, made possible by luck or a commodity boom, as seen in countries such as Nigeria and Russia.[14]

[13] Pritchett *et al.* (2018) distinguish between episodes of "sustained accelerated growth," which are rare, and "non-persistent growth with episodes of boom, stagnation, and bust."

[14] In *Why Nations Fail*, Acemoglu and Robinson attribute China's development without the apparent right institutions to "a critical juncture" (Mao died and Deng took over), a coalition of reformers, and "some luck" (Acemoglu and Robinson 2012, 427). But this is hardly a satisfactory explanation for a country that has sustained transformative development for four decades and in which development is still ongoing. Many poor

The durability and gigantic scale of Chinese economic expansion, juxtaposed with reports of "rising" and "explosive" corruption,[15] cannot simply be brushed away by assertions of imminent collapse, even amid the current slowdown.[16] How China has come this far – from an impoverished communist regime to a capitalist superpower rivaling the United States, despite a crisis of corruption that its leadership sees as "grave" and "shocking" – must be explained. This is the task of my book.

THE LIMITS OF EXISTING ACCOUNTS

Studies on Chinese corruption are voluminous enough to fill a library. Many books on the subject describe the evolving forms and severity of corruption in the reform era.[17] By exposing corrupt practices, this line of work presents a necessary counter-narrative to positive accounts of Chinese officials as "developmental" and "entrepreneurial."[18] Yet it does not explain how China has prospered in the midst of endemic corruption.

One popular argument is that the Chinese economy and regime will soon collapse due to rampant corruption.[19] Casting the CCP state as "incapacitated" and "predatory," Minxin Pei warned in 2006: "The international community should start preparing ... for the unpleasant prospect that China may ... descend into long-term stagnation." A decade later, he repeated his prognosis: "The inevitable consequence of crony capitalism is the decay of the Leninist regime."[20] But Pei's dark portrayal

countries have reform-minded leadership but are still hobbled by corruption. And "luck" is not an explanation in any context.

[15] Hao and Johnston (1995); Sun (2004); Wedeman (2005a; 2012).

[16] Chang (2001); Pei (2006; 2016); Acemoglu and Robinson (2012).

[17] Examples include *Cadres and Corruption* (on bureaucratic corruption), *Taxation without Representation* (on corruption in rural China), and *Anxious Wealth* (on deal-making and moral decay among businessmen and officials). See Lü (2000); Bernstein and Lü (2003); Osburg (2013).

[18] Blecher (1991); Oi (1992; 1999); Walder (1995b); Duckett (1998); Blecher and Shue (2001); Whiting (2001).

[19] Back in 2001, Chang predicted in *The Coming Collapse of China* that the CCP regime had only five years left. "No government, not even China's, can defy the laws of gravity forever," he asserted (Chang 2001).

[20] Pei (2006; 2016).

only deepens the puzzle – if things are so bad, why hasn't China already collapsed?

Others argue that following market reform, China's economy grew so fast that corruption could not dent it. Wedeman, whose account is the most comprehensive to date, explains with an analogy: "In China the hen was increasingly robust and capable of laying more eggs than the Chinese foxes [officials] could grab." But there is no reason to believe that rapid growth immunizes countries against graft and theft, especially given Wedeman's insistence that China suffered "very significant levels of overtly predatory corruption."[21] Indeed, many thriving economies tanked under corrupt governments; the Philippines under Ferdinand Marcos is a case in point.[22]

A third explanation, also from Wedeman, is that the Party's anti-corruption campaigns "prevented corruption from reaching even higher levels or spinning out of control."[23] But this is contradicted by President Xi's emphatic statement in 2012 that weak checks allowed corruption to fester to an alarming level. Other studies concur that crackdowns prior to Xi's arrival in office were episodic and ineffective.[24]

A final set of accounts imply that Chinese corruption did not impede rapid growth because it was "less destructive" than corruption in other countries. According to Sun, "corruption tends to be somewhat less costly in China than in Russia," as big bang reforms unleashed lawless corruption in Russia, whereas Chinese "arrangements of profit-sharing … [turned] potential opponents of reform into participants."[25]

This theory is plausible but suffers from a few crucial flaws. First, Sun uses the term "profit-sharing" only as an analogy; she does not spell out the mechanisms or demonstrate how such arrangements work. Second, comparative arguments about the nature of corruption in China are based on subjective impressions, which are often contradictory.[26]

---

[21] Wedeman (2012, 8).   [22] Overholt (1986); Kang (2002b).   [23] Wedeman (2012, 8).

[24] According to Manion (2004), disciplinary inspectors lacked independence and prioritized political unity over anti-corruption. Penalties dealt to offenders were also lenient. In addition, the Party avoided alienating high-ranking members of the regime even as it tried to check corruption (Cai 2015).

[25] Sun (2004, 198). See also Blanchard and Shleifer (2001).

[26] For example, Wedeman sharply disagrees with Sun's perception of China's corruption as less damaging than Russia's. Instead, he insists that Chinese corruption conforms to "the worst examples of endemic and economically destructive corruption elsewhere in the developing world" (Wedeman 2012, 5).

Without systematic data, we cannot tell who is right or wrong. Third, Sun's claim that China's corruption is of a less destructive variety is not supported by evidence. Instead, throughout her book, she proves the opposite – "the weakening of state institutions and capacities" resulted in "worsening corruption"[27] – which takes us back to square one: if corruption is indeed bad and getting worse, why has China prospered?

In short, despite an abundant literature, the paradox remains unresolved. To advance a satisfactory explanation, this book offers a different approach centered on "unbundling corruption," and it has four key features. First, rather than accept the conventional wisdom that all corruption retards growth, I unpack and revise this assumption. Second, rather than assert that China's structure of corruption is of a certain type on the basis of anecdotes or subjective impressions, I establish objective standards and collect data to compare corruption structures in China and other countries. Third, rather than lump more than 50 million functionaries in China's gigantic bureaucracy into one homogeneous group, my theory distinguishes between political elites and rank-and-file bureaucrats, who engage in different forms of corruption.[28] Fourth, my study deploys a range of data, both qualitative and quantitative, within China and across countries, to support my explanation.

UNBUNDLING CORRUPTION

Corruption is conventionally defined as the abuse of public office for private gain. This broad definition encompasses many varieties of corruption, but global indices, including the CPI and the World Bank's Control of Corruption Index, present bundled scores – one number for every country. This approach obscures the fact that not all corruption is equally damaging. Indeed, I contend that certain kinds of corruption may stimulate growth in the short term yet produce serious risks and distortions.

To revisit the relationship between corruption and capitalism, we must first unbundle corruption into qualitatively distinct types. Any

---

[27] Sun (2004, 8). See Wedeman (2005b).
[28] Macro political-economy theories of deals and corruption model only national political elites (Khan 2010; Acemoglu and Robinson 2012; Pritchett *et al.* 2018).

useful typology must strike a balance between nuance and parsimony, that is, neither too few nor too many categories. Keeping this in mind, I propose a typology along two dimensions: (i) corruption with exchanges vs. theft, and (ii) corruption involving elites vs. non-elites.

TWO DIMENSIONS. First, I distinguish between corruption involving two-way exchanges between officials and social actors[29] – including but not limited to bribery – and corruption involving theft, such as embezzlement or extortion. Classic models of corruption focus on bribery.[30] To give two examples from a long list, Shleifer and Vishny's seminal article on corruption considers only bribery,[31] and Fisman and Golden's primer on corruption opens with the problem of "whether to pay a bribe to receive a government benefit or service."[32] But this omits an important form of corruption: state actors who steal from public coffers, or who extort without providing any benefit in return.[33]

Second, I highlight the difference between corruption involving elite political actors, such as politicians and leaders, and non-elites: regular civil servants, police officers, inspectors, customs officers, and front-line providers of public services. This dimension captures corruption that occurs among high- and low-level actors, which some term "grand" and "petty" corruption, respectively.[34] Political elites can grant special deals, block access, or control public coffers. This kind of corruption, therefore, involves high monetary stakes and the allocation of valuable resources such as land and legislations. Conversely, rank-and-file

---

[29] Whereas corrupt exchanges involve citizens or businesses giving benefits to state actors in exchange for their favors, clientelism entails state actors dispensing benefits to citizens in return for their votes or political support (Hicken 2011).

[30] For a non-exhaustive list of influential corruption studies focusing on bribery, see Rose-Ackerman (1978; 1999); Besley and McLaren (1993); Bardhan (1997); Gray and Kaufman (1998); Ades and Di Tella (1999); McMillan and Zoido (2004).

[31] In Shleifer and Vishny (1993), the term "corruption with theft" does not refer to embezzlement, but rather to bribery that results in a loss of public revenue, e.g., bribing customs officers to waive customs taxes.

[32] Fisman and Golden (2017). But note that the authors subsequently discuss whether corruption should include influence peddling and legal practices.

[33] One notable exception is Reinikka and Svensson's (2004) study on the theft of government education funding in Uganda, where they estimate a leakage rate of 87 percent.

[34] Rose-Ackerman (1999; 2002); Jain (2001); Bussell (2012).

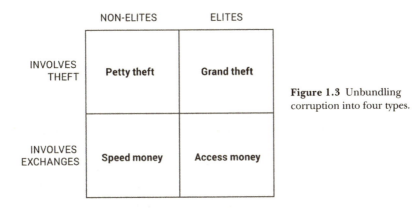

Figure 1.3 Unbundling corruption into four types.

bureaucrats exercise discretion only within their limited job scope, for example, processing permits or assigning school enrollment slots.

FOUR VARIETIES OF CORRUPTION. Dividing corruption along these two dimensions generates a matrix of four categories, as shown in Figure 1.3.

To illustrate each of the four categories, consider these distinct acts of corruption.

- **Petty theft**: In Bangkok, Thailand, complaints about police shake-downs are on the rise. As an anti-corruption politician puts it, "If you go to Sukhumvit Road, you can see the police looking for tourists who are smoking or drop a cigarette butt, then they ask for their passport and make them pay 2000 baht [just over US$60]."[35]
- **Grand theft**: Sani Abacha, the military dictator of Nigeria, siphoned an estimated US$4 billion from the central bank into his overseas accounts, which is nearly 10 percent of the country's entire GDP of $55 billion in 1998, the year he left office. Recently, Swiss authorities recovered and returned US$300 million of the "Abacha loot" to the Nigerian government.[36]

[35] Ian Lloyd Neubauer, "Tourists Are Reporting a Dramatic Surge in Harassment by Thai Police," *Time*, 25 January 2015.
[36] Bukola Adebayo, "Former Nigerian Dictator's $267 Million Seized from Jersey Account," *CNN*, 5 June 2019.

- **Speed money**: In India small shops shutter despite a booming retail market because, as one retailer lamented, "It's not possible to do business without greasing palms, without paying bribes." A typical supermarket must obtain a daunting list of 40 permits, forcing retailers to bribe many officers in order to get these permits faster, which cuts into their thin profit margins.[37]
- **Access money**: Turning to China, Ji Jianye, former Party secretary of Yangzhou city, received hefty gifts, bribes, and company shares from his long-time cronies in exchange for near-monopoly access to government construction and renovation projects. Within six years of Ji's tenure, their company's profits multiplied 15-fold. But as soon as Ji was investigated for corruption, its share price fell.[38]

From these examples, it's clear that corruption manifests itself in extremely diverse ways, which makes lumping them into a single category or score misleading. Generically described, each of the four categories in Figure 1.3 encompasses the following.

- **Petty theft** refers to acts of stealing, misuse of public funds, or extortion among street-level bureaucrats.
- **Grand theft** refers to embezzlement or misappropriation of large sums of public monies by political elites who control state finances.
- **Speed money** means petty bribes that businesses or citizens pay to bureaucrats to get around hurdles or speed things up.
- **Access money** encompasses high-stakes rewards extended by business actors to powerful officials, not just for speed, but to access exclusive, valuable privileges.

Whereas petty theft, grand theft, and speed money are almost always illegal, access money can encompass both illegal and legal actions. Illegal forms of access money entail large bribes and kickbacks – which are common in China – but they can also include ambiguously or completely legal exchanges that omit cash bribes, for example, cultivating political connections, campaign finance, "revolving door" practices (moving

---

[37] Nandita Bose, "Speed Money Puts the Brakes on India's Retail Growth," *Reuters*, 5 May 2013.
[38] This case is examined in detail in Chapter 5.

between leadership posts in private and public sectors), and influence peddling.[39]

Much of the literature on bribery centers on "speed money" but neglects "access money."[40] The popular analogy of "greasing the wheels" implies overcoming friction or cumbersome regulations, which is equivalent to speed money in my typology.[41] Access money, on the other hand, buys special deals and lucrative rights, making it more sludge than grease.

As Max Weber said, ideal-types are "border cases . . . of indispensable analytical value, and bracket historical reality which almost always appears in mixed forms."[42] Indeed, the four categories in my framework often mix and overlap. For example, corruption schemes among Chinese political elites may combine grand bribery, forged loan agreements, insider trading, and collusion with thugs. But precisely because reality is messy, we need to highlight the dimensions that matter most to our inquiry.[43]

NOT ALL CORRUPTION HARMS IN THE SAME WAY

While corruption is never good, not all forms of corruption are equally bad for the economy, nor do they cause the same kind of harm. The best analogy is drugs (Table 1.1). Within my typology, petty theft and grand theft are equivalent to toxic drugs – they are the most economically damaging as they drain public and private wealth.[44] Even worse, such

[39] Although influence peddling is not illegal, it may be considered corruption, as Fisman and Golden state: "There are cases in which public opinion holds behavior to be corrupt, even if the law does not" (Fisman and Golden 2017, 48). Several prominent legal scholars concur (Issacharoff 2010; Nichols 2017; Lessig 2018).

[40] Leff (1964); Nye (1967); Scott (1972); Rose-Ackerman (1978); Manion (1996). This distinction between "speed money" and "access money" builds off my historical analysis of the coevolution of corruption and the economy (Ang 2016, Chapters 1 and 5).

[41] Kaufmann and Wei (2000); Méon and Sekkat (2005); Chen *et al.* (2013).

[42] Weber (1968).

[43] As Collier and Adcock (1999) advise: "How scholars understand and operationalize a concept can and should depend on what they are going to do with it" (cited in Bussell 2015).

[44] According to Wedeman (1997), looting is the most damaging form of corruption as "it creates incentives for corrupt officials either to consume their illegal incomes immediately or to send them abroad for safekeeping." Likewise, Sun states that corruption with theft "entails absolute loss for an economy" (Sun 2004, 110).

TABLE 1.1 *Analogously to drugs, different types of corruption harm in different ways*

	Theft or exchange	Elites or non-elites	Legality	Economic effects	Analogy
Petty theft	Theft	Non-elites	Illegal	Growth-damaging	Toxic drugs
Grand theft	Theft	Elites	Illegal	Growth-damaging	Toxic drugs
Speed money	Exchange	Non-elites	Illegal	Shortens delays but imposes cost	Painkiller
Access money	Exchange	Elites	Legal and non-illegal	Stimulates growth but generates distortions, risks, and inequality	Steroids

corruption subverts law and order, deterring investors, tourists, and even foreign aid donors.[45]

The effects of exchange-based corruption are more ambiguous. Some argue that speed money (petty bribery) enhances efficiency by allowing citizens to overcome administrative hurdles and delays.[46] As Huntington wrote, "Corruption may be one way of surmounting traditional laws or bureaucratic regulations which hamper economic expansion."[47] But this kind of corruption still imposes a cost – and thus constitutes a tax – on citizens and businesses.[48] Particularly for the poor, even small bribes are crushing burdens. So, although speed money is not as debilitating as petty and grand theft, it does not spur growth. Alternatively, think of speed money as painkillers: although they lessen pain, they don't give health benefits, and consuming them in excess is harmful.

Access money, on the other hand, is the steroids of capitalism. Steroids are known as "growth-enhancing" drugs, but they come with serious side effects. And countries both rich and poor, in the West and the East, can fall prey to its temptation. From a businessperson's point of view, access money is less a tax than an *investment*. For example, Chinese entrepreneurs are willing to bribe their way into legislative congresses because the benefits of networking with Party-state bosses more than

---

[45] Kenny (2017).   [46] Leff (1964); Huntington (1968); Scott (1972).
[47] Huntington (1968, 69).
[48] On bribery as a tax or worse than taxation, see Shleifer and Vishny (1993); Bardhan (1997); Gray and Kaufman (1998); Wei (2000); Fisman and Svensson (2007).

offset the expense.[49] Likewise, in the United States, big corporations sink billions of dollars into lobbying every year because returns exceed costs.[50] By enriching capitalists who pay for privileges and by rewarding politicians who serve capitalist interests, access money can perversely stimulate commercial transactions and investment, which translates into GDP growth.

Yet this does not mean that access money is "good" for the economy – on the contrary, it distorts the allocation of resources, breeds systemic risks, and exacerbates inequality. For example, in China, bank loans are disproportionately allocated to politically connected companies,[51] forcing cash-strapped entrepreneurs to borrow from shadow banks at usurious rates, while connected companies, flush with excess credit, spend irresponsibly and speculate in real estate. Such distortions, however, are not captured in standard linear regressions that examine only annual income levels or growth rates.[52]

The harm of access money blows up only in the event of a crisis. The Chinese leadership is aware that such a danger is real and is struggling to keep its balance.[53] Elsewhere, the eruption of crises linked to corruption was preceded by euphoria: America's first great depression of 1839 (triggered by risky public financing and state-bank collusion),[54] the 1997 East Asia financial crisis, and the 2008 US financial crisis.[55]

---

[49] See Chapter 5. See also "Hunan City's Top Cadres Hit with Massive Vote-Buying Case," *South China Morning Post*, 30 December 2013, which is examined in the Appendix. Also see Li *et al.* (2006).

[50] Econometric studies of companies in the United States find a positive, robust relationship between lobbying expenditures, corporate financial performance, and future excess returns (Kim 2008, Chen *et al.* 2015). See also Fisman and Golden (2017, 44–46).

[51] Li *et al.* (2008); Chen *et al.* (2013). But this is not unique to China – listed companies in the United States with politically connected board members, too, secure bank loans at significantly lower cost (Houston *et al.* 2014).

[52] Perhaps this is why the perception of economies fueled by access money is typically exuberance followed by shock when a crisis erupts. As Kang writes about South Korea in the aftermath of the East Asian financial crisis: "While numerous observers profess to be shocked – Shocked! – at the revelations [of corruption], in reality such scandals are a recurrent theme in Korean political history" (Kang 2002a, 177).

[53] At the opening of the National People's Congress in 2019, Premier Li Keqiang warned of "tough challenges" and "a graver and more complex environment."

[54] See Wallis (2001, 2005); Ang (2016, Chapter 7).

[55] While multiple factors led to the 2008 financial crisis, regulatory capture and influence peddling was among them (Baker 2010; Igan *et al.* 2011, cited in Fisman and Golden 2017, 45–46; White 2011).

Through an "unbundled" approach, my study draws a clear distinction between the *quantity* and *quality* of corruption. Wealthy economies may have low quantities of aggregate corruption, as measured by standard cross-national indices, but it doesn't mean that they have no corruption; rather, their corruption may be of a different quality – concentrated in access money, which is difficult to capture and not immediately growth-retarding. Contrary to popular beliefs, the rise of capitalism was not accompanied by the eradication of corruption, but rather by the evolution of the quality of corruption from thuggery and theft toward sophisticated exchanges of power and profit. Compared with countries that prospered earlier, China is still a relative newcomer on this evolutionary path.

EXPLAINING THE PARADOX

Why has China prospered alongside vast corruption? I offer a four-part explanation. First, the dominant type of corruption in China is access money – elite exchanges of power and wealth – rather than petty bribery or outright theft, as I will show in Chapter 2. The standard argument for how corruption impedes growth, in Mauro's words, is that "corruption . . . lowers private investment, thereby reducing economic growth."[56] What this argument misses is that access money may actually *raise* private investment[57] – and even spur *over*-investment, as seen in China's real estate sector – thereby *increasing* growth, at least until the onset of a crisis.

Why has corruption in China primarily taken the form of access money, rather than outright looting? Since market opening, China's political system has followed a profit-sharing logic, where both elites and non-elites benefit from wealth creation in their jurisdictions. The entire Chinese bureaucracy is incentivized to promote development, even as officials engage in rampant deal-making. To understand how this works, we must distinguish between the mechanisms of profit-sharing among political elites, a corps of about 500,000 high-ranking officials

---

[56] Mauro (1995).

[57] As we will see in Chapter 5, the capitalist cronies who bribe politicians for deals are usually private sector bosses.

who are directly appointed by the Party, and rank-and-file employees in the bureaucracy, numbering about 50 million in total.[58]

Political elites have both career and financial incentives to enthusiastically foster development. It is often said that the promotion of local leaders is tied to economic growth,[59] but in reality, the small number of seats for promotion means that not all leaders may aspire to higher office.[60] The surer incentive, therefore, is financial: the more prosperous the local economy, the more local leaders will profit.[61] Successful Chinese politicians typically kill two birds with one stone: by spurring development and awarding projects to favored businesses, they achieve political targets and garner bribes (Chapter 5). And, unlike democratically elected politicians, authoritarian local leaders can bulldoze old properties, order new projects, and mobilize vast amounts of resources at will.

Among rank-and-file bureaucrats, profit-sharing operates through remuneration. Although their formal salaries are standardized at abysmally low rates, they are supplemented by an array of fringe benefits, such as allowances, bonuses, gifts, and free meals, which, as Chapter 4 shows, comprise about three-quarters of bureaucratic compensation. These fringe components are pegged to financial performance: the more tax revenue a local government generates and the more non-tax revenue (such as fees and service charges) individual offices collect, the more fringe benefits they can provide to their staff members. To borrow a term from economics, fringe compensation in the Chinese bureaucracy functions as an "efficiency wage"[62] – it not only incentivizes revenue-making effort but also deters bureaucrats from resorting to petty corruption.

Why did profit-sharing take root in the Chinese government but not in other poor, predatory states? I would point to Deng Xiaoping's historic decision to open markets while maintaining the Party's monopoly rule

---

[58] On the size of Chinese public employment, see Ang (2012). Walder defines China's political elite as "all cadres at the rank of county magistrate or division chief [*chu*] and above" (Walder 2004, 195).

[59] Li and Zhou (2005); Huang (2017).   [60] Kostka and Yu (2014).

[61] Oi's "local state corporatism" (Oi 1992; 1999) centers on the legal financial incentives for local governments through tax-sharing arrangements, whereas I examine corruption and rents as rewards.

[62] Becker and Stigler (1974).

and giving communist officials a personal stake in capitalist growth.[63] Corruption (rents) rewards their effort and participation.[64] This stood in sharp contrast to the former Soviet Union, where sudden political and economic liberalization (*Perestroika* and *Glasnost*) prompted the apparatchiks to defect en masse.[65] To use Olson's famous analogy of banditry, profit-sharing arrangements made Chinese officials "stationary bandits" who are invested in promoting collective welfare, as they can fleece off a percentage of gains, rather than "roving bandits" who just rob and flee.[66]

A third explanation is that the government has curtailed forms of corruption that directly inhibit entrepreneurial growth. This is a crucial part of the story that abundant accounts of "crony capitalism" and "rising corruption" missed.[67] Corruption may induce communist officials to enthusiastically embrace market reforms, but the central government has to steer them away from corruption that damages growth and undermines state performance – theft and extortion.[68] In Chapter 3, I show that although bribery has indeed exploded since 2000, embezzlement and misappropriation of public funds – which constitutes "corruption with theft" in my framework – has simultaneously declined. Arbitrary extortion of fees and fines, which had been rampant during the 1980s and 1990s, became less frequent than before. In addition, my survey in Chapter 2 shows that speed money (petty bribery) is less prevalent in China than in highly corrupt countries such as India and Russia.[69]

---

[63] Contrary to Nee's prediction that market reform will erode the power of the administrative elite, Walder shows that party-state membership fetched consistently high returns (Nee 1989; Walder 1996b; 2002). At the macro level, see Shirk's theory of "playing to the provinces" (Shirk 1993).

[64] On the role of corruption in maintaining political order, Huntington observes, "Corruption itself may be a substitute for reform and both corruption and reform may be substitutes for revolution" (Huntington 1968, 64).

[65] Solnick (1996); Åslund (2013); Walder (2003).   [66] Olson (2000).

[67] Hao and Johnston (1995); Hilton (1996); He (2000); Gong (2002); Sun (2004); Wedeman (2012); Pei (2016).

[68] Shleifer and Treisman (2000) offer a similar insight in Russia's context. Although rents are necessary for buying political support, the problem is how to induce actors to accept less costly rents. Unlike in China, the Russian government did not employ capacity-building measures to deal with this problem.

[69] This is consistent with the Global Corruption Barometer 2011, which found that only nine percent of Chinese citizens reported having paid a bribe in the past year, compared with 54 percent in India, 64 percent in Nigeria, and 84 percent in Cambodia.

These forms of corruption – petty theft, grand theft, and speed money – were brought under control through an ambitious program of capacity building, which began in 1998 under Premier Zhu Rongji and is still being expanded.[70] The program includes establishing a Civil Service Law, standardizing tax rates, strengthening oversight through budgeting and accounting reforms, replacing cash payments of fees and fines with direct electronic deposit, consolidating public bank accounts, and more. Because these reforms are dry and unsensational, the media and even much of the academic literature ignores them. Yet their practical effects are real: they have increased state capacity to monitor and penalize non-transactional forms of corruption and "speed money" payments.

Fourth, in China regional competition substitutes for electoral competition in checking predatory corruption. Facing fierce contestation for projects and investors, local leaders are motivated to curb "grabbing hands" among rank-and-file bureaucrats. Such efforts sometimes reached a point of religious fervor, as reflected in the leadership's slogan in a county of Hubei: "Investors are Gods, prospectors of investors are heroes, bureaucrats are humble servants, and those who harm corporate interests are sinners."[71] That's not all – deal-making is part of fervent growth promotion, too. Leaders compete to offer "preferential policies" (a common policy term) to selected businesses. To stay ahead, they must also project competence and upgrade their development strategies by strategically positioning their locales, crafting commercial niches, and branding, as Chapter 5 shows.

To summarize, my explanation for the Chinese paradox boils down to four elements.

- The dominant type of corruption in China today is access money, which stimulates growth but generates distortions and risks.

---

[70] Yang (2004); Ko and Weng (2012); Ang (2017).

[71] Interview B2013-334. This book draws on 375 interviews conducted with primarily local bureaucrats from 2006 to 2015, and a separate set of 42 interviews with regulatory officers in 2012. To maintain the anonymity of my respondents, I do not identify their names or particular location. Instead, I identify the interviewees by the year in which the first interview was conducted, followed by an ID assigned to each interviewee. For more on the coverage of these interviews by region and department, please see Appendix B in *How China Escaped the Poverty Trap* (Ang 2016).

- Access money dominates because China's political system runs on a profit-sharing model, where the rewards of leaders and bureaucrats are linked to economic performance.
- Beginning in the 2000s, capacity-building reforms have curtailed corruption with theft and speed money.
- Regional competition checks predatory corruption, spurs developmental efforts, and ratchets up deals.

Together, these elements not only explain the Chinese paradox, but also help to reconcile contradictions in China's political economy. Chinese growth is impressive yet imbalanced and risky. Local officials are corrupt yet worship the pursuit of development. China's regime is authoritarian and politically centralized, yet its regions are economically decentralized and highly competitive.

TWO GILDED AGES

Many of the features outlined above could also describe nineteenth-century America. As the economic historians Glaeser and Goldin remind us, "The irony [of the period] may be that corruption was large as a fraction of government ... but that economy prospered nationally and locally."[72] Bribing legislators, insider trading, political patronage, and so on, were all rampant. And yet America's economy soared for reasons quite similar to China.

American state governments were fiscally independent and eager to promote development, both to win elections and to get rich. Access money intertwined with the financing of major infrastructure projects that paved the way for economic boom while vastly enriching a handful of tycoons.[73] Ultimately, the risks inherent in such corruption erupted in the Crisis of 1893, leaving banks insolvent and forcing reforms.[74] From there, America continued to evolve. By the Progressive Era (1890–1920), as one historian noted, "The most striking aspect of embezzlement is how little it occurred."[75]

---

[72] Glaeser and Goldin (2006). [73] Wallis (2005). [74] Leahy (2010).
[75] Menes (2006).

To say that contemporary China and nineteenth-century America are similar does not mean that they are identical. China is a single-party autocracy whereas the United States is a democracy. As Menes underscores, in the United States, "even during the most corrupt periods, the corrupt mayors and council members could be voted out of office."[76] Transparency mandates, muck-raking journalists, and crusading prosecutors were central ingredients in America's battle against graft in the Progressive Era. Xi, on the other hand, spurns bottom-up measures, opting instead to stamp out corruption through the strong arm of the Party apparatus,[77] while expanding the state sector and tightening political control.[78]

Although the threats facing China today – over-investment and excessive debt, fueled by access money – recall America's Gilded Age, this doesn't mean the country will inevitably collapse. This is because, unlike the obliviousness preceding the American or East Asian financial crises, the dangers in China are widely known and under the constant glare of scrutiny. Long-standing Western expectations of Chinese failure have perhaps unintendedly kept the regime alert.[79]

At present, the Chinese leadership is desperately trying to "derisk" the economic and financial system while maintaining economic growth. This is a high-wire act, made all the more precarious by the United States–China trade war. Whether the leadership can keep its balance will determine not only China's fate but the global balance of power in the twenty-first century.

DATA

Existing books on Chinese corruption often rely on a single source: ethnography in one location,[80] prosecutorial statistics and cases,[81] various news reports and secondary literature,[82] and, most commonly, scandals reported in the Chinese media.[83] This is understandable – corruption is difficult to study in any setting, even more so in an authoritarian regime.

---

[76] Menes (2006).   [77] Stromseth *et al.* (2017).   [78] Economy (2018); Lardy (2019).
[79] Philip Pan, "The Land That Failed to Fail," *The New York Times*, 18 November 2018.
[80] Osburg (2013); Hillman (2014).   [81] Sun (2004); Wedeman (2012).
[82] Lü (2000); Pei (2006).   [83] Pei (2016).

Nevertheless, because the data we use shapes the conclusions we get, we must be particularly cautious about relying solely on media stories of corruption.[84] Using only scandals paints a skewed picture, as I show in Chapter 5.

This book strives to deploy mixed methods and a wide variety of data to shed light on the paradox of prosperity and corruption. Each chapter of my book will address a different research question with a different and appropriate data source, including the first expert survey that measures perceptions of distinct types of corruption across 15 countries including China (Chapter 2), official statistics on investigated corruption cases (Chapter 3), text analysis of media mentions (Chapters 3, 5, and 7), in-depth profiles of fallen leaders over the course of their careers (Chapter 5), an original dataset on county-level bureaucratic compensation and incentive structure (Chapter 4), and another original dataset on the downfall of city leaders during Xi's anti-corruption campaign (Chapter 6). Last but not least, by incorporating more than 400 interviews that I conducted with Chinese bureaucrats and businesses, my study delivers voices on the ground to readers.

ROADMAP

The rest of *China's Gilded Age* is divided into six chapters. Chapter 2, "Unbundling Corruption across Countries," critiques conventional bundled measures of corruption and presents an alternative – the Unbundled Corruption Index (UCI). This is an original expert survey that measures the prevalence of the four categories of corruption in my framework: petty theft, grand theft, speed money, and access money. It provides preliminary but systematically collected evidence that China's corruption is indeed distinct from other typically predatory states.

Chapter 3, "Unbundling Corruption over Time," examines how access money came to dominate China's structure of corruption. Contrary to popular claims of "rising" corruption, I show that since the 2000s, only

---

[84] As Howson (2017) points out in a careful review of Pei's *China's Crony Capitalism*, scandals reported in the Chinese media are usually not independent investigations, but rather "central-level propaganda" to shame and warn corrupt local officials. Interpreting this material as evidence of regime decay, therefore, is ironic.

bribery has exploded, both in frequency and in scale, while embezzlement, misappropriation of public funds, and bureaucratic extortion have declined. Two forces drove this evolution: the expansion of markets after 1993 and the central government's rollout of capacity-building measures in 1998.

In Chapter 4, "Profit-Sharing, Chinese-Style," I explain the little-understood mechanisms of profit-sharing within China's vast bureaucracy, which are frequently dismissed as "organizational corruption." Drawing on extensive interviews and an original dataset, I show that in the Chinese bureaucracy, fringe compensation is pegged to financial performance, making it an unusual variant of profit-sharing in the public sector. Furthermore, I demonstrate that the golden goose maxim – restraint today yields long-term benefits – is not just a parable but a reality, thus distinguishing China's bureaucracy from myopic, predatory states elsewhere. For the global development community, this chapter sheds light on how poor-and-weak countries can escape the vicious cycle of poverty and corruption through what I term "transitional administrative institutions."

Moving up the hierarchy, Chapter 5, "Corrupt and Competent," turns to national and local leaders. Profit-sharing among leaders follows a different logic: the more economically prosperous the locality, the more personal rents they can collect as massive graft. By unpacking the career paths of two infamously fallen officials – Bo Xilai (provincial Party secretary of Chongqing) and Ji Jianye (city mayor of Nanjing) – this chapter reveals why deal-making corruption was compatible with aggressive growth promotion. It also fleshes out the structural distortions and risks brought about by access money.

Since its launch in 2012, Xi's anti-corruption campaign has gripped the world's attention. How will this crackdown affect China's economic and political prospects? Chapter 6, "All the King's Men," examines the determinants of downfall among city-level leaders during Xi's campaign. My analysis finds a remarkably high turnover rate, indicating extraordinarily stressful conditions and heightened political risks for local leaders. In addition, I find that patronage, not performance, predicts the likelihood of downfall. Facing harsh scrutiny, volatility, and mounting demands, bureaucrats feel paralyzed, precipitating a new problem in Chinese politics – inaction.

In Chapter 7, "Rethinking Nine Big Questions," I review my key arguments and revisit the comparison of reform-era China to America's Gilded Age using historical data on reported corruption to highlight their similarities and differences. Finally, I explore the implications of this book for big questions in Chinese political economy and in corruption and capitalism more broadly.

CHAPTER 2

Unbundling Corruption across Countries

I N PRINCIPLE, WE SHOULD MEASURE WHAT WE VALUE, YET THE reality is often the opposite – we value what we can measure. Perhaps nowhere is this statement truer than in the study of corruption, which is inherently difficult to gauge and quantify. Our understanding of corruption and its relationship to economic prosperity has been profoundly shaped by the way it is conventionally measured – as a one-dimensional problem.

Standard indices of corruption assign a single score to each country and rank them annually. These indices are hugely influential, especially the Corruption Perception Index (CPI), which is produced by Transparency International (TI).[1] The media covers the release of CPI like a pageant, praising the countries on top and chastising those which lag behind. Multinational companies rely on the CPI to gauge risks when investing in foreign countries.[2] Researchers deploy it in statistical analyses to test the impact of corruption on investment and growth.[3] And China observers cite the CPI liberally when assessing the country.[4]

---

[1] Other perception-based, cross-national measures of corruption include the World Bank's "Control of Corruption" Index and Business International's Corruption Index.

[2] As advisors at Baker McKenzie, a multinational law firm, wrote, "The CPI is the leading global indicator of public sector corruption ... It has been used as an important gauge by companies in managing corruption risks when conducting businesses in foreign countries." See "China Continues to Improve in Transparency International's 2017 Corruption Perception Index," 22 February 2018, www.bakermckenzie.com/en/insight/publications/2018/02/china-improve-corruption-perception-index (accessed 21 November 2019).

[3] Mauro (1995; 1996); Treisman (2000); Wei (2000); Mo (2001); Montinola and Jackman (2002); Gerring and Thacker (2004); Bose *et al.* (2008).

[4] Pei (2006); Cole *et al.* (2009); Cai (2015); Manion (2016); Walder (2018); Zhu (2018).

But measuring corruption on a single scale is misleading. First, these indices do not distinguish among qualitatively different types of corruption. For instance, taking cash bribes, stealing public funds, and placing family members on corporate boards are all examples of corruption, but of different kinds with vastly different consequences.

Second, conventional measures predominantly capture the obviously illegal forms of corruption that afflict the poorest countries, such as bribery and outright looting of state assets.[5] Meanwhile, transactional corruption among the rich and the powerful, which is more cleverly disguised, even legitimized, in wealthier states, tends to fall off the radar.[6] As a result, when researchers plot bundled scores like the CPI with national income, poor countries appear to be riddled with corruption while rich countries look clean.

Unbundling corruption is a necessary first step toward revising assumptions about its relationship to capitalist wealth. While earlier studies have proposed an abundance of corruption typologies,[7] attempts to measure the different forms are rare, particularly across countries.[8] In this chapter, I begin to fill this crucial gap. Using a perception-based survey of experts in 15 countries, including China, I measure the four varieties of corruption identified in this book: petty theft, grand theft, speed money, and access money. This survey provides a systematic basis for comparing not only the perceived levels of corruption across countries, but also and more significantly, their varying composition.

Some types of corruption are immediately lethal while others poison over time. In examining the impact of corruption on growth, researchers must first identify what kind of corruption dominates. Although China is reputed to face a mounting crisis of corruption, my survey shows that its structure of corruption is distinct from other notoriously corrupt countries, including Nigeria and Russia. Chinese corruption is dominated by

---

[5] "The World's Most Corrupt Countries," *The New York Times*, 9 December 2016.

[6] Whyte (2015); Lessig (2018).

[7] For example, see Wedeman (1997); Rose-Ackerman (1999); Kang (2002b); Johnston (2008); Bussell (2015).

[8] One notable exception is V-Dem, which asks respondents to rate corrupt exchanges and embezzlement in the executive branch and public administration separately. Their questions, however, are still broadly worded, and they do not disaggregate within each category, as I do in this survey.

access money, the same type of corruption as in South Korea and the United States.

WHAT STANDARD MEASURES MISS

Many hold up the CPI as an authoritative gauge of corruption. Even slight perturbations from year to year are interpreted as if CPI scores were temperature readings on a thermometer. In 2014, when China's CPI score dropped from 40 to 36, headlines on CNN blared, "China slips down corruption perception index, despite high-profile crackdown."[9] Two years later, when China's score nudged back up to 40, commentators declared that the country's anti-corruption efforts were paying off.[10]

Despite its wide usage, however, users rarely ask how standard corruption perception scores like the CPI are produced. When I raised this question with my students, most of them guessed that TI conducts original surveys in every country. This would be ideal, but too costly and time-consuming. Instead, TI gathers surveys conducted by third parties (for example, the Economist Intelligence Unit and Political Risks Services Guide) and combines them to construct a single score for each country. In the analogy of sausage-making, the CPI is made from many different meats but none of the meat is produced in-house.[11]

Critics, including the CPI's creator, Johann Lambsdorff, have pointed to a number of problems with amalgamated corruption indices.[12] Because the CPI is compiled from third-party surveys, TI has no control over the design or quality of the sources used. Country scores may change from year to year simply because TI selects different sources or the sources themselves have changed. In addition, CPI scores reflect first-world bias. Almost all the surveys TI consults are conducted by Western-

---

[9] Euan McKirdy, "China Slips Down Corruption Perception Index, Despite High-Profile Crackdown," *CNN*, 3 December 2014.

[10] Mini vandePol and Vivian Wu, "China's Anti-corruption Efforts Pay Off," *China Business Review*, 24 March 2017.

[11] For its World Governance Indicators (WGI), including its Control of Corruption Index, the World Bank employs a similar method: it combines results from third-party surveys to create a single score for each country.

[12] Alex Cobham, "Corrupting Perceptions: Why Transparency International's Flagship Corruption Index Falls Short," *Foreign Policy*, 22 July 2013; "Johann Lambsdorff Retires the Corruption Perceptions Index," *Global Integrity*, 18 September 2009.

based institutions, most of which are business-oriented, such as the Economist Intelligence Unit.[13] These studies survey first-world business expatriates, who may be predisposed to perceiving foreign low-income countries as corrupt while overlooking influence-peddling back home.

A third problem, not previously noted by critics, is the wording of existing surveys. For instance, the World Competitiveness Yearbook, one of the CPI's sources in 2016, asked senior business leaders a single terse question:

> Bribery and corruption: exist or do not exist.

Other surveys bundle many different types of corruption into an overall score. The Political Risk Services Guide, another CPI source, asked respondents to evaluate a country's corruption on a scale of 0 to 6 using this paragraph-long guideline, which appears to be the equivalent of rating a forest by roughly averaging all the animals that live within it:

> This is an assessment of corruption within the political system. The most common form of corruption met directly by businesses is financial corruption in the form of demands for special payments and bribes connected with import and export licenses, exchange controls, tax assessments, police protection, or loans. The measure is most concerned with actual or potential corruption in the form of excessive patronage, nepotism, job reservations, exchange of favors, secret party funding, and suspiciously close ties between politics and business.

Overly broad wording presents a validity problem: the surveys may not measure what they intend or claim to measure.

Despite the flaws highlighted here, bundled scores such as the CPI and the World Bank's Control of Corruption Index do provide a convenient metric for comparing perceived levels of corruption across countries every year, which is difficult and expensive to do using in-house surveys. TI also deserves credit for using these indices to push for anti-corruption efforts around the world. My point isn't that we should discard corruption indices entirely, but that we should interpret and use them mindfully.

---

[13] A description of the sources used to construct the CPI in 2016 can be downloaded from TI's website: www.transparency.org/news/feature/corruption_perceptions_index_2016 (accessed 21 November 2019).

Furthermore, researchers should strive to improve existing measures, as this study tries to do.

THE UNBUNDLED CORRUPTION INDEX (UCI)

The structure of a country's corruption – what types dominate and to what degree – may have a larger effect on economic and social outcomes than aggregate levels of corruption. To capture this qualitative variance, we need a different measurement strategy.

To the best of my knowledge, this study presents the first indicator of qualitatively distinct typologies of corruption across countries – what I call the Unbundled Corruption Index (UCI). The UCI is based on an original survey of country experts that measures the perceived prevalence of the four categories of corruption identified in my framework: access money, speed money, grand theft, and petty theft (see Chapter 1 for the theory).

WHY EXPERT SURVEYS? Analysts regularly use expert surveys to measure institutional or political contexts at the country level. Examples include the various surveys that comprise the CPI and the World Bank's World Governance Indicators, Global Integrity's Africa Integrity Indicators, Varieties of Democracy, and Banerjee and Pande's study of political corruption. These surveys target experts because individuals who study, report on, or do business in a country are more likely to have a bird's-eye view of the entire political economy. Citizens' experiences, by contrast, are usually limited to daily encounters with petty corruption.[14]

My UCI survey, which I conducted in 2017 and 2018, measured responses from these experts: academics with area expertise, journalists, and business leaders and professionals with at least 10 years of experience in a given country. To partially counter the problem of first-world bias in standard business surveys, 45 percent of my expert respondents are natives of the country they scored.

---

[14] Global Corruption Barometer, a survey conducted by TI with citizens around the world, focuses on the payment of bribes to access public services, which is equivalent to speed money in my typology.

TABLE 2.1 *Unbundling four corruption categories into sub-categories*

	Non-elites	Elites
Involves theft	**Petty theft**	**Grand theft**
	Street-level bureaucrats privately pocket illegal fees; extort street vendors for protection money; agencies coerce companies to pay for their services; take group vacations on public funds	Top officials illegally siphon public funds into private accounts; create ghost payroll for family members; illegally keep state-subsidized properties for themselves; executives in state-owned companies collude to embezzle funds
Involves exchanges	**Speed money**	**Access money**
	Citizens pay police bribes to avoid penalties; tips to receive basic medical services; private payments to expedite medical services; small bribes to speed up licensing process; excessive regulations to extract bribes	Businesses directly pay massive bribes for deals; pay for politician's family expenses for deals; allocate corporate positions to family members of politicians; politicians build clientelist network for indirect bribe-taking; lobbying for favorable regulations; revolving door; loose oversight and bailouts with impunity

CATEGORIES AND COUNTRIES. Following my framework, my survey unbundles each of four categories into sub-categories for a finer measurement, as listed in Table 2.1. The responses for each sub-category sum to a category score, which add up to the UCI total corruption score. My survey yielded both category-specific and aggregated scores for 15 countries, including China.

These 15 countries include a mixture of low-income (Bangladesh, Ghana, India, Indonesia, Nigeria), middle-income (Brazil, China, Russia, South Africa, Thailand), and high-income (Japan, Singapore, South Korea, Taiwan, the United States) countries. Following V-Dem, an award-winning expert perception survey of dimensions of democracy across countries,[15] I consulted a minimum of four country experts for each country.[16] Six

---

[15] V-Dem received the Lijphart/Przeworski/Verba Dataset Award from the American Political Science Association in 2016.

[16] The V-Dem project states in their methodology section that they "endeavor to find a minimum of five Country Experts to code each country-year for every indicator," but that this is sometimes impossible for some historical periods or understudied countries. See Michael Coppedge, John Gerring, Carl Henrik Knutsen *et al.* 2018. "V-Dem Methodology v8." Varieties of Democracy (V-Dem) Project, www.v-dem.net/media/file r_public/5a/f1/5af198e9-f3e8-4619-b9fd-a8387fdc22a5/v-dem_methodology_v8.pdf (accessed 21 November 2019). In my survey, I strove for a minimum of five country

countries, including China, received seven or more expert responses (Appendix: Chapter 2 provides more methodological details.)

METHODOLOGICAL INNOVATIONS. My survey features a few methodological innovations. First and foremost, this study directly measures the four distinct categories of corruption that my theory identifies. Although many previous studies advanced typologies of corruption,[17] none, to my knowledge, measured them across countries.

Second, my survey makes a targeted attempt to measure the elusive category of access money – the purchase of lucrative privileges, both illegal and legal. Bribery and embezzlement are obviously illegal and morally reprehensible, but practices such as moving between leadership positions in the private and public sectors (the revolving door) and regulatory capture through lobbying are more ambiguous. As a result, existing perception surveys usually exclude them. Yet including them is necessary to capture what Lessig calls "institutional corruption."[18] My survey makes a first-known empirical effort to bring access money to the surface and capture its wide universe of forms, as listed in Table 2.1.

A third innovation is the use of vignettes to more accurately capture perceptions of corruption. Most surveys ask respondents to assess corruption in broad terms, for example:[19]

Rate: state capture by narrow vested interests.

Are there general abuses of public resources?

Is the government free from excessive bureaucratic regulations, registration requirements, and other controls that increase opportunities for corruption?

Any of these statements can be interpreted in multiple, even conflicting, ways. Respondents are likely to have different definitions or scenarios in

---

experts, but because of difficulties in getting responses in a few countries, I decided on a minimum of four.

[17] For a review, see Bussell (2015).

[18] Lessig (2018). I thank John Padgett for emphasizing this point.

[19] These three survey questions are from the African Development Bank Governance Ratings 2015, Economist Intelligence Unit Country Risk Ratings 2016, and Freedom House Nations in Transit 2016, respectively. All three were CPI sources in 2016. See www.transparency.org /news/feature/corruption_perceptions_index_2016 (accessed 21 November 2019).

mind when asked to evaluate "state capture" or "general abuses of public resources." Again, this presents a validity problem: vague questions may not measure what they claim to measure.

To improve measurement validity, my survey asks respondents to evaluate corruption using stylized vignettes, designed to be concrete and yet generic enough to represent a class of similar corrupt activities. The vignettes are based on real events reported in scholarly work or the media. For example, inspired by the saga of the Chinese politician Bo Xilai (see Chapter 5), one question captures "crony capitalism" in this way:

> By cultivating close ties with a powerful official and paying for his family's expenses, a businessperson gains monopoly access to public construction projects.
>
> How common do you think this *type* of scenario is in [country] today?[20]

Another survey question, inspired by the case of Zhou Yongkang – a high-ranking Chinese politician who was netted for corruption in 2014 – is presented in this vignette:

> A top politician is linked to an extensive network of former associates, protégés, and/or family members, who monopolize power in certain sectors of the economy. While the politician himself never or rarely accepts bribes, a massive amount of bribes flows through his network.
>
> How common do you think this *type* of scenario is in [country] today?

A third vignette captures conflict of interest among influential actors who have a foot in government and another in corporations. It is inspired by a *New York Times* article on "a revolving door between Washington and Wall Street," which revealed that the chief architects of America's housing policies were or became heads of lobby groups or big banks.[21]

> Major figures move back and forth between the public and private sector, and there are no laws forbidding this practice.
>
> How common do you think this *type* of scenario is in [country] today?

[20] Respondents rate the prevalence of each type of corruption on a five-level Likert-type scale, ranging from "extremely common" to "never occurs."

[21] Gretchen Morgenson, "A Revolving Door Helps Big Banks Muscle out Fannie and Freddie," *The New York Times*, 7 December 2015.

Previous studies used vignettes to "anchor" respondents with potentially divergent understandings of survey questions.[22] My vignette-focused survey, while not identical, is also designed to overcome cultural and other biases regarding what constitutes corruption, a perennial challenge in measuring corruption.[23] As Rose-Ackerman writes, "One person's bribe is another person's gift."[24] Note that my survey questions do not ask respondents to judge or determine whether a particular scenario is corrupt; I simply ask them to rate how commonly it occurs. Using vignettes ensures that respondents are rating the same scenarios. In this way, my measurement strategy improves coder consistency.

UPGRADING PERCEPTION MEASURES. To sum up, my survey design presents a number of advantages over standard measurements (Table 2.2). The most significant difference is that it allows researchers to examine distinct strands of corruption both in isolation and in theoretically relevant bundles, yielding portraits that are simultaneously fine-grained and parsimonious. As my survey will show, two countries with the same CPI scores (for example, China and India) can feature divergent dominant modes of corruption. In addition, this survey captures the elusive category of access money in its varied forms, both legal and illegal.

TABLE 2.2 *Advantages of the UCI over standard perception measures*

Problems with standard measures like CPI	How the UCI addresses these problems
Single bundled scores mask the composition of corruption, reinforcing the idea that corruption is a homogeneous problem that varies only in quantity, not in quality.	The UCI allows us to examine qualitatively distinct forms of corruption on their own and in theoretically relevant bundles. This measurement strategy offers both nuance and parsimony.
Existing surveys tend to under-capture sophisticated, non-illegal forms of corruption, particularly in the category of access money.	The UCI is designed to measure the prevalence of four distinct types of corruption, including the elusive category of access money.
Respondents are either unsure of what is required or have different scenarios in mind when asked to rate broad concepts such as "state capture" or "misuse of public resources for private gain."	The UCI uses stylized vignettes to ensure that respondents evaluate the same scenario, thereby increasing coder reliability and measurement validity.

---

[22] King *et al.* (2004); King and Wand (2007).
[23] Davis and Ruhe (2003); Nichols and Robertson (2017).   [24] Rose-Ackerman (1999).

Finally, it improves measurement validity by using vignettes instead of vague descriptors.

Skeptics may contend that perception-based surveys are inherently flawed and should be abandoned because perceived corruption may not align with experiences.[25] Yet for cross-national comparisons, expert perception-based indices of corruption remain the most widely used and influential measure.[26] Global indicators such as the CPI determine foreign aid allocation,[27] guide corporate investment decisions and reform policies, receive widespread media coverage, and affect the image of governments. Thus, improving expert perception measures, regardless of their limitations, has huge impact.

COMPARING BUNDLED AND UNBUNDLED CORRUPTION

Having introduced my survey method, we may now explore the results. Table A2.1 in the Appendix lists the UCI scores in four typological clusters (petty theft, grand theft, speed money, access money) on a scale of 0 to 10, with 10 indicating the highest perceived level of corruption. The sum of the four categories is the UCI total score, which ranges from 0 to 40. To facilitate analysis, the scores are visualized in a format shown in Figure 2.1, which displays the total UCI score (listed below country name), and the distribution of this aggregate score across four categories. The category that takes up the highest proportion of score is interpreted as the dominant mode, shaded in dark gray.

Each country's total and unbundled scores are visualized in Figure 2.2, from the most to the least corrupt. The overall UCI ranking is consistent with casual observation. The most corrupt country is Bangladesh (No. 1) and the cleanest is Singapore (No. 15). Singapore, Japan, Taiwan, and South Korea, known collectively as the East Asian "developmental" states,[28] all rank among the least corrupt, followed by the United States.

---

[25] Seligson (2006); Olken (2009); Razafindrakoto and Roubaud (2010).

[26] Moreover, in the real world, perceptions often matter more than reality. Investors make decisions that are based on perceived risks. Citizens support politicians primarily on the basis of impressions (Grimmer *et al.* 2014).

[27] Kenny (2017).   [28] Evans (1989); World Bank (1997a).

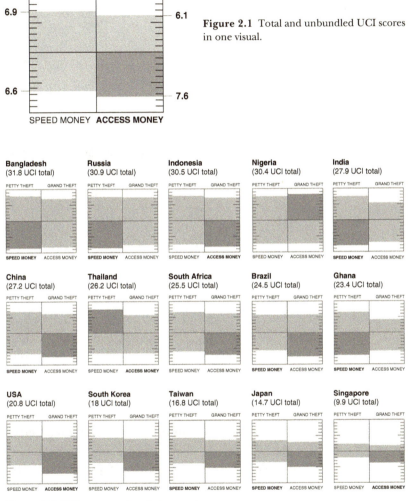

Figure 2.1 Total and unbundled UCI scores in one visual.

Figure 2.2 UCI scores and ranks by country.

At No. 6, China is perceived as more corrupt than Brazil and South Africa, but less corrupt than Russia, Indonesia, and Nigeria.

But, on comparing UCI with the countries' CPI rank in 2017, there are some notable deviations. I find that the ratings and rankings of moderately corrupt countries such as China are more sensitive to different

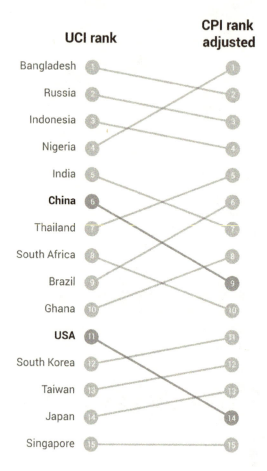

UCI rank

CPI rank adjusted

Bangladesh
Russia
Indonesia
Nigeria
India
China
Thailand
South Africa
Brazil
Ghana
USA
South Korea
Taiwan
Japan
Singapore

Figure 2.3 Comparing the UCI and CPI ranks.

measurement methods than those of countries on the extreme ends. Figure 2.3 compares the two indices, where 1 is the most corrupt and 15 is the least corrupt in both.[29] At the extremes – the most and least corrupt countries – the rankings are consistent across the UCI and CPI; but there is notably less consistency in the rankings of moderately corrupt countries, including China. For example, according to my survey, China is more corrupt than Thailand, Brazil, and Ghana. But in the CPI, China is ranked as less corrupt than all three countries. The UCI ranks Nigeria

[29] For ease of comparison with my survey, I inverted the CPI ranking of the 15 countries based on their CPI scores in 2017, such that 1 is the most corrupt and 15 is the least corrupt.

as less corrupt than Russia and Indonesia, but in the CPI, it is rated the most corrupt among the 15 countries in my survey.

A second divergence is that the CPI rates the United States more favorably than the UCI. As Figure 2.3 shows, according to the CPI, the United States (No. 14) is less corrupt than South Korea (No. 11) and Japan (No. 13). My survey, however, shows the reverse. Why might this be the case? One possibility is cultural bias. The CPI's sources are predominantly surveys of business expatriates conducted by Western business advisory firms; these respondents may be inclined to view the United States as less corrupt.

Then I turn to a different pair of comparisons. What if, instead of obtaining the UCI total score by aggregating individual responses from 20 sub-categories, we asked respondents to rate their overall impression of the severity of corruption in a single question. My survey posed this question first: "How do you grade the problem of corruption in [country] today on a scale of 0 to 10, with 10 being most severe?"[30] This is a commonly asked question in business surveys used to generate the CPI.[31]

Figure 2.4 compares the two methods of scoring: one by the UCI method and the other by asking for a single bundled perception. It indicates that when respondents are asked for their overall impression of corruption, this survey design *under*-counts forms of corruption commonly found in wealthy economies while *over*-counting those in poor countries. The United States and Singapore are perceived as more corrupt by the UCI aggregated score than by overall impression. One possible explanation is that when respondents are asked to evaluate corruption in a single question, they overlook non-illegal manifestations of access money, such as influence peddling and regulatory capture. When perceptions are unbundled, however, these activities are factored into the total.

Conversely, Nigeria and Ghana are perceived as more corrupt by overall impression than by UCI aggregated scores. This could be because the forms of corruption that dominate in Ghana (speed money) and

---

[30] This question was asked at the beginning of the survey, so that respondents will not be influenced by the unbundled questions that follow.

[31] For example, the Political and Economic Risk Consultancy, one of the CPI's sources in 2016, poses this question: "How do you grade the problem of corruption in the country in which you are working?"

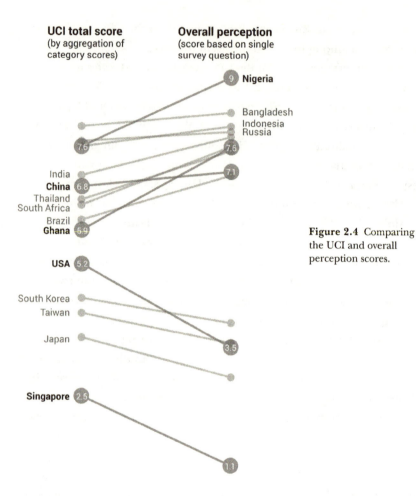

UCI total score
(by aggregation of
category scores)

Overall perception
(score based on single
survey question)

Figure 2.4 Comparing
the UCI and overall
perception scores.

Nigeria (grand theft) are visible to the public or widely condemned. China is also rated as slightly more corrupt by the CPI than by my unbundled method, which might reflect the influence of wide media coverage of its worsening corruption and the fact that its leadership speaks openly about corruption as a crisis.

WHICH MODE OF CORRUPTION DOMINATES?

Another advantage of the UCI is that we can disaggregate the scores to examine which mode of corruption dominates in each country. Instead of subjectively selecting countries to represent various typologies, my survey allows us to examine the relative weight of each category. The category that makes up the highest share of the UCI aggregate score may be interpreted as the dominant mode of corruption. This feature is visualized in Figure 2.2, with the dominant mode of each country highlighted in a darker shade.

The results are striking. In China the dominant mode of corruption is *access money*, which puts it in the same league as all five high-income economies (Japan, Singapore, South Korea, Taiwan, and the United States) and three large emerging markets (Brazil, Indonesia, and South Africa). In contrast, Bangladesh, Ghana, India, and Russia are dominated by *speed money*, which suggests that bribes are more commonly paid to avoid harassment and delays than to buy privileges. Consistently with most qualitative accounts,[32] Nigeria's corruption is defined by *grand theft*, elite embezzlement of public funds and resources. In Thailand, *petty theft*, malfeasance among low-level public officers that does not involve exchanges, emerges as most prevalent.[33]

CHINA VS. RUSSIA. The empirical efforts in this chapter allow observers of China to *objectively* assess a long-standing question: is corruption in China different from other countries – and, if so, how?

I begin with a paired comparison of China and Russia. Students of post-communist societies have long wondered why economic liberalization brought about vibrant capitalist growth in China but regime collapse in the former Soviet Union and economic stagnation in Russia. Both China and Russia experienced an explosion of corruption over the course of transition toward capitalist markets. Why are their economic outcomes so different?

One popular explanation is that corruption is "more devastating" in Russia than in China.[34] Blanchard and Shleifer argue that unlike Russia, which abruptly introduced market reforms under a dysfunctional democracy, China did so under the CCP's centralized rule. As

---

[32] Joseph (1987); Kohli (2004).

[33] This appears consistent with recent media reports. See "Tourists Are Reporting a Dramatic Surge in Harassment by Thai Police," *Time*, 25 January 2015.

[34] Larsson (2006).

a result, corruption in China did not degenerate into chaos and lawlessness.[35] Echoing this argument, Sun agrees that whereas Russia is wrecked by lawless "looting," China is marked by "rent-seeking" and "profit-sharing."[36] But Wedeman disagrees: "It is wrong, I conclude, to argue that corruption in China was distinct from corruption in post-communist Russia because of greater levels of profit-sharing corruption versus greater levels of looting, as Sun argues. China had plenty of both."[37]

Beyond the academy, business executives also offer anecdotal comparisons. Dan Harris, an attorney who has worked in both countries, blogs:[38] "I have been to China probably five times as often as I have been to Russia and yet I have been shaken down for bribes by police officers in Russia more than once and that has never happened to me in China." He also asserts that Chinese authorities are less likely than their Russian counterparts to demand speed money – bribes or fees to expedite the processing of licenses. In his words, "[In Russia] what they're essentially telling you is if you don't pay the fee to expedite your trademark application, your company trademark application is going to go into that 'dark corner' over there. And that generally does not happen in China."

Is Harris' personal observation shared by other expert respondents? Is Sun or Wedeman correct? The UCI provides an objective basis to assess various observational claims, which, expressed in my typology, translate into three research questions.

- Does China have lower levels of *grand theft* than Russia, which Sun and Wedeman refer to as "looting"?
- Does China have higher levels of *access money* than Russia, which Sun terms "rent-seeking" and "profit-sharing"?
- Does China have lower levels of *speed money* than Russia, in Harris' terms, "a fee to expedite things" and "shakedowns for bribes" by police?

---

[35] Blanchard and Shleifer (2001); see also Walder (2002; 2003). [36] Sun (1999).
[37] Wedeman (2012).
[38] Dan Harris, "Why China Is Better Than Russia for Business," China Law Blog, 15 December 2013, www.chinalawblog.com/2013/12/why-china-is-way-better-than-russia.html (accessed 21 November 2019).

Figure 2.5 China vs. Russia's UCI scores.

Figure 2.5 presents my answers to these questions. First, I find that China has lower levels of *grand theft* than Russia. In my survey, China scores 6.1 out of 10 on grand theft, lower than Russia's 7.2. Under grand theft, one sub-category question asked how common it is for political leaders to siphon large amounts of embezzled funds overseas. The mean response in China is 2.8 out of 5 (which translates into "sometimes occurs"), lower than Russia's score of 3.8 ("commonly occurs").

Second, does China have higher levels of *access money* than Russia? No, in that the two countries have almost identical scores. But the most dominant mode of corruption in China is access money, whereas in Russia it is speed money. Is Wedeman's insistence that China has "plenty of" both types of corruption – grand theft and access money – correct? Here, it depends on what "plenty" means. It's true that China has both types of corruption, and the frequency of both grand theft and access money in China is above average. But compared with Russia, grand theft (or looting) in China is less prevalent.

Does China have lower levels of *speed money* than Russia? Yes, China's level of speed money (6.6) is lower than in Russia (8.6), being closest to Thailand (6.4) in my survey. In my dataset, Russia ranks second only to Bangladesh (8.7) in the prevalence of speed money. This supports Harris' impression that paying bribes "to expedite things" or to avoid shakedowns is common in Russia and certainly more so than in China. For a fine-grained view, we can further compare their scores on two sub-categories of speed money (Table 2.3): petty bribes to avoid police penalties and bribes

TABLE 2.3 *China vs. Russia on speed money*

Category	Survey question	China's score	Russia's score
Speed money	Police officers release drivers who are stopped for speeding once a bribe is paid on the spot.	2.7	4.5
	To speed up the process of obtaining permits, businesses pay minor bribes to approving officials.	3.5	4.1

that speed up the process of obtaining permits. In both, China scores lower than Russia, but the gap is wider in the first sub-category.

While my survey is by no means perfect, it provides some systematically collected evidence that the structure of corruption in Russia is indeed distinct from China's. I find that not only does Russia have a higher aggregate level of corruption than China, but also it exhibits more damaging types of corruption – grand theft, speed money, and petty theft – that inhibit business activities and deplete public wealth. The evidence suggests that whereas abrupt political liberalization in Russia unleashed all types of corruption, China has been more effective at curbing growth-damaging corruption. It also appears to exercise more discipline over street-level bureaucrats and police officers.

CHINA VS. INDIA. Bundled scores of corruption can mask important structural variances, as a comparison of China and India vividly demonstrates. Although the two nations are political opposites – China is the world's largest autocracy while India is the largest democracy – both have sprawling territories with multiple levels of government. They also display nearly identical aggregate levels of corruption according to standard indices. In 2017, China's CPI score was 41 and India's was 40. In my survey, China and India rank next to each other, too. Yet as Figure 2.6 shows, their composition of corruption diverges.

In terms of the structure of corruption, China and India are virtually mirror images of each other. Petty extortion and speed money – corruption involving street-level bureaucrats – are more prevalent in India than in China by a margin of 0.7 points and 1.4 points, respectively. On the other hand, grand theft and access money – corruption involving elites – are more widespread in China, by 0.6 points in each category.

Figure 2.6 China vs. India's UCI scores.

A comparison of China and India sharply illustrates the distinction between speed money (bribes to overcome administrative barriers or delays) and access money (graft for buying privileged access). For a nuanced breakdown, Table 2.4 compares China's and India's score on four survey questions, two about speed money and two about access money. Although Chinese citizens do complain about arbitrary fee extraction and petty bribery,[39] these problems are even more endemic in India. For example *The New York Times* reported that hospital staff in India routinely demand petty bribes to deliver even basic public services, from providing wheelchairs to allowing parents to carry their newborns.[40] It is also more common for businesses in India (4.5) than in China (3.5) to pay petty bribes to accelerate the process of obtaining permits, a classic example of speed money.

This finding is consistent with the Global Corruption Barometer (GCB), an original survey that TI conducts across countries and separate from the CPI, focusing on citizens' personal experiences with petty corruption. The latest GCB, conducted between 2015 and 2017, asked respondents whether they had to pay a bribe during the last 12 months in order to access public services.[41] The survey found that petty bribery was

[39] Lü (2000); Bernstein and Lü (2003).
[40] Celia Dugger, "When a Cuddle with Your Infant Requires a Bribe," *New York Times*, 30 August 2005.
[41] Website of the Global Corruption Barometer, www.transparency.org/whatwedo/pub lication/people_and_corruption_asia_pacific_global_corruption_barometer (accessed 21 November 2019).

TABLE 2.4 *China vs. India on speed money and access money*

Category of corruption	Survey question	China's score	India's score
Speed money	At public hospitals, patients are expected to pay hospital staff "tips" or small bribes for even the most basic services, from having wheelchairs to seeing newborn infants at nurseries.	3.1	3.7
	To speed up the process of obtaining permits, businesses pay minor bribes to approving officials.	3.5	4.5
Access money	By cultivating close ties with a powerful official and paying for his family's expenses, a businessperson gains monopoly access to public construction projects.	4.1	3.3
	A top politician is linked to an extensive network of former associates, protégés, and/or family members, who monopolize power in certain sectors of the economy. While the politician himself never or rarely accepts bribes, a massive amount of bribes flows through his network.	4.3	3.7

highest in India, where 69 percent of respondents reported paying a bribe, compared with only 26 percent in China. According to the GCB, petty bribery is less frequent in China than in Vietnam (65 percent), Thailand (41 percent), and Indonesia (32 percent).

Although China may have less of a problem with petty bribery than India, access money flows abundantly in the middle kingdom. The scandal of Zhou Yongkang, a former member of the Standing Committee of the Politburo who fell during Xi's anti-corruption campaign, revealed that top Chinese politicians cultivate an extensive network of clientele through which massive bribes flow, even if the patron doesn't personally take bribes.[42] My survey finds that this style of elite, network-based bribery is more prevalent in China than in India. Plying the family members of political leaders with perks in order to cultivate close ties with them, as Bo Xilai's saga exposed, is also more common in China.

To sum up, in India, people pay bribes to override obstacles; in China, graft buys lucrative business deals. If the former is analogous to grease, then the latter is more like sludge. This difference stems from the two

---

[42] Lucy Hornby, "Zhou Yongkang: Downfall of a Patron," *Financial Times*, 31 March 2014.

countries' contrasting political regimes.[43] In the Chinese developmental autocracy, power is concentrated in the hands of individual leaders who can easily waive restrictions and open doors. By contrast, the system of checks and balances in India's fragmented democracy gives numerous authorities the power to block decisions but not to unilaterally approve requests or extend deals. Bardhan insightfully illustrates this with a quote from a high-level official in New Delhi: "If you want me to move a file faster, I am not sure if I can help you. But if you want me to stop a file, I can do it immediately."[44]

The economic and social effects of access money and speed money are starkly different. In India "nickel-and-dime bribery ... infects everyday life,"[45] to use the words of Swati Ramanthan, co-founder of I-Paid-A-Bribe. Such corruption directly stifles growth by imposing delays, inefficiencies, and costs on businesses. Worst of all, the burden of petty bribery falls most heavily on the poor. By contrast, access money fuels China's capitalist machine, enriching capitalists who pay for deals and rewarding communist officials for promoting rapid growth; yet it can produce serious harm in the long term by sharpening inequality and distorting policies and capital allocation (Chapter 5).

My comparison of authoritarian China and democratic India prompts a rethinking of the way we study the relationship between regime type (democracy or autocracy) and corruption. According to existing cross-national regressions, which all rely on bundled corruption scores, democracy measures do not consistently correlate positively or negatively with corruption.[46] My analysis brings attention to a different dimension: the effects of regime type on the dominant *type* of corruption, rather than its overall level. But existing corruption indices fail to capture qualitative variation, as Stephenson pointedly observes: "reliance on perception

---

[43] But not all nascent democracies are equal. Differences in the stability of party systems can affect how governments manage the distribution of rents and private sector development (Pitcher 2012).

[44] Bardhan (1997; 2010).

[45] Stephanie Strom, "Website Shines Light on Petty Bribery Worldwide," *CNBC*, 6 March 2012.

[46] See review by Stephenson (2015). Furthermore, as democracies tend to be rich countries, it's hard to separate the effect of democracy on corruption from that of wealth (Fisman and Golden 2017, 177).

index scores may cause a change in the form of corruption to be mis-interpreted as a change in the level of corruption."[47] The way to correct this problem is to develop an index of different types of corruption, as I do here.

CHINA VS. THE UNITED STATES. We now come to a third, intri-guing comparison: China and the United States. In terms of aggre-gate corruption scores, the two countries are miles apart. The United States is ranked among the least corrupt countries in the world, rated No. 16 (out of 180 countries) by the CPI in 2017, whereas China trailed at No. 77. Unlike China, the United States does not confront daily corruption scandals among its top officials, nor do middle-class American citizens normally encounter bribe-taking pub-lic officers.

Yet the two countries have something in common: access money is the dominant mode of corruption. To be sure, the level of corruption in China is much higher than in the United States across all four categories, but the gap narrows when it comes to access money. Indeed, the US score on access money (6.9) is above average in my dataset of 15 countries, higher than Thailand (6.5), South Korea (6.1), and even Ghana (5.8). This striking statistic would be obscured if we relied solely on bundled scores.

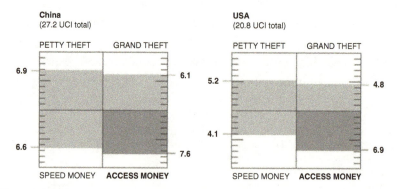

Figure 2.7 China vs. the United States' UCI scores.

[47] Stephenson (2015, 108).

TABLE 2.5 *China vs. the United States on access money*

Survey question	China's score	United States' score
A top politician is linked to an extensive network of former associates, protégés, and/or family members, who monopolize power in certain sectors of the economy. While the politician himself never or rarely accepts bribes, a massive amount of bribes flows through his network.	4.3	3.0
Major figures move back and forth between the public and the private sector, and there are no laws forbidding this practice.	3.3	4.4
To influence laws and regulations in favor of their industry, major corporations collectively employ lobbyists or professional middlemen, who supply policymakers with various perks, but not cash bribes.	3.5	4.6

Even more interesting is that different forms of access money dominate in China and the United States. To illustrate, Table 2.5 compares their scores on three survey questions. The first vignette represents the practice of cultivating extensive client networks for bribe-taking, in which China clearly dominates. Yet when we turn to revolving door practices and regulatory capture through lobbying – the second and third vignettes – the United States dominates. This suggests that access money in the US capitalist democracy is institutional, which is consistent with arguments made by several American scholars.[48] Pointing to Congress as an example, Lessig observes, "We could imagine an institution that is corrupt even when no one within that institution is also corrupt."[49] In short, whereas access money in the United States today is primarily institutional, in China it is enmeshed within personal relationships and still involve bribes and illegal actions. One might say China has a backward version of access money.

REVISITING THE CORRUPTION–GROWTH NEXUS

One of the most widely cited analyses of the impact of corruption on economic growth is Mauro's 1995 article "Corruption and Growth." The author's regression analysis of 70 countries uses bundled indices of corruption and red-tape from Business International (BI). He concludes

[48] Stockman (2013); Teachout (2014); Lessig (2018).   [49] Lessig (2018, Kindle 231).

that "the negative association between corruption and investment, as well as growth, is significant, both in a statistical and in an economic sense."[50] More recent statistical studies generally support Mauro's finding,[51] although a few do not.[52]

My study highlights two main problems with this approach. Mauro and others rely on bundled scores of corruption, which under-measure or ignore access money. In fact, this type of corruption can be salient among high-income countries, as demonstrated by the case of the United States. A second problem is that standard regression analyses only capture the effects of corruption on a cross-section of income levels or growth rates. They do not capture lag effects or tipping points, whereby the accumulation of risks and distortions erupts in a major fallout, such as the 2008 financial crisis.

My dataset of observations on 15 countries is too small to make causal inferences; nevertheless, exploring the correlations between unbundled corruption scores and economic growth may yield some useful insights. Figure 2.8 shows a clear negative relationship between the UCI score and GDP per capita across the countries in my dataset. Consistently with prior studies, wealthier countries are less corrupt.

But when we break up the UCI aggregate score into speed money and access money, as shown in Figure 2.9, we observe that although wealthy countries consistently have lower levels of speed money than poor countries ($r^2 = 0.76$), they do not always have lower levels of access money ($r^2 = 0.31$).

In other words, we need to qualify the assertion that wealthier countries are less corrupt by asking what type of corruption is in question. The standard practice of combining bundled corruption scores and GDP measures in cross-national regressions has produced a flawed yet powerful consensus: corruption always impedes growth. Imagine what regression results might look like if the UCI were extended across a large number of countries. We would be able to examine the relationship

---

[50] Mauro (1995).   [51] La Porta *et al.* (1999); Treisman (2000; 2007); Mo (2001).

[52] Svensson (2005) replicates Mauro's study using updated data and finds that even though the estimated coefficient of corruption on economic growth is negative, the results are not statistically significant.

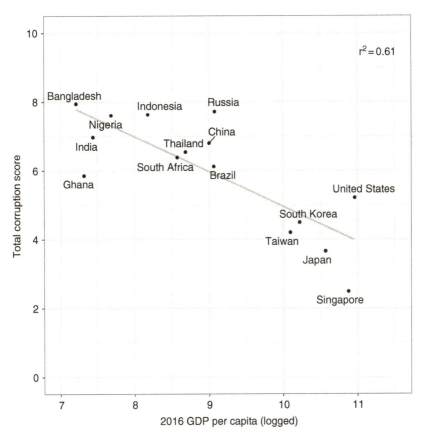

Figure 2.8 UCI scores and income levels are negatively correlated.

between types of corruption and wealth levels, instead of fixating on overall levels of corruption.

ADVANCING SYSTEMATIC QUALITATIVE COMPARISONS

Apart from improving quantitative indices of corruption, my survey serves to advance *systematic* qualitative comparisons across countries. While there is an abundance of excellent qualitative studies on corruption, this literature is constrained by subjectivity. Observers can have vastly different opinions on the dominant type of corruption in each country. Consider, for example, two competing characterizations of Chinese corruption.

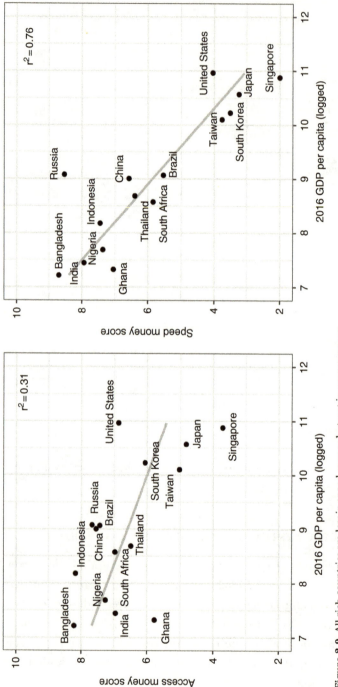

Figure 2.9 All rich countries are low in speed money but not in access money.

- Wedeman: "Corruption in China was similar to many of the worst examples of endemic and economically destructive corruption elsewhere in the developing world."
- Huang: "Corruption in China helped to navigate around excessive regulations and controls in an overly centralized bureaucracy."[53]

Which of these conflicting descriptions is correct? With data on corruption structures, we can evaluate these statements *objectively*. Is China's corruption similar to "economically destructive corruption elsewhere in the developing world," as Wedeman claims? My survey indicates that it is not – as an example, just compare the level and structure of China's and Nigeria's UCI. Was corruption in China primarily about "navigating around excessive regulations and controls" (the equivalent of speed money in my typology), as Huang perceives? My survey shows that speed money in China is moderate, at a level similar to Thailand, but its most prevalent type of corruption is in fact access money – graft for buying special deals.

My approach can apply beyond China to any cross-national comparative study. In qualitative comparisons, the standard practice is to illustrate each typology with a country case. For example, Johnston selects four countries to represent four varieties of corruption: Japan as "influence markets," South Korea as "elite cartels," India as "oligarchs and clans," and China as "official moguls."[54] A clear problem is that different analysts may classify the same cases in different categories, depending on their focus or judgment.[55] This problem is exacerbated in large and fast-evolving countries, exemplified by China.[56] Another problem with this conventional method of national classification is the assumption that all countries have only one type of corruption[57] – in fact, as the UCI shows, each country has a combination of multiple types in varying degrees.

---

[53] Wedeman (2012, 5); Yukon Huang, "The truth about Chinese Corruption," *Diplomat*, 29 May 2015.

[54] Johnston (2008).

[55] For example, see Alice Evans' review of *Deals and Development*, in *LSE Review of Books*, 9 January 2018.

[56] In China studies, this is known as the "blind men and elephant" problem (Ang 2016; 2018c).

[57] This method is applied not only in the study of corruption but also in seminal frameworks in political economy. For example, see North *et al.* (2009); Khan (2010); and Pritchett *et al.* (2018).

CONCLUSION

Corruption is not a homogeneous problem, as the UCI visualizes. Standard bundled indices like the CPI mask important structural variances across countries. For example, China and India have identical aggregate corruption scores, yet access money dominates in China while speed money prevails in India. Wealthy countries with low aggregate corruption scores may have higher levels of access money than low-income countries; the United States is a case in point. Unlike standard measures, the UCI makes a clear distinction between the *quantity* and *quality* of corruption. Each UCI visual (Figure 2.1) simultaneously displays the quantity of corruption (in each of the four categories and in total) and where corruption is most concentrated.

The UCI should be viewed as a pilot, and much more work is needed to refine its design and implementation. The patterns in the survey are only suggestive, and future research is necessary to confirm or disprove them. Nevertheless, by specifying a clear, common set of criteria for measuring corruption structure, analysts may now debate procedures of data collection rather than opinions and impressions. This is a big step forward.

Below I highlight three comparative patterns that my analysis suggests.

- *The structure of corruption matters as much as the overall level of corruption.* Corruption in China is less damaging than in Russia because of divergence in composition. Both countries are rife with cronyism, but China has lower levels of corruption that directly stifles growth: speed money, petty theft, and grand theft.

- *Regime type affects which type of corruption dominates.* In authoritarian China, capitalists court politicians for their power to make sweeping decisions, whereas in India's fragmented democracy, state actors extract rents by blocking approvals. Hence, bribery assumes different dominant forms in the two developing countries. The effect of democracy on corruption, however, appears to be moderated by levels of economic development and state capacity. Although the United States is also a democracy, access money dominates, as the government successfully brought petty bribery under control through more than a century of administrative and political reform (see the section "Two Gilded Ages" in Chapter 7).

- *Not all systems of access money are the same.* Compared with institutional corruption in the United States, China's style of access money is crude in that elite exchanges are enmeshed with personal relationships, mostly illegal, and still involve bribes.

The findings in this chapter supplied the first important clue to the Chinese paradox of corruption and growth – access money, rather than corruption with theft or speed money, dominates. Although access money poses long-term economic risks and undermines the CCP's legitimacy, it does not deter private investment and business activities in the short term. But how did China arrive at its present pattern of corruption? What was the corruption landscape like in the early decades of market liberalization, and why did it change over time? Chapter 3 will trace the evolution of Chinese corruption.

CHAPTER 3

Unbundling Corruption over Time

CHINA'S CORRUPTION IS "RISING," "GETTING WORSE," AND "spiraling out of control"[1] – or so the media breathlessly reports. But observers rarely look below the surface. China is not corrupt in the same manner as other notoriously corrupt states, as I showed in Chapter 2. Unlike India and Russia, where petty bribery (what I term speed money) is most rife, or Nigeria, where state elites brazenly looted state coffers (grand theft), China's corruption is distinguished by an abundance of access money – elite exchanges of money and power.

How did China arrive at its present structure of corruption? This chapter traces the evolution of corrupt practices from the beginnings of market reform in 1978 to the present day. A temporal analysis shows that access money, specifically in the form of bribery, has indeed become not only more widespread but grander, involving larger stakes and more powerful players. At the same time, levels of non-transactional corruption, such as embezzlement, misappropriation of public funds, and bureaucratic extortion, have been declining since the 2000s. Thus, corruption in China is not "rising" across the board – in fact, it is shrinking in some areas even as cronyism and graft flourish.[2]

I highlight two forces driving the present pattern of corruption in China. The first is the leadership's monumental 1993 decision to replace

---

[1] "China Slips Down Corruption Perception Index," *CNN*, 3 December 2014; "What Motivates Chinese President Xi Jinping's Anti-corruption Drive?," *NPR*, 24 October 2017; "Xi's Corruption Crackdown," *The National Interest*, 3 April 2014.

[2] My findings are consistent with an excellent earlier study by Ko and Weng (2012) that employed data prior to 2008; since then, I find, bribery grew larger in scale and evolved more sophisticated forms.

central planning with a "socialist market economy," that is, a market economy in which the state plays a dominant role. Communist officials became active promoters of private businesses and new industries, while still maintaining control over key resources.[3] This gave them considerable power over a massive emerging market, attracting a surging class of private capitalists to buy their favors. The second factor is the central government's rollout of comprehensive administrative reforms, beginning in 1998, which quietly raised the state's ability to monitor public finances and deter non-transactional malfeasance. Although the rise of crony capitalism in China is widely known,[4] this second development is overlooked.[5]

Corruption was both a product and a driver of China's transition from a command to a market economy. To unpack the coevolution of the economy and corruption, I first review the history of China's reform process. I then show the evolving patterns of corruption by drawing on the best available source of data for this purpose: official statistics on corruption prosecutions. To supplement this analysis, I also look at media mentions. Jointly, my examination reveals a clear reversal of trends in transactional and non-transactional corruption: after 2000, the former spikes while the latter drops.

CHINA'S EVOLVING LANDSCAPE OF CORRUPTION

"China changes too quickly!" is a common refrain among my interviewees. As China has transformed so rapidly and dramatically over the past four decades, any description of the country at any point in time is only a fleeting snapshot.[6] In the 1980s, 1990s, 2000s, and 2010s, the state's role in the economy changed, as did the dominant modes of corruption. My analysis will try to capture this moving picture in several distinct stages, each punctuated by a change in national leadership, crisis, or major

---

[3] Such key resources include land and finance (Huang 2017).
[4] Pei (2016); "China's Decentralized Kleptocracy," *Democracy Digest*, 18 October 2016.
[5] Notable exceptions are Yang (2004); Ko and Weng (2012).
[6] Drawing conclusions from a single snapshot is partial – even misleading; analysts must take further steps to trace a whole causal chain of mutual feedbacks, or what I term coevolution (Ang 2016).

policy break. By necessity, I focus only on those parts of history relevant to corruption and skip over many details.[7]

THE 1980S: GROWING OUT OF THE PLAN. Corruption existed during the Maoist era, but the scale was small and the forms rudimentary. Petty bribes were given in-kind through food and gifts in exchange for access to state-allocated goods such as ration coupons and housing.[8] Corruption was limited under Mao not because bureaucrats were morally upright, as fervent Maoists believe, but because people were impoverished and punishments were harsh. As one official recounted, "During the [Maoist era], people were summarily executed for even a bit of corruption. Nobody dared to be corrupt."[9] Moreover, although monetary corruption was scarce, abuse of power was rampant, as Bachman points out: "Authorities could extract 'favors' – such as sex in exchange for recommendations to attend university – or when quotas came down for people to purge, officials would purge individuals whom they disliked."[10] When markets opened and the economy sputtered to life, however, the currency of corruption shifted from brute power to money.

Following Mao's death in 1976, Deng Xiaoping finally emerged as the nation's paramount leader, who, in December of 1978, launched the Party's "second revolution" – reform and opening. As Walder points out, the transition from plan to market generates "new opportunities for elite enrichment," but how such enrichment occurs and its consequences depend on the extent of regime change.[11] Unlike the Soviet leadership, who simultaneously unleashed economic and political reform, Deng chose cautiously to embark on market liberalization while maintaining the monopoly rule of the Chinese Communist Party (CCP).[12] The

---

[7] Vogel (2011); Coase and Wang (2012); Ang (2016); Naughton (2018).

[8] Andrew Wedeman, "Growth and Corruption in China," *China Research Center (Website)*, 30 December 2012.

[9] Interview B2013-326.   [10] Bachman (2017).

[11] Another factor was constraints on the appropriation of state assets by political insiders. In China this process was mitigated by a delayed process of privatization, along with growth of a large private sector, whereas in the Soviet Union assets were rampantly converted by elites into private wealth (Walder 2003, 901).

[12] Although Deng spurned Western-style democracy, he did reform the political system – just not in the manner that Western observers expected. Deng unveiled a host of bureaucratic reforms, such as mandatory retirement and changing bureaucratic targets,

reformist leadership maintained tight appointment and disciplinary control over officials, even as it extended economic and fiscal autonomy to local governments.[13] This sent a clear signal to party apparatchiks that they would benefit from market reforms so long as they played by the party's revised rules.[14] Thus, whereas market transition in the Soviet Union spawned lawless corruption and rampant looting of state assets, which soon eroded the regime, in China corruption spread but with restraints.[15]

On the economic side, Deng and his compatriots also maintained a gradualist approach by introducing market activities on the margins of a planned economy – also known as "growing out of the plan."[16] In the countryside, the CCP partially revived private farming. In the cities, state-owned enterprises (SOEs) could sell goods to consumers once they had met their quotas. Township and village governments set up their own factories, known as Township and Village Enterprises (TVEs), which flourished like "sprouts after a spring rain" once the Party officially endorsed them. The state retained price controls but gradually reduced their scope.[17] All of these market reforms supplemented rather than replaced central planning.

As markets emerged in the 1980s, so did corruption. The forms of corruption that proliferated were particular to a mixed economy with central planning at its core. For example, managers of state-owned enterprises acquired goods cheaply at planned prices and sold them at higher prices on the market. Another example was the discretionary use of extra-budgetary funds. To incentivize local governments to promote economic growth and industrialization, central authorities allowed them to keep all profits generated by locally based collective enterprises as "extra-budgetary revenue."[18] But the absence of central oversight

---

which injected a dose of accountability, competition, and partial limits on power into the massive bureaucracy (Ang 2018).

[13] Oi (1992; 1999); Montinola *et al.* (1995); Walder (1995b).

[14] China's gradualist approach contrasted with "shock therapy" in Russia and Eastern Europe that sought to rapidly dismantle communism and strip communist officials of power and privilege (Walder 1996a).

[15] Walder (2003).   [16] Naughton (1995).

[17] This is known as dual-track pricing. The dual-track logic also appeared in bureaucratic compensation practices, as documented in Chapter 4.

[18] Oi (1992; 1999).

encouraged widespread misuse and illegal diversion of public funds. Within each locality, agencies all of stripes also joined the mad rush to generate extra-budgetary revenue by collecting fees, fines, and levies, and by running side businesses. Their income was stashed away in unauthorized accounts known as "small treasuries."[19]

During the 1980s and well into the 1990s, the spread of extractive profiteering led to widespread complaints about "the three arbitraries" (*sanluan*): arbitrary fees, arbitrary fines, and arbitrary levies. The third item – *tanpai* – refers to various charges that local agencies imposed through coercive means.[20] For example, in addition to collecting fees and fines, regulatory agencies pressured businesses to pay for overpriced magazines that they published or to sponsor events solely for the purpose of wining and dining. Lu labels these actions "organizational corruption," that is, collective actions taken by agencies "to achieve monetary or material gains for the agency as a whole."[21] Petty bribery among individual bureaucrats spread, too, as an emergent and politically weak class of private entrepreneurs were forced to pay speed money to overcome bureaucratic hurdles and red-tape.[22]

Yet this flourishing of petty corruption did not impede economic growth. Granting local governments and local agencies the right to generate and retain extra-budgetary revenue may be understood as part of a nationwide "profit-sharing" scheme: public employees took a cut of the revenue produced by their organizations, be it taxes, fees, or profits (more details can be found in Chapter 4).[23] This incentivized the entire bureaucracy to embrace market reforms and dive headlong into making money. It also relieved the state's formal budgetary burden by allowing Party-state organizations and public service providers to "self-finance," topping up their own salary at a time when formal pay was abysmally low and state funding was scarce. In this particular context of profit-sharing, it may be said that the economy took off because of – rather than despite – corruption. Yet this system produced clear drawbacks: excessive discretion, bureaucratic

---

[19] Lü (2000); Wedeman (2000); Tsai (2004).

[20] During this period, arbitrary and excessive extraction of fees from farmers by township and village cadres was also rampant in the countryside, provoking mass protests (Bernstein and Lü 2003).

[21] Lu (2000).   [22] Sun (2004); Tsai (2007a).   [23] Ang (2016).

extortion, petty bribery, and profiteering. Such corruption also burdened businesses and stoked public resentment.

Even though Deng only partially introduced markets on the margins of a planned economy, the 1980s achieved commendable economic results: GDP per capita grew 7.5 percent annually. But this progress was violently interrupted in 1989 when mass protests broke out in Tiananmen Square in Beijing and then spread to other cities. Corruption was one of the rallying calls for political change. Tragically, the protests ended in a bloody crackdown on 4 June 1989. Shortly afterward, the conservative faction clamped down on liberal policies, and, at this critical juncture, China could have reverted to Maoism.

But Deng turned the tide around. In 1992, he went on his famous Southern Tour, urging the nation to continue market reform. Deng's political maneuvers succeeded in large part because the 1980s was a golden decade of broad-based development that economists termed "reform without losers."[24] Living standards improved across all walks of life, particularly among farmers. In other words, there was incipient popular demand for rekindling the flames of reform, and Deng's swan song was to light the match. By the end of the Southern Tour, the 88-year-old patriarch had set China on a firm path toward an accelerated phase of market liberalization (Figure 3.1).

FROM 1993 TO 2000: BUILDING A SOCIALIST MARKET ECONOMY.
China's reform is popularly equated with Deng's slogan of "crossing the river by touching the stones." In fact, this mantra applies only to the 1980s, when reforms were bottom-up and experimental without a clear vision of what lay across the river. But in 1993, that vision became clear when the new leadership under President Jiang Zemin and Premier Zhu Rongji announced the Party's decision to establish a "socialist market economy." It was this post-1993 phase that propelled China to phenomenal growth.

What is a socialist market economy?[25] Western observers may dismiss the slogan as ceremonial, but the choice of words is revealing: "socialist"

---

[24] Lau *et al.* (2000).

[25] As Hu Shuli, editor of *Caixin*, points out: "Don't forget, the word socialism was already in use, but it was the first time that the concept of market economy was proposed by the central government." See interview with Hu Shuli, "Changing China's Market

Figure 3.1 Banner in Shenzhen, showing Deng Xiaoping and the words "Stick firmly to the Party's fundamental path for 100 years."

is an adjective appended to the goal of achieving a "market economy." Building a socialist market economy meant replacing central planning with market mechanisms and drastically reducing state ownership in the economy. Beijing scrapped state-allocated production quotas and price controls after 1993. "The orthodox planning system disappeared with barely a whimper, scarcely noticed," Naughton wrote.[26] This was accompanied by a massive wave of state enterprise downsizing and reform in the 1990s, known as "grasping the large but letting go of the small." Tens of thousands of small SOEs shuttered during the 1990s,[27] while the largest SOEs in strategic sectors consolidated, yielding behemoths such as China Mobile and China National Petroleum Corporation – the poster children of state capitalism today.[28]

Framework," *The China Boom Project*, http://chinaboom.asiasociety.org/thread/36/189 (accessed 24 November 2019).

[26] Naughton (2018).

[27] Employment in SOEs dwindled from 76 million in 1992 to 43 million in 2005 (Naughton 2018).

[28] Hsueh (2011).

Meanwhile, TVEs and collective enterprises, a hybrid between state and private enterprises that proliferated during the 1980s, were privatized en masse. Although this process enabled corruption by allowing political insiders and former managers to buy collective assets cheaply, it also sponsored the first broad wave of private entrepreneurs across the country, especially in rural areas.[29] Compare this with Russia, where the overnight privatization of SOEs spawned an oligarchic concentration of wealth.[30]

As the state sector receded, the private sector flourished. From 2000 to 2009, the number of registered private companies grew by 30 percent annually. By 2010, non-state-owned enterprises were estimated to account for 70 percent of China's GDP.[31] The party leadership bolstered this development with its progressively warmer embrace of private entrepreneurs.[32] This support was enshrined in 1999, when the Party wrote into the constitution that the private sector is "an important component of the socialist market economy."

In addition to embracing the private sector, China dramatically opened up to global markets after 1993. Foreign direct investment (FDI), which had previously been allowed only in special economic zones, was now welcomed throughout the country. In 2001, China's entry into the World Trade Organization (WTO) accelerated the adoption of many international best practices and standards, solidifying China's integration into the global economy.

As the economy dramatically privatized and opened up, central reformers rebooted the country's institutions. Unlike the 1980s approach of tinkering on the edges, the post-1993 reform featured the design and implementation of a comprehensive institutional framework, covering fiscal and tax policies, banking and finance, corporate governance, and administrative reforms. For the leadership, reforming governance was a top priority as it needed state capacity to carry out the regulatory functions of the central government, as well as to foster a conducive environment for private businesses.

---

[29] See my historical case study of Blessed County in Zhejiang province (Ang 2016, Chapter 6).
[30] McFaul (1995); Walder 2003; Fisman and Wang (2014).
[31] "Let a Million Flowers Bloom," *The Economist*, 10 March 2011.
[32] Tsai (2007a); Dickson (2008).

Figure 3.2 President Bill Clinton listens as Chinese Premier Zhu Rongji makes a statement on the South Lawn of the White House in 1999.

At the helm of this administrative modernization campaign was Zhu Rongji (Figure 3.2), a leader famous for his fiery temper and iron resolve. Starting in 1998, the central government pushed through a wide range of reforms that included standardizing budget planning and implementation, establishing a single treasury account system, adopting procurement rules, separating accounting firms from government agencies, divesting the military of its side businesses, promulgating a new Civil Service Law, and more (see Chapter 4 for more details). Although these technical reforms received scant attention in the scholarly literature and none in the media, they had real effects in "strengthening the fiscal and regulatory sinews of economic governance," Yang emphasizes.[33]

Why did this modernization drive progress quickly only in the 1990s? Yang argues that it was the combination of "changing economic conditions, leadership, and crises" that catalyzed the process. In 1993, the Jiang–Zhu leadership was under pressure to pull the country forward after the Tiananmen crisis. The preexisting communist bureaucracy was

[33] Yang (2004).

designed for a planned economy; the embrace of a global market economy, however, must be complemented by a modern administrative state. According to Yang, the Asian financial crisis of 1997 "gave the final push for a modern rationalization drive," as leaders scrambled to stabilize the economic and banking system.[34] Another key factor I would add is that it was in the interests of local leaders throughout China to cooperate with these reforms. Modernizing administration and controlling petty corruption enhances their ability to attract investments and expand markets, yet these reforms would not restrain them from collecting grand transactional rents.

Taking these developments into account, it is no surprise that China's economy boomed after 1993. For the next two decades, China clocked up a spectacular average GDP growth rate of 10 percent. In 2010, it surpassed Japan and clinched the spot of the world's second-largest economy. Given these statistics, one might also expect that the country drastically reduced corruption, but in reality, the opposite occurred. Investigations of corruption spiked from the 1990s onward. And corruption scandals, which previously had involved only a few thousand Yuan of arbitraged goods or petty bribes, morphed into the stuff of political thrillers, featuring massive graft, mistresses, mafia, and even murder. In 2017 these stories were made into a hit TV series called "In the Name of the People." In the eyes of the public and the leadership, the problem of corruption grew more and more severe.

Why is that? The post-1993 reforms did not diminish the role of the state in the economy; they changed it. During the 1980s, the government's primary job was still to plan and command, deciding what to produce, how much, and at what price. After central planning was dismantled in 1993, Party-state officials took on new roles: fostering new industries, promoting investment, borrowing funds from the market, urban planning, demolishing and building at a frenzied pace. These roles gave communist officials new sources of power, "in ways that were never possible in the Soviet system," Walder stresses.[35]

Hence, although centrally led administrative reforms increased state capacity and curbed non-transactional forms of malfeasance, new

---

[34] Yang (2004, 2, 36).   [35] Walder (2018).

varieties of corruption flourished, including the stripping of state assets by political insiders,[36] collusion with smugglers and thugs,[37] the sale of government offices,[38] and, above all, extensive networks of massive graft.

THE 2000S: BONANZAS AND BUBBLES. The value of political and regulatory power spiraled further in the 2000s, as land-based public finance proliferated.[39] Although land cannot be sold, local governments can lease time-limited rights for "land transfer fees" that go directly to local coffers. Nationwide, land-related proceeds ballooned from 51 billion Yuan in 1999 to an estimated 3.2 trillion Yuan in 2012.[40] This spawned an extremely lucrative market in real estate, where developers readily offered officeholders large kickbacks in exchange for prized parcels of land.

Land proceeds financed a bonanza of public infrastructure construction in the 2000s and onward (Figure 3.3). Between 2007 and 2017, the length of Chinese highways more than doubled from 54,000 to 130,000 kilometers, "enough to go around the world three times," the State Council boasted on its website.[41] Every year since 2011, another 10,000 kilometers has been added to this network. The frenzied construction of subways was just as spectacular. In 2009 alone, central regulators approved metro projects in 19 cities totaling 2,100 kilometers, an investment of 800 billion Yuan. Today, the length of subways in Beijing and Shanghai exceeds that of New York City, London and Tokyo.[42]

Although the physical expanse of Chinese infrastructure is dazzling, the way it was financed is deeply troubling. Funds for these projects were funneled through a proliferation of non-transparent "investment vehicles" (*rongzi pingtai*), shell companies set up by local governments and agencies to borrow loans. In 2008, to cushion the blow of the US financial

---

[36] Ding (2000); Sun (2004); Wedeman (2012).   [37] Sun (2004); Pei (2006).

[38] Zhu (2008).

[39] In 1994, Zhu's policy of fiscal recentralization drastically tightened the budgetary constraints of local governments. In this context, land use rights provided a crucial source of alternative income.

[40] World Bank and DRC of State Council (2014).

[41] "China has 130,000 km of highways, the most in the world," Website of the State Council, News Section, 27 August 2017.

[42] Hans-Ulrich Riedel, "Chinese Metro Boom," *International Railway Journal*, 19 November 2014.

Figure 3.3 Land proceeds financed an infrastructure boom in the 2000s, including high-speed rail, as seen here in Hangzhou.

crisis, the Hu–Wen leadership announced a US$586 billion stimulus package, the largest in the country's history. Much of this capital fell into the hands of SOEs, which invested profligately in local government vehicles and further accelerated the pace of infrastructure construction.[43] The result was rapidly mounting debt. In 2011 the National Audit Office released the results of its audit for the first time, estimating local government debts, excluding townships, to be 11 trillion Yuan.[44] In 2018, total debt ballooned to 18.4 trillion Yuan, about 20 percent of gross GDP.[45]

China is often perceived as exceptional, but the situation today closely parallels the "taxless (public) financing" in America during the nineteenth century, when state governments built massive projects such as the Erie Canal by selling bonds through investment companies and charters

[43] Lardy (2019, 79).

[44] "China's Local Government Debts Exceed 10 Trillion Yuan," *China Daily*, 26 June 2011.

[45] Frank Tang, "China Local Government Forced to Rob Peter to Pay Paul," *South China Morning Post*, 3 April 2019.

(monopoly rights) to businesses instead of raising taxes on residents. Taxless financing led to widespread corruption and incurred contingent liabilities (debt that manifests itself when projects fail to generate expected revenue). These accumulated risks eventually imploded in 1837 – America's first great depression.[46] China today faces a similar problem. Shadow financing massively increased its stock of physical infrastructure, but it has also created a hotbed of shady deals and graft.

The influence that Chinese officials exercised over a burgeoning economy and new financing instruments was amplified by the concentration of personal power in an authoritarian regime. At the local levels, the making of important development policies need not undergo legislative debates or public consultation. Instead, leaders can "slam the table" (*paiban*) and make unilateral decisions with far-reaching consequences. Ji Jianye, former party secretary of Yangzhou and later mayor of Nanjing, is an archetypal case (see Chapter 5). Ji's nickname was "Mayor Bulldozer." In Nanjing, his "Operation Iron Wrist" razed an astonishing 10 million square meters of unlicensed buildings within a year, equivalent to 66 Forbidden Cities, making it the largest scale of demolition in the city's history. It is unimaginable for democratically elected politicians to behave as Mayor Bulldozer did without provoking a vigorous public backlash and losing votes.

Authoritarian power paired with a single-minded focus on economic growth spurred rapid urbanization and development, but also created ample room for corruption. As a leader, Ji could designate chosen plots of land for commercial purposes, acquire plots of land cheaply from farmers and resell them at high prices to developers, grant preferential tax breaks, and distribute a bounty of procurement and construction projects to family members and cronies. Because they outrank local banks and financial institutions, local leaders can also direct them to extend credit to favored companies. When Ji was finally netted for corruption in 2013, he was charged for taking more than 10 million Yuan in bribes.

Set against this backdrop of titanic emerging markets, an expansive state role in the economy, and trillions worth of slush funds are extensive

---

[46] Ang (2016, Conclusion); Wallis (2005).

personal networks that coagulate around figures of power. Politicians form tight relationships of mutual dependence among themselves, family members, and private capitalists.[47] The result, Walder incisively notes, is "super-clientelism," the creation of a "much more powerful, wealthy and resourceful Party elite" than anything imaginable in the previous decades,[48] a hierarchy where webs of power and wealth extend from the very top down to the lowest level.

FROM 2012 TO THE PRESENT: THE POST-REFORM ERA.
President Xi Jinping's coming to power in 2012 marked the beginning of a new era. As Minzner pronounces, "China's reform era is ending."[49] Just a few decades ago, China was one of the poorest countries in the world. Now it is a high-middle-income economy. But, although it commands more resources and greater confidence on the world stage, China faces a daunting set of new development challenges, including rising labor costs, shrinking demographic dividends, and an ongoing trade war with the United States.

Warning that corruption would "doom the party and the nation," Xi has made fighting corruption a keystone of his administration. In 2012, he launched the most far-reaching anti-corruption drive in the Party's history (more details are given in Chapter 6), subjecting more than 1.5 million officials to disciplinary action, including some of the Party's most senior leaders. The first to head this crackdown was Wang Qishan, a famously competent top official whom admirers nicknamed "the best premier China never had" (Figure 3.4).[50]

---

[47] The China field saw a boom of studies on the value of "political connections" in the last decade. Political connections are found to exert significant impact across a range of economic activities, from obtaining loans, resolving disputes, to corporate performance (Li *et al.* 2008; Wang 2013; Ang and Jia 2014; Jia 2014).

[48] Walder (2018; 30).

[49] Minzner (2015). Although the dominant view of Xi is that of a strongman who has broken ranks with past institutional norms, some disagree. Solinger argues that rather than having invented a new style of rule, "Xi is engaged in an exploitation of tried approaches for his own purposes" (Solinger 2018, 5). Walder points out that, contrary to popular belief, Xi is not like Mao, as he is "a lifelong bureaucrat for whom political stability and economic progress are the highest goals – an orientation that Mao scorned" (Walder 2018, 21).

[50] Tom Mitchell, Gabriel Wildau, and Henny Sender, "Wang Qishan: China's Enforcer," *The Financial Times*, 24 July 2017.

Figure 3.4 Chinese President Xi Jinping and other top leaders. On the far right is Wang Qishan.

Meanwhile, however, his administration's stance on the state's role in the economy remains contradictory. In 2013, Xi lifted hopes when he declared that markets should play a "decisive" role in allocating resources, but he also said that the state will maintain the "leading" role. As Yukon Huang incisively concludes, "Squaring that circle can be tricky."[51] In fact, under Xi, China saw a deceleration of economic reforms and the resurgence of state dominance in the economy. In 2016 the share of private investment declined relative to state investment in the previous 10 years.[52] Two years later, profit among private industrial companies shrank 27.9 percent from the previous year while that of SOEs grew by 28.5 percent.[53] Private investors became increasingly unnerved by instances of illegal state seizures of private assets and Xi's call for "the Party to exercise leadership over all endeavors in every part of the economy."[54] Facing market tremors in 2018, the Chairman held a high-

---

[51] Yukon Huang, "China's Economy Is not Normal," *The New York Times*, 13 March 2018.
[52] Lardy (2019, 19).
[53] Orange Wang, "Beijing Tilts toward State-Owned Enterprises," *South China Morning Post*, 21 September 2018.
[54] Lardy (2019, 20).

level symposium to assure top private bosses that their property rights would be protected, although it remains to be seen whether he will keep his promise.

CHINA'S GILDED AGE. The Western media often portrays China's political economy as "state capitalism," characterized by *The Economist* as state ownership of giant companies.[55] For the public, this label gives the misimpression of China as still a centrally planned, state-owned economy. In fact, China's economy is predominantly driven by the private sector, which, according to the latest statistics, accounts for 60 percent of GDP, 70 percent of innovation, 80 percent of employment, and 90 percent of new jobs and businesses.[56] Moreover, compared with Russia, the looting of state assets was much more restrained and rents less concentrated in China.[57] Although the Chinese apparatchiks grew richer over the course of market transition, so did millions of newly minted private entrepreneurs. In addition, as described earlier, the central government pushed through vast institutional changes to improve monitoring capacity and align the regulatory apparatus with a capitalist economy.

Perhaps the best way to understand the sources of corruption in contemporary China is to look to America's Gilded Age. Both countries underwent a wrenching structural conversion from rural to urban and closed to global markets, producing once-in-a-generation opportunities for the politically connected and the enterprising (or, in many cases, those with a combination of both qualities) to acquire fabulous wealth. The excesses of America's Gilded Age, however, are intensified in China's single-party autocracy, where the personal powers of elite officials are not checked by elections, civil society, or a free press.

Yet another parallel between the two cases is that their governments did not let all forms of corruption run amok. In the late nineteenth

---

[55] "The Rise of State Capitalism," *The Economist*, 21 January 2012. See also John Bussey, "Tackling the Many Dangers of China's State Capitalism," *Wall Street Journal*, 27 September 2012, which points to the dangers of "tens of thousands of state owned enterprises that dominate half of China's economic output."

[56] "China's Private Sector Contributes to Economic Growth," *Xinhua*, 6 March 2018. See also Lardy (2014).

[57] McFaul (1995); Hoffman (2002); Walder (2003).

century, the Gilded Age in America gave way to the Progressive Era, a period of sweeping political and administrative reforms that subsequently curtailed petty corruption and embezzlement.[58] What's different in China is that a Gilded Age and a Progressive Era collided within a 20-year period. Hence, corruption in China did not rise across the board – it exploded in some areas but shrank in others.

DATA AND ANALYSIS

In this section, I will trace the patterns of corruption highlighted in the historical review by examining the official statistics on corruption investigations, as reported by the procuratorate,[59] a source widely used by other China scholars.[60] In China the two key bodies in charge of investigating corruption are the Party's discipline inspection committees (*jiwei*) and the procuratorate (*jiancha yuan*). Disciplinary actions meted out by the disciplinary committees range in severity from warnings to expulsion from the Party. Where formal criminal charges are pressed, the cases are sent to the procuratorate.

The limitations of official statistics should be acknowledged at the outset. First and foremost, the concept of corruption has changed drastically since market opening. In 1979 as market reforms began, Chinese Criminal Law (CCL) recognized only three acts of corruption: embezzlement, bribery, and dereliction of duty. By 1997, the CCL had expanded its definition of corruption to seven forms and stated that penalties should be linked to the amount of money involved.[61] But, given how quickly corruption evolved, prosecutors struggled to keep pace with the changes, so they stuffed new species of corruption into ambiguous categories such as "possessing large sums of unaccounted income."

Complicating matters further, the government changed the definitions used in official statistics. Prior to 1997, "large-sum" corruption cases

---

[58] Glaeser and Goldin (2006).

[59] Specifically, I drew on the Procuratorate Yearbooks (*jiancha nianjian*) and Law Yearbooks (*falv nianjian*).

[60] Wedeman (2004); Guo (2008); Ko and Weng (2012); Wedeman (2012).

[61] Ko and Weng (2012). In a detailed description of the "phenomenology of reform-era corruption," Sun lists 10 common acts of corruption and four acts of misconduct (Sun 2004).

were defined as embezzlement or bribery involving more than 10,000 Yuan; after 1997, the cut-off point for both categories was raised to 50,000 Yuan, and for misuse of public funds, the threshold was raised from 50,000 to 100,000 Yuan.[62] This means that official statistics before and after 1997 are not comparable. Another significant concern about this data is that it indicates the level of exposed corruption, rather than actual corruption.[63] Indeed, periodic cycles of anti-corruption campaigns may influence the official statistics;[64] my data finds that more cases are reported following Xi's crackdown on corruption in 2012.

Despite these limitations, however, data compiled by the prosecutorial apparatus still provides a useful indicator of corruption trends over time. Moreover, the objective of my analysis is to unpack the composition of corruption, not to use quantitative measures to run regressions. Although anti-corruption campaigns are likely to affect the number of reported cases, they are unlikely to affect the reported *structure* of corruption. No leader has expressed a preference for indicting certain types of corruption over others.

UNBUNDLING CORRUPTION USING OFFICIAL STATISTICS

Many reports have pointed to China's "rising corruption."[65] In fact, in terms of the total number of prosecuted cases and individuals, corruption displayed a cyclical pattern (see Figure 3.5).[66] With the onset of Xi's crackdown in 2012, the figures swept up again. Although only a minority of corruption is committed by high-rank (deputy mayor and above, see Box 3.1) officials, who are few in absolute number, this proportion has steadily risen from 4.5 percent in 1998, to 6 percent in 2011, to 8.4 percent in 2015. Consistently with Wedeman's observation of "intensification," corruption has escalated

[62] Ko and Weng (2012)

[63] Wedeman (2004); Guo (2008); Ko and Weng (2012); Wedeman (2012).

[64] According to Manion (2004), the last anti-corruption campaign before Xi's took place in 1995, which is before the time period of my data in this analysis.

[65] *Wall Street Journal*, 11 January 2012; *New York Times*, 24 August 2011. See also Wedeman (2012).

[66] In 1998, prosecutors investigated slightly more than 35,000 cases of corruption, involving 40,162 officials. This figure reached a peak of 45,266 cases (50,292 officials) in 2001 – coinciding with the implementation of centrally mandated administrative reforms nationwide – before tapering off to an all-time low in 2009.

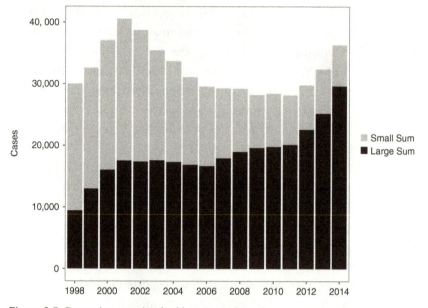

Figure 3.5 Corruption cases involved larger sums over time.

over time to encompass ever larger sums and a higher proportion of high-rank officials.[67] But we must look beyond aggregate numbers, as they obscure a yet more important feature: changes in the structure of corruption over time.

To examine the evolving structure of corruption, I unbundle the prosecutorial data into different qualitative categories. Another constraint of this data source is that prosecutorial statistics record only acts of corruption that involve sufficiently large monetary value or political impact. This means that they do not capture petty corruption or organizational malfeasance at the agency level, such as street-level bureaucrats taking small bribes, arbitrary extraction of fines and fees, and local agency extortion (*tanpai*). Following my theoretical framework – which unbundles corruption into petty theft, speed money, grand theft, and access money – the analysis in this section compares just the last two categories, which involve *elites* (as summarized in Table 3.1.)

Although this section looks solely at elite corruption, unbundling this category still reveals some structurally significant patterns.

[67] Wedeman (2004).

TABLE 3.1 *Official statistics capture only two of four corruption categories in my theory*

	Non-elites	Elites
Involves theft	**Petty theft** Excluded from official statistics	**Grand theft** Recorded in official statistics as embezzlement, misuse of public funds, asset stripping
Involves exchanges	**Speed money** Excluded from official statistics	**Access money** Recorded in official statistics as bribery, abuse of office, misuse of office for private gain

- Beginning in 2000, transactional corruption rose sharply and consistently, while non-transactional corruption declined.
- By 2006, bribery was the most prevalent mode of elite corruption, exceeding embezzlement and misuse of public funds.
- But only high-stakes bribery increased in frequency, while low-stakes bribery declined.
- Corruption cases involving large sums of money grew across all categories.
- Particularly among officials at the highest ranks ("mega-tigers"), corruption involved big-stakes access money, not grand theft.

We begin with the theoretically significant comparison of "corruption with exchanges" and "corruption with theft." As I argue, the latter harms the economy more directly than the latter.[68] As summarized in Table 3.1, I classify bribery under "corruption with exchange" and embezzlement and misuse of public funds under "corruption with theft." In Chinese prosecution statistics, these are the three largest categories of corruption, which together made up 78 percent of all cases in 2015. Embezzlement refers to theft of public funds (e.g., diverting disaster relief funds into private accounts), whereas misappropriation involves the unauthorized use, transfer, or borrowing of funds.[69]

As we can clearly see from Figure 3.6, the trends of corruption with theft and corruption with exchange have *reversed* since 1998. In 1998, the

---

[68] Wedeman makes a similar argument: "While [transactional] corruption often involves exchanges that are mutually beneficial to those directly involved, plunder attacks the economy's vitals by rendering property rights insecure and encouraging capital flight." See Andrew Wedeman, "Growth and Corruption in China," *China Research Center (Website)*, 30 December 2012.

[69] In Appendix: Chapter 3, I translate the legal definition of each category into English.

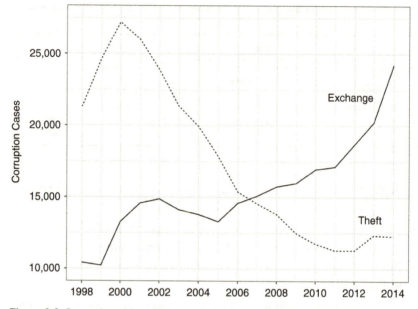

Figure 3.6 Corruption with exchange exploded but corruption with theft shrank.

number of cases involving theft was more than twice that of cases involving exchange. It grew sharply between 1998 and 2000, perhaps reflecting the rollout of administrative reforms in 1998, which enhanced the detection of embezzlement and misuse of public funds through increased internal transparency and precision in tracking fiscal flows. The deterrence effects of these reforms appear to set in after 2000. From then on, cases of corruption with theft progressively declined, hitting their lowest point in 2012, a 59 percent reduction from a peak in 2000. After Xi launched a sweeping anti-corruption drive in 2012, the incidence of corruption with theft picked up modestly, but it still remains far below the level of transactional corruption. By contrast, corruption with exchange began in 1998 at slightly over 10,000 cases, increased 50 percent by 2002, and then doubled by 2013. By 2014, there were almost twice as many cases of transactional corruption as there were of non-transactional corruption.

Next, in a modified presentation of the data used in Figure 3.6, I provide a more detailed breakdown of corruption into three forms – embezzlement, misuse of public funds, and bribery – with the total

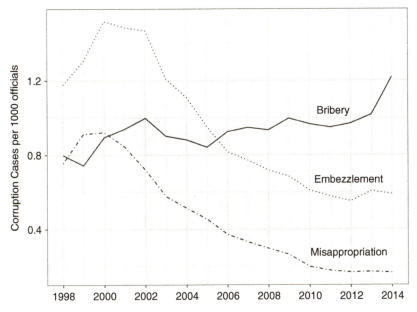

Figure 3.7 Bribery rose while embezzlement and misuse of funds declined.

number of cases divided by the number of officials, to account for the bureaucracy's growing size (see Figure 3.7).[70] This analysis follows that by Ko and Weng, who examined earlier data from 1998 to 2007.[71] Extending their analysis to 2014, I find a consistent pattern: embezzlement and misappropriation of funds fell while bribery rose. By 2006, bribery had become the most prevalent mode of elite corruption among the three categories, rising in share from only a quarter in 1998 to 60 percent by 2014 (see Figure 3.8).

For a finer comparison, Figure 3.9 looks at bribery (a form of transactional corruption) and embezzlement (a form of non-transactional corruption) by monetary size, which the CCL classifies as "small-sum" and "large-sum," where large-sum corruption involves more than 50,000 Yuan.[72] This breakdown reveals some interesting patterns. First, from 1998 to 2013, small-sum bribery steadily declined, falling to a third of its starting level, whereas large-sum bribery increased, rising more than ninefold to a peak of 17,435 cases in 2013. In other words, while

[70] Ang (2012).   [71] Ko and Weng (2012).   [72] Ko and Weng (2012, 727).

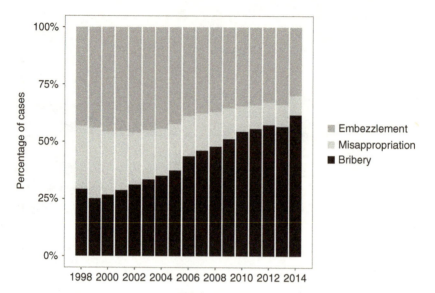

Figure 3.8 Bribery took up a growing share of corruption over time.

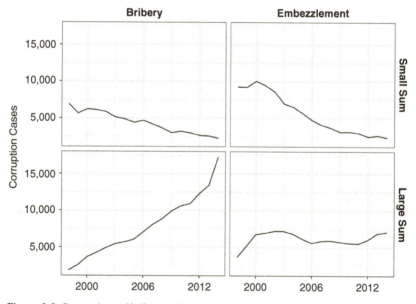

Figure 3.9 Comparison of bribery and embezzlement trends by monetary value.

low-stakes bribery came under control or fell out of fashion, high-stakes bribery exploded.

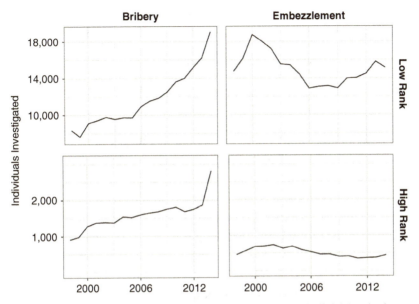

Figure 3.10 Comparison of bribery and embezzlement by rank of officials involved.

Turning to non-transactional corruption, small-sum embezzlement dropped sharply from its peak in 2000, whereas large-sum embezzlement fluctuated slightly over the years. This suggests that the monitoring and control measures instituted since 1998 are more effective at curtailing petty than grand forms of non-transactional corruption. One reason could be that grand embezzlement is usually committed by high-level officials who are powerful enough to circumvent institutional controls. One example is Chen Liangyu, former Party secretary of Shanghai, who, in addition to taking bribes, was charged for embezzling millions from Shanghai's social security fund,[73] through the aid of his network of underlings.

Next, in Figure 3.10, I unbundle bribery and embezzlement by the seniority of officials involved, whom official statistics divide into low-rank and high-rank, or "flies" and "tigers" in Xi's terminology (see Box 3.1). Bribery spread among both low- and high-rank officials over time.

---

[73] "上海已全部收回社保违规资金 [Shanghai Has Reclaimed Embezzled Funds]," *Xinhua*, 29 January 2007.

Numerous exposés feature township and even village leaders at the lowest levels who took massive bribes from businesses in exchange for deals.[74]

Box 3.1 Who Are the "Tigers" and "Flies" in Xi's Anti-corruption Campaign?

Xi's anti-corruption campaign is famous for its professed goal of hunting both "tigers" and "flies," popularly interpreted as high- versus low-level officials. What few realize is that this distinction between tigers and flies is extremely coarse and sometimes mislead- ing because the Chinese bureaucracy has many layers. From the highest to the lowest levels, including Party-state organs and public service providers, the bureaucracy has more than 50 million personnel.[75]

Who are the tigers and the flies? In the Chinese Party-state apparatus, officials who hold leadership positions are divided into 10 ranks, from highest to lowest: *guojia zheng, guojia fu, shengbu zheng, shengbu fu, tingju zheng, tingju fu, xianchu zheng, xianchu fu, xiangke zheng,* and *xiangke fu.*

The procuratorate defines "high-rank" as officials at the deputy *ting* level and above, which includes, for example, the deputy mayor of a city government or the division chief of a central-level ministry. All officials at the *chu* level and above are directly appointed by the Party and rotated across offices.

By this definition, a fly is any bureaucrat who is not a tiger, which is a massive residual category of officials and civil servants, ranging from as powerful as county Party secretaries (the first-in-command in county governments) to police officers and clerks at the street level. Yet, in reality, not all "flies" are trivial characters. County Party secretaries exercise supreme authority on economic and social

---

[74] Between 2012 and 2017, disciplinary authorities punished 278,000 village party secretaries and chiefs nationwide. See "Work Report of the 18th Central Discipline Inspection Commission," Website of the Central Discipline Inspection Commission, 29 October 2017.
[75] Ang (2012).

Box 3.1 (cont.)

affairs in their jurisdictions (see the case of Guo Yongchang in the Appendix to Chapter 5). Some of them are nicknamed "local emperors."

To distinguish between political elites above *chu* rank (e.g., deputy mayors and higher) and the remainder, Manion refers to the former as "mega-tigers" and the latter as "tigers." Others refer to upper-middle-tier officials as "wolves."[76]

Embezzlement, however, shows a different pattern. Far fewer high-rank officials are involved in embezzlement than low-rank officials. Even at its peak in 2002, only 732 high-rank officials were investigated for the crime, compared with over 17,000 low-rank officials. This suggests that "tigers" engaged much more frequently in bribery than in embezzlement. In 2015, six times more tigers were investigated for bribery (3,145) than for embezzlement (579). In the same year, 15 percent of all officials caught for bribery were tigers, compared with only 4 percent in embezzlement. In the language of my framework (see Table 3.1), for those at the top echelons of China's political hierarchy, corruption primarily involved big-stakes access money, not grand theft.

One final pattern stands out (Figure 3.5). Across all categories, large-sum corruption has increased. In bribery, the share of large-sum cases leapt from 28 percent in 1998 to 90 percent to 2015. As for embezzlement, its share grew from 28 percent to 77 percent. By 2014, more than three-quarters of all investigated cases involved large sums.

UNBUNDLING CORRUPTION USING MEDIA MENTIONS

Having reviewed the structural evolution of corruption in China using official statistics, I now turn to the media as a supplementary source of

---

[76] Manion (2016); Conversation with Christopher Buckley, 2 July 2018.

information. In this section, I will report the frequency of media mentions of corruption in the *People's Daily* from 1988 to 2012.

One advantage of media mentions over official statistics is that they allow us to approximate agency-level extortion practices (what Lu describes as "organizational corruption"). Recall that official statistics capture only cases of corruption committed by individual bureaucrats that are illegal and sufficiently severe to merit prosecution. Analysis of media mentions also lets us explore longer temporal patterns, going back to as early as 1988 (compared with the prosecutorial statistics that begin in 1998). Of course, this source has limitations, too, as it measures what the media chooses to cover rather than actual levels of corruption. Still, we can have greater confidence about observed trends when they are consistent in both the media and official statistics. Additionally, media mentions in the *People's Daily*, the Party's official outlet, reflect national policy priorities and concerns, allowing us to explore how discussions about corruption evolved.

For this analysis, I searched for the following commonly used terms that fall under the categories of transactional and non-transactional corruption, respectively.

- Transactional corruption:[77] bribery, bribe-giving, hidden rules, rent-seeking, elegant bribery, vote-buying, naked official, money laundering.
- Non-transactional corruption:[78] bureaucratic extortion, arbitrary extraction of fees, arbitrary extraction of fines, misuse of public funds.

I then produced raw counts of articles that match the term searches, normalized by the number of articles published in that year.[79] Figures 3.11 and 3.12 illustrate their trends.[80]

---

[77] The Chinese translations for these terms are as follows: bribery (*huilu*), bribe-giving (*xinghui*), hidden rules (*qianguize*), rent-seeking (*xunzu*), elegant bribery (*yahui*), vote-buying (*huixuan*), naked official (*luoguan*), and money laundering (*xiqian*).

[78] The Chinese translations for these terms are as follows: bureaucratic extortion (*tanpai*), arbitrary extraction of fees (*luanshoufei*), arbitrary extraction of fines (*luanfakuan*), and misuse of public funds (*nuoyong gongkuan*).

[79] Note that all the plots are of normalized frequency and the y scales are allowed to float, which means that we can only compare the frequencies of each term with themselves across time, rather than with one another. Absolute frequencies (i.e., with a pinned y axis), make the plots difficult to interpret, as terms with few media mentions relative to popular ones show up as flat lines, and are therefore not shown here.

[80] The plots in Figures 3.11 and 3.12 visualize the frequency of media mentions by smoothing them with a loess regression.

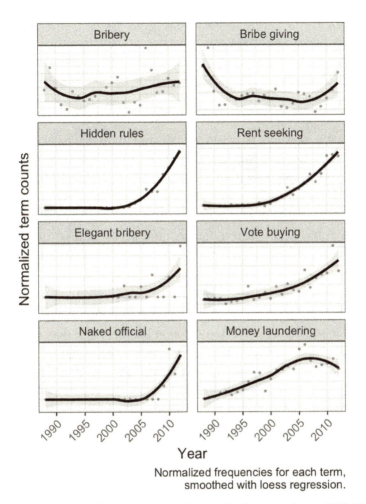

Figure 3.11 Media mentions of transactional corruption, by year and term, 1988–2012.

First, let's look at transactional forms of corruption. Recall that, prior to 1993, markets were only partially liberalized. During this period, there was some discussion of "bribery" and "bribe-giving," but in a downward direction from 1988. The concepts of "rent-seeking" and "hidden rules" were almost completely absent from the *People's Daily*.

The period from 1993 to 2000 saw a qualitative change in the discussion of corruption. During this foundational stage of building a "socialist market economy," two new corruption terms emerged: "vote-buying" and "money laundering." Although China does not hold nationally competitive elections, it introduced elections for village leaders in 1988, which continue to this day and were subsequently extended to some townships.[81] Money laundering also became increasingly relevant, as bribery spread and as the central government began targeting illicit financial flows through administrative reforms.

Recall from Figure 3.6 that 2000 was the year in which non-transactional corruption began to fall and transactional corruption climbed. The words "rent-seeking" and "hidden rules" were first mentioned in 2000, and their frequency has since soared. Although western political economists have used the term "rents" (*zu*) for more than a century since Weber, it is a new addition to Chinese corruption lingo. "Hidden rules" (*qian guize*) refers to informal behavioral norms. For example, to cultivate good will within a political network, businesses may be obliged to participate in rigged biddings for government procurement projects. Another example is developers who offer discounts on properties to government officials, which is technically not a cash bribe.[82]

From around 2005 onward, corruption became even more elaborate. While mentions of "bribery" and "bribe-taking" plateaued, those of "rent-seeking" and "hidden rules" climbed. At the same time, two new terms surfaced: "naked official" and "elegant bribery."[83] "Naked official" (*luoguan*) refers to individuals who possess no wealth domestically but whose family members enjoy lavish lifestyles overseas. Instead of giving cash bribes, business sponsors pay for the education of an official's children and their family members' expenses abroad (see Chapter 5 for Bo Xilai's case). Others seeking favors from government officials give works of art in lieu of cash, a practice known as "elegant bribery" (*yahui*). Art has the advantage of subjective value, making it harder to trace and prosecute as bribery. One notorious example is Wen Qiang, formerly Chongqing's deputy police chief, who fell in connection with Bo. When the authorities raided his home, they found a museum of collectables, including a painting by the famous Chinese artist Zhang Daqian, worth 3.6 million Yuan, and even fossil dinosaur eggs.[84]

[81] Pastor and Tan (2000).   [82] Interview B2007-93.
[83] Anthony Ou, "The Chinese Art of Elegant Bribery," *Open Economy*, 25 June 2011.
[84] "文强受贿物品曝光 [Wen Qiang's Corrupt Booty Exposed]," *Sohu News*, 4 February 2010.

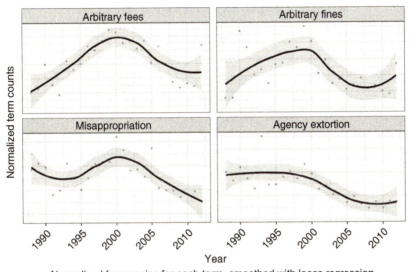

Normalized frequencies for each term, smoothed with loess regression.

Figure 3.12 Media mentions of non-transactional corruption, by year and term, 1988–2012.

It is also worth noting that mentions of "vote-buying" have steadily increased over the past two decades. This likely reflects the connection of vote-buying with illegal or contested land takings that arose in the 2000s,[85] where leaders buy votes from villagers in order to sell land and assets to developers and then usurp the lion's share of the windfall.

On non-transactional forms of corruption (Figure 3.12), the media frequently discussed "bureaucratic extortion" (*tanpai*) from 1986 to 1998, but mentions sharply dropped off afterward. "Arbitrary extraction of fees" and "arbitrary extraction of fines" peaked in 2000, and then similarly declined. Likewise, "misappropriation of public funds" peaked in 2000 and has since dissipated. This indicates that bureaucratic extortion and "organizational corruption" were nationally rampant only in the 1980s and 1990s, although they are still prevalent in poor localities today.[86] Clearly, it is high time to update our impressions of Chinese corruption.

---

[85] Zhao (2018). See also Susan Whiting, "Land Rents and Vote Buying in China's Village Elections," Lecture at Stanford University Freeman Spogli Institute, 7 March 2018.

[86] See my historical analysis of Humble County in Hubei province (Ang 2016, Chapter 6).

WHAT'S MISSING IN EXISTING ACCOUNTS?

A systematic review of the evolution of corruption allows us to concretely reevaluate some existing accounts. Temporal context matters, especially in a fast-evolving China. As I have shown, China in the 1980s, China in the 1990s, China in the 2000s, and China post-2012 are dramatically different Chinas. Confusion results when observers make arguments about corruption in the present day that are based on outdated impressions or data from the 1980s and 1990s,[87] which would be the equivalent of testing theories about smartphones using data on landlines.

Consider Fan *et al.*'s article "Embezzlement vs. Bribery," which was published by the National Bureau of Economic Research in 2010, and received coverage in the *Wall Street Journal.*[88] Proposing a formal model, this article argues that "China's political leaders deliberately tolerate a great deal of relatively small-scale embezzlement in order to reduce the incentive for officials to extract bribes."[89] In other words, they argue that central authorities permit corruption with theft in order to divert officials from bribery. As evidence, they cite Sun's study set in the 1990s, which reported that the post-1992 period saw a surge of embezzlement and misappropriation whereas bribery was small in scale.[90]

Sun's observations are correct, but what Fan and his collaborators fail to notice is that her findings are based on prosecutorial data from 1993 to 1997, before the onset of radical administrative reforms and accelerated market expansion. During Sun's period of study, there were indeed fewer cases of bribery than embezzlement (see Figure 3.7). In the present day, however, the pattern is reversed, as I show in this chapter.

My analysis shows the exact opposite of what Fan *et al.* argue. China's leaders do not "tolerate" embezzlement, let alone deliberately so. In fact, since 1998, they have taken strong, methodical measures to combat non-transactional forms of malfeasance.[91] As a result, although corruption with theft sharply declined over time, bribery has exploded.

---

[87] Failing to specify the time period in question will also aggravate the "blind men and the elephant" problem: multiple studies produce apparent contradictions that are in fact observations of different periods.

[88] Fan *et al.* (2010). See "What's Worse, Bribery or Embezzlement?," *Wall Street Journal,* 23 November 2010.

[89] Fan *et al.* (2010).   [90] Sun (2004).   [91] Yang (2004); Ko and Weng (2012).

My approach in this chapter also highlights the importance of tracing temporal patterns across *all* types of corruption. For example, Pei highlights the grave problem of "crony capitalism," but he ignores changes in other types of corruption. As a result, his study fails to note that embezzlement and predatory practices have in fact fallen. Even though the CCP struggles to guard its own elites from exploiting their power for personal enrichment, it is capable of disciplining rank-and-file bureaucrats and deterring outright theft.

CONCLUSION

Why has China's economy prospered despite rampant corruption? Building on Chapter 2, this chapter revealed a second key to the puzzle: the structure of corruption changed over time. Starting in 2000, corruption with exchange, particularly bribery, exploded, but corruption with theft steadily fell. Two factors drove this structural evolution: first, the Party's embrace of a global market economy in 1993, after which the value of political connections multiplied astronomically; and second, the central government's rollout of modernizing administrative reforms on a scale that parallels America's Progressive Era.

For comparative political economists, the evolutionary perspective in this chapter cautions against the assumption that countries have stable patterns of corruption – China evidently does not. As I discussed in Chapter 2, the conventional approach in small-n, comparative studies is to classify entire countries into a single typology of corruption.[92] Not only does this approach suffer from subjectivity, but also it neglects the possibility that a given country may witness dramatically different structures of corruption over time. Analysts, therefore, must specify the time period of observation, especially in fast-evolving nations. China must be unbundled into temporally distinct cases.

This chapter also raises comparative-historical questions for further research. Have other countries also experienced significant structural changes in corruption patterns? The United States experienced

---

[92] For example, Kang (2002b); Johnston (2008); Sun and Johnston (2010); Wedeman (2012).

transformative structural shifts, from a period of heady growth and rampant corruption in the Gilded Age to a professionalized bureaucracy in the Progressive Era.[93] If we unbundle corruption over time in countries such as India, Russia, and South Korea, what might we find? Although such a comparative project is outside the scope of this book, I hope the efforts here will stimulate interest among other social scientists to pursue it.

---

[93] Glaeser and Goldin (2006); Parrillo (2013).

CHAPTER 4

Profit-Sharing, Chinese-Style

O NE OF THE MOST INTRACTABLE PROBLEMS OF DEVELOPMENT is the trap of "corruption-causing-poverty-causing-corruption."[1] In other words, countries are poor because they are corrupt, and they are corrupt because they are poor. As Chapter 2 shows, poor countries typically exhibit the most economically debilitating forms of corruption, including petty bribery and extortion. Once such corruption becomes endemic – settling into an "equilibrium," as social scientists say – is it possible to break free?

Chapter 3 sheds some light on this question from a macro-historical perspective, focusing on two forces that shaped China's structure of corruption: an overhaul of the economy paired with nationwide procedural reforms. This chapter turns to a micro perspective, going *inside* the tens of thousands of Party-state agencies across China that run the machinery of governance. This allows us to home in on a question pertinent to all developing countries: how can the state keep poorly compensated public agents from harassing businesses for petty gains and induce them to support long-term development goals?

The scholarly literature proposes two solutions to this problem. The first is to "skip straight to Weber" by replicating the best practices of first-world public administration in developing countries.[2] Pay is too low? Raise it. Bureaucracy is overstaffed? Slash it. Petty corruption is rampant? Vow to punish it. Although these measures appear correct in principle, in

---

[1] Fisman and Golden (2017).
[2] The term "skip straight to Weber" was coined by Pritchett and Woolcock (2004) in their critique of blindly copying best practices.

practice, they routinely fail and may even backfire, raising administrative costs and undermining public sector morale.[3]

The second solution, as Fisman and Golden underscore, is to "trigger a change in social norms."[4] Social norms are important, and muck-raking journalism and public protests can help citizens hold corrupt elites accountable. But norms cannot fill empty stomachs. Poorly paid bureaucrats often steal, extort, or moonlight in order to subsist.[5]

Reform-era China charted an unusual pathway out of this vicious cycle. Its solution was to allow street-level bureaucrats to extract some payments to top up their paltry formal salaries, while also aligning their financial incentives with long-term economic development objectives. Essentially, the state applied a profit-sharing model to the communist bureaucracy. Public employees in China are entitled to a slice of the revenue generated by the local government and the particular department to which they belong.

In China's opaque bureaucracy, compensation practices are often vilified as "organizational corruption."[6] This chapter employs a mixture of qualitative and quantitative evidence to shed a different light on these incentive structures. On top of extensive interviews with local bureaucrats, I analyze a first-of-its-kind dataset that measures the actual amount of compensation – both formal and fringe – among county governments.

My core finding is that in China the golden goose maxim – restraint today yields long-term benefits – is not just a parable but a *reality*. Extracting fees, fines, and levies enriches local bureaucrats in the short term, but increasing compensation in the long run requires expanding the formal tax base by recruiting and retaining businesses. The Chinese bureaucrats whom I interviewed would regard this as self-evident, but in fact, outside of China, the norm of public administration is that civil service pay is divorced from economic performance.[7] This is the first study to demonstrate the systematic links between public compensation and financial outcomes in the Chinese bureaucracy.

---

[3] Olowu (2010); Pritchett *et al.* (2013).   [4] Fisman and Golden (2017).

[5] Matthew Rosenberg and Jawad Sukhanyar, "Afghan Police, Often Derided, Face Another Drawback: Missing Pay," *The New York Times*, 12 January 2014.

[6] Lü (2000).

[7] As Mookherjee (1997) states, "Civil servants have little personal stake in the social implications of their efforts."

PAYING BUREAUCRATS THROUGH PROFIT-SHARING

As Max Weber points out, all public officials in pre-modern states were de facto entrepreneurs. Although they received little or no formal pay from the state treasury, they were allowed to generate income through the prerogatives of public office by extracting taxes and fees from local residents, running monopoly trades, or accepting gifts in exchange for services (what we now regard as bribes). Weber termed these rights "prebends" or rents.[8] In modern economic terms, prebendalism is a form of *profit-sharing* that allows public agents to keep a full or partial share of the revenue their offices collect.

In pre-modern times, prebendal practices brought certain advantages, but they also created problems. On the one hand, by allowing public administrators to "self-finance," rulers did not have to pay regular wages in money, which was especially burdensome in the absence of fully monetized economies and stable tax collection. On the other hand, entrepreneurial officials often seized as much as they could, resulting in excessive predation and even popular revolts. As Weber explains, facing these risks, modern governments gradually replaced prebendalism with "fixed salaries paid in money" – a norm of public administration that we now take for granted in the first world.[9]

In Western Europe and the United States, the transformation of public administration from prebendal to state-funded and from profit- to service-oriented took centuries to complete,[10] whereas in contemporary developing countries, this transition is still in progress. But standard theories of public administration are ahistorical and first-world-centric; they posit norms in present-day industrialized democracies as universal. In fact, notions of profit and practices of profit-sharing, which are "ruled out" in Western public administrations, still exist in the Chinese bureaucracy.[11]

---

[8] Tax-farming, in which officials directly retain a share of taxes collected, is a variant of prebendalism.

[9] Weber (1968).   [10] Brewer (1988); Parrillo (2013).

[11] Scholars of American bureaucracy assume that the notion of "profit" is irrelevant to *all* public bureaucracies, as Moe (1984) states: "Incentive plans that give employees a share of the 'profit' in partial payment for their effort are also ruled out." But in the Chinese bureaucracy, profit exists insofar as individual offices can rightfully retain a share of

Classical theories of public sector wage incentives build on Becker and Stigler's seminal 1974 article,[12] which argues that in the presence of effective monitoring and disciplinary mechanisms, higher "efficiency" wages will deter public employees from abusing their power for personal gain. Adapting this notion, Besley and McLaren identify a second public compensation scheme that they call "capitulation wages," where formal salaries are so low that bureaucrats are expected to be corrupt.[13] This, they claim, is the norm in most developing countries.

These theories suffer two limitations. First, they ignore history, depicting incentive structures in static terms and providing no insight into processes of change. The second limitation is that they consider only two types of income for public agents – formal salaries and corrupt monies (such as bribes), ignoring a third category: perks and allowances that are neither formalized nor illegal. Yet such practices are common in developing countries. For example, according to a World Bank report, in Zambia[14]

> Fringe benefit and monetary allowances have progressively been used as a major vehicle for increasing compensation, particularly for upper-middle level and senior civil servants. The allowances have included: acting, special duty, hardship, responsibility, non-practicing, commuter, transport, risk, security, extraneous duty, field, overtime, honoraria, accommodation leave, transfer, entertainment, telephone, utility, mileage, subsistence, settlement, uniform among others.

Because standard policy prescriptions ignore this amorphous category of public compensation, they focus on raising only *formal wages* to deter corruption. Yet China's experience shows that this intermediate category of "fringe benefit and allowances," which as we will later see, make up 76 percent of total compensation among county-level bureaucrats, can function as a variety of "efficiency wages" under certain circumstances.

---

revenue earned (Ang 2016). Also, see Oi (1992; 1999) on her discussion of "surpluses" in the context of central-local fiscal sharing arrangements.
[12] Becker and Stigler (1974).   [13] Besley and McLaren (1993).
[14] World Bank (2004, 118).

CHINESE BUREAUCRACY 101

Before diving into the details of compensation practices, it helps to know some basic facts about the Chinese bureaucracy. Although China is a unitary political regime, it has one of the world's most economically and administratively decentralized public administrations.[15] While the central government lays out the national vision and broad policy parameters, subnational governments exercise tremendous autonomy over their own economic and social development plans.[16] They also fund and deliver the bulk of essential public services such as education, health, public safety, pensions, and urban infrastructure, at levels exceeding many federal governments, including the United States.[17]

The Chinese bureaucracy is massive. By 2007, the Party-state apparatus, excluding the military and state-owned enterprises, consisted of 50 million employees,[18] roughly the size of South Korea's entire population. This corps must be divided into at least three layers, as summarized in Table 4.1. The top one percent – roughly 500,000 officials at the *chu* rank and

TABLE 4.1 *Three layers of China's bureaucracy*

Layer	Approximate share of personnel size	Characteristics	American equivalent[a]
Leaders and elite officials	Top 1 percent	Officials at *xianchu* rank and above	Political appointees
		Directly appointed by party	
		Rotated across locales and offices	
Civil servants (*gongwuyuan*)	19 percent	Perform management roles in Party-state agencies	Mid-level managers
		Not rotated; managed by personnel department	
Non-civil service public employees (*shiye renyuan*)	80 percent	Directly deliver services to and interact with citizens on daily basis	Street-level operators
		Not rotated; managed by personnel department	

[a] Wilson (1989).

[15] OECD (2006); Landry (2008).   [16] Ang (2016, Chapter 3).

[17] OECD (2006); World Bank and DRC of State Council (2014).

[18] According to the Local Financial Statistics Yearbook, the exact number is 49.8 million. See Ang (2012).

above – make up China's "political elites."[19] A middle layer of civil servants – roughly 19 percent of personnel – perform management roles in party or state agencies.[20] The remaining 80 percent are non-civil service public employees, such as clerks, inspectors, police officers, health-care workers, and township cadres, who directly deliver services to citizens. Whereas political elites are appointed and rotated across offices by the Party, most bureaucrats are stationed for life in one location under the supervision of the personnel departments of the administrative branch.[21]

Elite officials are evidently powerful figures in China's authoritarian hierarchy, but the remaining 99 percent of the administration should not be dismissed as trivial. Far from it, this group runs the daily machinery of governance and implements policies at the street level. As Lipsky emphasizes, "Although they are normally regarded as low-level employees, their actions actually constitute the 'services' delivered by government."[22] Moreover, in the reform era, rank-and-file officers, clerks, inspectors, and even school teachers are more than just public service workers – they are potential entrepreneurial agents. In the early stages of economic take-off, local governments mobilized public employees to recruit investors through their personal networks.[23] Street-level bureaucrats can be either "grabbing" or "helping" hands.[24] They can inhibit entrepreneurial growth by arbitrarily extracting fees and fines and harassing businesses

---

[19] Walder (2004). They include party secretaries, chief administrators, central ministerial officials, and division chiefs.

[20] The passing of the Civil Service Law in 2006 gave these bureaucrats the formal title of "civil servants" (*gongwuyuan*). Previously, they were referred to, in communist lingo, as "cadres" (Ang 2012).

[21] At the city and county levels, the party secretary, the head of government, and members of the Party committee (who usually hold concurrent leadership posts in key departments like organization) are appointed on terms lasting five years each (B2011-236; B2011-241). However, vice-leadership posts (e.g., vice-county chief) are not subjected to term limits, and it is not uncommon for their holders to serve in the same locale for a lifetime (B2011-237). The notion of term limits does not apply to the remaining posts, such as chiefs of the various departments, who generally work in the same locale until they retire. Only rarely are these county cadres rotated to other counties (B2011-237; B2011-239; B2011-240). Further, the non-leading cadres are overwhelmingly natives of the particular locale in which they work (B2011-236; B2011-22; B2011-222; B2011-225; B2011-239; B2011-240; B2011-237).

[22] Lipsky (1980). [23] Ang (2016, Chapters 1 and 5).

[24] On the "helping hand" model, see Walder (1995a). On the "grabbing hand," see Frye and Shleifer (1997); Shleifer and Vishny (1998); Brown *et al.* (2009).

Box 4.1 At Your Service, Investors!

Chinese local bureaucrats often go to great lengths to attract and serve investors. One example is an urban district (equivalent to township) government in Chengdu, which faced exciting prospects after the arrival of a new pro-business leader.

As one of the district's officers described it, "We hope to forge a friendly business environment by providing all-round services, for example, applying for permits, filling out paperwork, coordinating among various departments, parking, schooling, taking care of the surrounding sanitation, and so on. We want to serve businesses well, because every business has a thick network behind it, including friends and business associates. If we serve one investor well, we can access and mobilize these resources and attract more investors, thereby promoting our district's economic development and tax revenue base."[25]

Apart from enjoying increased tax revenue and staff bonuses, the district office benefited from a business-sponsored refurbishment. As the district leader recounted, "Our office used to be so shabby, even the walls are not painted. Last year, because we served an enterprise well, it donated more than 100,000 Yuan to renovate our office and also bought computers for our staff members." He described this sponsorship as "an affectionate reciprocation of our excellent services."[26]

---

with excessive inspections, or they can foster the economy by connecting entrepreneurs with one another, providing amenities and personalized services for investors, organizing conventions, and more (Box 4.1).

With few exceptions, studies of political incentives in China have focused only on promotion incentives among elites (see Chapter 6 for a similar analysis of city leaders centered on their downfalls).[27] However,

---

[25] Interview B2011-230.   [26] Interview B2011-229.
[27] For some representative work, see Li and Zhou (2005); Landry 2008; Kung and Chen 2011; Shih *et al.* (2012); Lü and Landry (2014); Jia *et al.* (2015).

the top one percent and the remaining 99 percent are motivated by different sets of incentives. Leaders and elite officials aim for higher office, greater personal power, or both. But, for most bureaucrats, the chances of ascending to elite ranks are exceedingly small.[28] Mid-level managers and street-level operators care less about rising to power than mundane things such as salary and perks. As one officer stated, "Incentives for regular folks like me are quite simply incentives supplied by material benefits."[29] This chapter's analysis of bureaucratic compensation centers on this neglected bulk of "regular folks," who rarely feature in media reports.

PAYING THE 99 PERCENT OF THE BUREAUCRACY

Like in many other developing countries, formal salaries in the Chinese bureaucracy are standardized at abysmally low rates across the country. Following a wage adjustment in 2006, the most junior civil servant (Grade 1) received only 290 Yuan (US$45) a month, rising to a maximum of 450 Yuan (US$67) with longer years of service.[30] In 2011, entry-level civil servants at a county government in Sichuan province received only 830 Yuan in official wages per month, less than the county's minimum wage of 850 Yuan for workers.[31] As part of Xi's fight against corruption, civil service pay was most recently increased in 2015, which raised the monthly salary of the lowest-ranking officer to 510 Yuan (US$82) and that of the highest-ranked to 5,250 Yuan (US$845).[32]

As Xu Songtao, a former Vice-Minister of Personnel Management acknowledged, formal public salaries have always been too low, too compressed, and woefully behind rapid inflation.[33] The central government has raised them several times since 1978, but the increases were small and failed to accommodate wide regional disparities (see

---

[28] Even among county leaders, there are extremely limited opportunities for promotion (Kostka and Yu 2014).

[29] Interview B2010-188.

[30] "Civil service pay by rank and grade" (*gongwuyuan jibie gongzi biaozhun*), issued in 2006 by the central government, document obtained during fieldwork.

[31] Interview B2011-235.

[32] "China Raises Wages for Government Workers," *Reuters*, 20 January 2015.

[33] Xu (2007).

Figure 4.3). On the surface, this scenario fits Besley and McLaren's description of "capitulation wages" – wages so low that governments in effect "abandon any attempt to solve either the moral hazard or adverse selection problem via wage incentives."[34] So why don't we see widespread petty corruption in China, as we do in Bangladesh and India (Chapter 2)?

It is because formal wages were only part of the story. Since the 1980s, local bureaucracies in China routinely topped up salaries with perks including overtime pay, bonuses, free meals, free vacations, subsidized housing, entertainment budgets, and daily necessities such as food, electricity, and gas.[35] They also supplied items of collective welfare, for example, spacious buildings, new office furnishing, and subsidized child care.

Observers dismissed these perks as "organizational corruption" or "non-transactional corruption,"[36] because they are associated with arbitrary extraction of fees and fines, departmental slush funds, discretionary spending, and other unsavory practices. In even harsher terms, Fan *et al.* describe the provision of fringe benefits as "embezzlement." According to them, "Consumption of the state budget by officials ... occurs on a massive scale, with surprisingly feeble attempts to stop it."[37]

Are Chinese bureaucrats really free to plunder public budgets? My fieldwork uncovers a different reality. Local bureaucrats are not on a rampage. Instead, the practice of topping up "capitulation wages" with extra benefits follows an internal set of rules. Chinese public employees are compensated in a "dual-track" manner: fixed formal wages combined with variable allowances and perks.[38] This structure may be found in other developing countries too,[39] except that, in China, the supply of fringe benefits was regulated and linked to financial performance, such that it functions as a monetary incentive.

---

[34] Klitgaard (1988); Besley and McLaren (1993).
[35] Whiting (2001); Burns (2007); Chan and Ma (2011).   [36] Lü (2000); Sun (2004).
[37] Fan *et al.* (2010).
[38] "Dual-track" pricing refers to a hybrid of centrally planned and market-based pricing, which was adopted during the initial phase of China's market liberalization and credited as an example of incremental reforms that worked.
[39] Colclough (1997); World Bank (2004).

In China allowances and perks are pegged to two sources of income: local tax revenues and the fees and fines extracted by individual agencies. Consider the hypothetical case of Cadre Li ("cadre" is a common Communist term for bureaucrat), who works for the Construction Bureau of Jade County. Cadre Li receives a nationally standardized formal salary. In addition, he receives allowances from the state budget of Jade County, which draws upon tax income generated and retained by the county. There is also a third stream of benefits from Li's home department, the Construction Bureau, which generates income by collecting fees, fines, user charges, and profits from subsidiary services. Drawing on this non-tax income, each department disburses staff benefits such as overtime pay, group vacations, free meals, and even gift cards.

Essentially, this is a profit-sharing scheme, where public employees take a cut of the revenue produced by their organizations. Normally, profit-sharing exists only in the private sector, and even then, it is usually limited in scale.[40] Reform-era China, however, practiced profit-sharing in the entire public administration.[41] Even more unusual is that it linked staff remuneration to both tax and non-tax income. The relationship of staff pay and perks to local tax income is akin to a *dividend system*, whereas its connection to the fees and fines collected by individual departments functions like a *commission*.

Why didn't the local states simply stop individual agencies extracting rents and pay them entirely through tax income? The reason is simple: most local governments cannot afford to do so. As one finance bureaucrat explained, "We don't have enough tax revenue to feed the bureaucracy and invest in economic development at the same time."[42] Another bureaucrat added that if the state removed the departments' rights to spend the fees, fines, and charges they collect, "they would have no motivation to generate revenue for themselves," and consequently, "the financial burden of our county would be too large."[43]

---

[40] Lazear (1995); Baker *et al.* (1998).

[41] Earlier theories studied local governments as aggregated units and highlighted only the growth-enhancing effects of revenue-sharing arrangements (Oi 1992; 1999; Montinola *et al.* 1995; Walder 1995b; Whiting 2001).

[42] Interview B2007-127.   [43] Interview B2007-114.

That is why budgetary authorities in many locales pledged to retain their "spending rights" (*shiyong quan*) despite the extractive risks of allowing departments to partially self-finance. This compromise between the budgetary authorities and individual departments is known as a "refund" (*fanhuan*). For example, one county government in Jiangsu guaranteed all its departments a universal 70 percent "refund," meaning they had discretion to spend up to 70 percent of their income on staff benefits and administrative expenses.[44] In this county, unused funds rolled over and accumulated, such that each department in effect "owned the means of administration," to use Weber's term.

One consequence of de facto profit-sharing is that gaps in actual compensation widened over the years even as formal salaries scarcely budged, because localities and departments possess vastly uneven capacity to generate income. Public employees in different localities, even ones that are geographically adjacent, may receive starkly unequal levels of remuneration (as my analysis in the next section will show). Within each locality, staff benefits also vary across departments. Agencies that enjoy access to rich streams of income through their regulatory power over booming economic sectors are known as "greasy agencies." Those with few means are dubbed "distilled water agencies." As one county-level bureaucrat mused, "Even an idiot knows the gap [in income and benefits] between the Construction Bureau and the Archives Office."[45]

GRABBING AND HELPING HANDS

Put succinctly, bureaucratic compensation is derived both from "helping" (attracting and retaining businesses) and from "grabbing" (extracting fees, fines, and payments). This institutional arrangement explains an abiding paradox in China: the coexistence of developmental and predatory behavior among street-level bureaucrats.[46] Existing theories focusing on promotion incentives may account for why local leaders

---

[44] Interviews B2007-111; B2007-114; B2007-115; B2007-116; B2007-117.
[45] Interview B2007-128.
[46] As Tsai (2004) observes, in her critique of the developmental state literature, we find in China "extractive behavior that seems unacceptably predatory for a local developmental state."

encourage growth,[47] but to explain the contradictory economic behavior of street-level state actors, we must turn to monetary incentives – particularly compensation practices.

That Chinese street-level bureaucrats obtain income both from "helping" and by "grabbing" from businesses raises a collective action problem: why wouldn't these bureaucrats choose only to "grab" (extracting fees, fines, and profits for their departments) and neglect pro-business efforts that would benefit the entire locale? The reasons, I found, are two-fold. One obvious factor is that local leaders, whose careers and self-enrichment are tied to prosperity, would not passively allow their subordinates to undermine business interests; they have incentives to institute controls, which I will discuss later. But there is a more interesting and less obvious restraint: street-level bureaucrats believed that curbing extractive behavior served their long-term self-interest. In their own words,

> Of course taking care of the big picture, that is, growing our local economy, is more important than departmental self-financing. This is because it is a healthier model of development. It promotes a healthy progression of our staff welfare and budgets. Activities that involve departments sourcing revenue for themselves are ultimately unstable. They are hungry one year and not hungry the next. It is not healthy.[48]

> If the overall economy prospers, then our departments will also benefit. Conversely, if each department only thinks about organizing or extracting revenue for itself, then, if our enterprises cannot survive, they will leave. Our local economy will be finished. Consequently, each department's finances will worsen. This will turn into a vicious cycle. Only when we all work together can we promote local economic development. In the long term, only this strategy can benefit every department.[49]

As Manion argues, "shared expectations" about the structure of payoffs shape the behavior of state actors.[50] In most poor countries, development outcomes are divorced from bureaucratic efforts, and time

---

[47] Li and Zhou (2005).   [48] Interview B2012-301.   [49] Interview B2012-302.

[50] Manion (2004). On the role of "cognitive maps" (ideas and beliefs) in structuring what political elites see as the possible range of policy choices and actions, see Mehta and Walton (2014); Sen *et al.* (2014).

horizons are short. What distinguishes China is that even street-level bureaucrats *know* they have a personal financial stake in economic performance, and that curbing extraction today will benefit them over the long term.

HYPOTHESES DERIVED FROM FIELDWORK. Field research is essential for uncovering phenomena that are unreported in the literature, as O'Brien emphasizes.[51] But are findings from interviews *falsifiable*? How do we know whether they are *generalizable* across larger groups of respondents? In the analysis that follows, I examine whether there is support for two qualitative findings.

- H1: In the short term, agency collections raise bureaucratic compensation more than tax revenue.
- H2: In the long term, however, tax revenue raises compensation more than agency collections.

In the regression analysis that follows, I aim to test whether patterns in numerical data support my narrative – if so, we may be confident that the remunerative practices and incentive logic uncovered through my fieldwork are not anecdotal, but generalizable.

NEW DATA ON FRINGE COMPENSATION

Topping up low formal public salaries with extra allowances and fringe benefits – which I will term "fringe compensation" – is a common practice across developing countries. For example, in Tanzania, in-kind benefits were estimated to constitute 400 percent of formal salaries among senior bureaucrats and 35 percent among regular public employees.[52] Yet previous analyses measured only formal salaries, relying on estimates made by country experts or formal wages reported in IMF sources and statistical yearbooks.[53]

Measuring fringe compensation is difficult because these practices are often scattered, unrecorded, and not monetized (for example, free

---

[51] O'Brien (2006).   [52] Olowu (1999).
[53] Evans and Rauch (1999); Treisman (2000); Van Rijckeghem and Weder di Mauro (2001); Di Tella and Schargrodsky (2003).

vacations and food hampers). In China, this component of remuneration is widespread yet secretive because authorities fear criticisms of corruption. My dataset breaks new ground by estimating levels of fringe compensation across county governments in one Chinese province – Shandong – which is more populous than the United Kingdom and Australia combined. This is the *first* dataset that measures fringe compensation not only in China, but in *any* developing country.

To construct this dataset, I leveraged a previously unavailable source: line-item budgets at the county level.[54] Other China specialists have employed only publicly posted yearbook budgets, which list public expenditure by broad categories (e.g., education, agriculture). These budgets do not indicate whether a given amount goes toward social spending, infrastructure, or the provision of cadre pay and benefits. Line-item budgets, on the other hand, disaggregate public spending into remunerative and non-remunerative items. Table A4.1 in the appendix details how I deconstructed these budgets into my dataset.

Specifically, my dataset is drawn from line-item budgets compiled by the Finance Bureau of Shandong, a province situated on the Northern coast. With 90 million residents, it is the second most populous province in China. Economically, Shandong is one of China's fastest-growing regions, though not as wealthy as Jiangsu or Zhejiang on a per capita basis. Within the province, there is wide variation in economic development, including some highly urbanized areas and many rural counties. Hence, although my data comes only from Shandong, this province is fairly representative of middle-to-high income provinces in China (Figure 4.1). The line-item budgets cover almost all the counties in the province, 136 in total, except for a few dropped due to redistricting, from 1998 to 2005.

This dataset suffers from several limitations. First, although my data source is much more detailed than conventionally analyzed budgets, the information is still aggregated and coarse compared with line-item budgets in developed democracies. The original data source lists line-item

---

[54] Recall that fringe compensation is a form of public spending; these are not individually collected bribes or stolen funds. Therefore, internal line-item budgets must reflect these amounts.

Figure 4.1 Zouping, one of the 136 counties in Shandong province where I did research.

spending only by county, not by departments within each county. We therefore cannot tell which department spent the listed items or which individuals benefited from them. Second, these budgets do not specify whether particular expenditures were financed by tax or non-tax revenue. Therefore, my empirical strategy is modest: I examine the correlations between the relevant revenue sources and overall compensation levels in order to draw inferences about the underlying incentive structure.

OPENING THE BLACK BOX OF PUBLIC COMPENSATION

Before proceeding to the regression results, it is useful to explore the descriptive patterns in my data, since no quantitative analysis to date has examined fringe compensation in China. (Note that all monetary values have been adjusted for inflation and are expressed in 1998 prices.) Figure 4.2 provides a disaggregation of total public compensation – formal and fringe – among the county governments in Shandong.

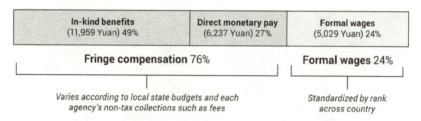

Figure 4.2 Fringe components made up 76 percent of compensation.

Table A4.3 in the Appendix provides a summary of descriptive statistics for the variables in my analysis.

An average county in Shandong had about 16,000 officials and public employees. Between 1998 and 2005, the mean value of total compensation was 23,226 Yuan (US$3,600) per employee per year. Not surprisingly, formal wages were low, averaging only 5,029 Yuan (US$770) per year, lower than average urban wages of 11,022 Yuan (US$1,695) in Shandong province during the same period.[55] Fringe compensation constituted 76 percent of the total, and came in two forms: direct monetary pay (such as bonuses and overtime pay) and indirect, in-kind benefits (such as entertainment and vehicles). Although bonuses were previously highlighted as a key monetary incentive,[56] they comprise only 1.4 percent of total compensation in my data. In-kind benefits took up the lion's share at 49 percent. The average amounts are not extravagant; they constitute a living wage.[57]

Patterns of geographic variation are consistent with my narrative. Formal wages varied little across the counties, reflecting the fact that formal public salaries are standardized. By contrast, regional variance in fringe compensation is much wider, as shown in Figure 4.3. In 2005, they ranged from as low as 4,752 Yuan to as high as 125,454 Yuan – a 26-fold difference. Compared with the Weberian norm of fixed and flat public

---

[55] Note that these monetary values are expressed in 1998 prices, which means they would be higher in today's prices. Numbers for average urban wages are from Shandong Statistical Yearbooks.

[56] Oi (1999); Edin (2003); Whiting (2004).

[57] In his study of county administration in the Qing dynasty, Reed (2000) makes a similar observation: "the annual incomes of yamen clerks and runners were considerably less than the extravagant amounts frequently cited in official and gentry sources, which, until quite recently, have largely been accepted at face value."

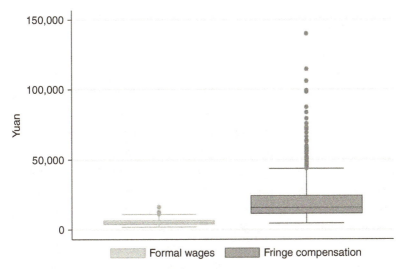

Figure 4.3 Fringe compensation varied far more widely than formal wages.

salaries in first-world countries, the finding of such gaps within a single province is striking. To put this pattern in context, imagine that public employees in one county of California were compensated 26 times more than their counterparts in another Californian county.[58]

My data includes three main sources of revenue for local governments: *tax revenue, agency collection,* and *fiscal transfers.* In China, local governments are not authorized to create their own taxes, but they are allowed to retain a certain portion of tax revenue according to tax-sharing rules. Most Chinese taxes are business-related taxes, such as the value-added tax. Expanding the tax base, therefore, requires attracting businesses. Agency collection amounts to the revenue collected by individual departments, mainly through fees and fines. Finally, fiscal transfers comprise financial aid and earmarked grants from higher-level governments. Although land proceeds occupy a growing share of local public finances, they are excluded from my analysis because they are an earmarked fund that can be legally spent only on land and construction purposes. Local leaders who misappropriate these funds to disburse staff allowances and perks will not only be criminally liable, but will also

[58] Although the pay of state governors in the United States varies across states and over time, the salaries of public administrators are generally flat (Di Tella and Fisman 2004).

compromise the infrastructure projects that are key to their political success.[59]

In addition to the county-level data used in this chapter, it is useful to look at longitudinal patterns from a separate dataset that measures actual compensation among sub-provincial (city and county) governments in Shandong, from 1979 to 2005. As we see in Figure 4.4, in 1979, when market reforms began, the majority of public compensation was in the fringe category, although the amount was meager in absolute terms. From 1979 to 1993, the initial phase of market liberalization, formal wages barely budged, whereas fringe allowances and benefits nearly doubled. From 1994 onward, central authorities raised formal salaries several times, but even by 2005, the effect was small.

The left plot in Figure 4.5 shows that formal public wages fell consistently below average urban wages in the province, which on the surface confirms a scenario of "capitulation wages." When fringe components are added, however, as shown in the plot on the right, an average civil servant earned considerably higher income than an average urban worker, and furthermore, this gap expanded over time.

PUTTING THE GOLDEN GOOSE TO THE TEST

The purpose of my regression analysis is not to prove that revenue causes spending (obviously, it does), but rather to test whether the correlation patterns are consistent with expectations of how profit-sharing operates in the Chinese bureaucracy. In particular, we wish to know whether the golden goose maxim holds in practice, as follows.

- H1: In the short term, agency collections raise public compensation more than tax revenue.
- H2: In the long term, however, tax revenue raises compensation more than agency collections.

Standard regressions estimate a composite effect of a given explanatory variable over an outcome, but they don't distinguish between

[59] Interview with Finance Bureau, Stanford–NDRC Joint Field Trip, August 2012.

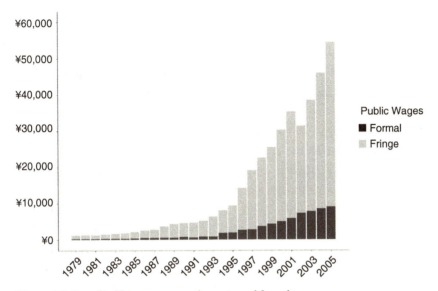

Figure 4.4 Growth of fringe compensation outpaced formal wages.

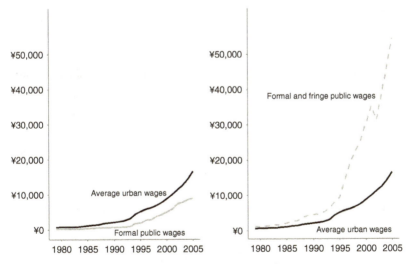

Figure 4.5 Total bureaucratic income exceeded average urban wages.

short- and long-term effects. The single-equation error-correction model (ECM), on the other hand, is designed to estimate the parameters of the short- and long-term effects of the explanatory variables (three sources of public revenue) on the dependent variable (levels of public compensation).[60]

In my analysis, the dependent variable of interest is total compensation (formal and fringe components combined) per public employee, or *comp*.[61] All fiscal variables are expressed in per capita terms. I condition on a number of factors: population size, share of urban population, and total number of public employees. To control for time-invariant unobserved effects across the county governments (for example, leadership idiosyncrasies), I include county fixed effects. To control for unit-invariant exogenous shocks, e.g., aftershocks of the Asian financial crisis, I also include year fixed effects. I ran a separate specification that also conditioned on GDP per capita, which is excluded from the final regression, as it does not change the direction or statistical significance of the results.[62]

An ECM requires that analysts specify the dependent variable as a differenced value, i.e., this year's value minus the previous year's value. In addition, the regression must include (a) the lagged dependent variable (value from the previous year), (b) lagged values of all explanatory and control variables, and (c) differenced values of all explanatory and control variables.

For *short-term* effects, we examine the differenced values of all explanatory and control variables. The coefficients indicate the estimated contemporaneous effects of a unit change in the explanatory variable on the outcome. In my case, this is an estimate of how changes in each revenue stream in a given year correlate with changes in bureaucratic compensation levels in the same year. For *long-term* effects, we examine the estimated coefficients of the lagged values. These coefficients are estimates of the long-term effect on compensation levels over multiple time periods. The

---

[60] Statistically, the basic idea of the ECM is that there exists a long-run equilibrium between two or more time-series variables, but with short-lived deviations from the equilibrium. Effects of changes in independent variables on the dependent variable may either be contemporaneous (i.e., they happen during the same period, T_0) or cumulative (i.e., distributed over future periods from T_1 to T_n) (De Boef and Keele 2008).

[61] Running the regressions with only fringe compensation as the dependent variable does not change my results.

[62] The only difference is that, because GDP per capita correlates highly with tax revenue, it slightly reduces its estimated coefficient in the model.

TABLE 4.2 *Linkages between revenue sources and compensation*

Revenue source	Dependent variable: total compensation
Fiscal Variables (short-term effects)	
D. *tax revenue* per capita	13.18*** (1.43)
D. *agency collections* per capita	20.21*** (2.06)
D. *fiscal transfers* per capita	4.51*** (1.44)
Fiscal Variables (long-term effects)	
L. *tax revenue* per capita	13.45*** (1.74)
L. *agency collections* per capita	2.52 (2.29)
L. *fiscal transfers* per capita	3.14** (1.46)
Control Variables	
D. *population*	170.76*** (34.70)
D. *urban share of population*	−7.23 (12.16)
D. *no. of cadres*	−1.43*** (0.13)
L. *population*	220.65*** (39.50)
L. *urban share of population*	−12.00 (18.71)
L. *no. of cadres*	−0.75*** (0.16)
Lagged DV (Error-correction term)	−0.41*** (0.04)
County fixed effects included?	Yes
Year fixed effects included?	Yes
Constant	5,239.08
N	952
R^2	0.50

Standard errors are given in parentheses. Note: * $p < 0.10$, ** $p < 0.05$, *** $p < 0.01$.

rate at which this long-term effect manifests itself is calculated using the error-correction term, which is the value of the lagged dependent variable. *Total effects* refer to the sum of short- and long-term effects.

Table 4.2 reports the results of my regressions. First, let's explore short-term effects, which are indicated by the differenced value of each variable, denoted in the table as D. The variables D. *tax revenue*, D. *agency collection*, and D. *fiscal transfers* each register a statistically significant and positive effect on *comp*, indicating that an increase in all three revenue streams raises compensation in the short term. But the magnitudes of their effects differ. *Agency collection* has the largest coefficient (20.21), compared with *tax revenue* (13.18) and *fiscal transfers* (4.51). This means that, consistently with H1, an increase in *agency collections* raises bureaucratic compensation more than *tax revenue* in the short term. Specifically, a unit increase in *agency collection* is correlated with an increase in compensation by 20 Yuan, whereas an equivalent increase in *tax revenue* will boost it by only 13 Yuan. Expressed in the plain language of a Chinese bureaucrat, this result verifies the following: "From a short-term perspective and the narrow view of one department, it appears that it makes so much more money this year by collecting more fees."[63]

When we examine long-term effects, however, the results are reversed. Long-term effects are indicated by the lagged value of each variable, denoted as L. In Table 4.2, L. *tax revenue* posts a statistically significant and positive coefficient, whereas the coefficient for L. *agency collection* is positive but not statistically significant. A unit increase in *tax revenue* registers a long-term effect of raising compensation by 33 Yuan, which, according to the ECM model, plays out over multiple time periods in percentages.[64] Simply put, consistently with H2, these results indicate that expanding the formal tax base raises public compensation over the long term, but extracting fees and fines for one's agency may not. It supports an earlier statement made by a Chinese bureaucrat: "Growing our local economy is more important than departmental self-financing ... because it promotes a healthy progression of staff welfare and budget."[65]

For a visual representation of the regression results, following the approach of King *et al.*,[66] I simulated the short-term and long-term effects of a unit increase in *tax revenue* versus *agency collections* on cadre compensation. This approach visualizes the distribution of possible values of Y (compensation levels) based on parameters and standard errors specified in Model 1. Figure 4.6 illustrates the short-term effects. In this figure, *agency collections* lies on the farther end of the x axis, indicating that on average *agency collections* increase compensation more than *tax revenue* in the short term. But the upper-bound parameters of *tax revenue* overlap

---

[63] Interview B2011-286.

[64] The magnitude of long-term effects cannot be directly read off the coefficients of the lagged fiscal variables. Instead, it is obtained by dividing the coefficient of the lagged independent variables by the negative value of the lagged dependent variable. Thus, the figure of 33 Yuan is obtained by taking the coefficient value of 13.45 (L. *tax revenue*) divided by the negative value of the ECM term. The statistical interpretation of an ECM model is that the long-term effect plays out over multiple time periods in progressive percentages. The ECM term of –0.46 tells us that 46 percent of the long-term multiplier effects are played out in T1, leaving 54 percent of the disequilibrium shock after T1, and so on.

[65] Interview B2012-301.   [66] King *et al.* (2000).

with the lower-bound values of *agency collections*, which means that, even in the short term, higher *tax revenue* may raise compensation levels more than *agency collection*.

Figure 4.7 simulates the long-term effects, in which we see a reversal of the patterns. Tax revenue lies on the farther right end of the x axis, which means that expanding the formal tax base correlates with substantively higher levels of compensation than extracting more fees and fines. Importantly, even the upper-bound predicted parameters of *agency collections* are lower than the lower-bound values of *tax revenue*, indicating that the long-term effects of *tax revenue* dominate those of *agency collection* at the 99 percent confidence level.

In sum, the empirical analysis supports my qualitative findings. Compensation rates in the county bureaucracies are directly tied to fiscal performance, both tax revenue and agency collections. In the short term, extracting fees, fines, and user charges is more financially rewarding for bureaucrats than tax growth. But, over the long term, growing the formal tax base by attracting and retaining investors generates higher remuneration and staff benefits than extracting rents.

CARROTS AND STICKS

Local Chinese bureaucrats know that it doesn't pay to kill the goose (the health of the local economy) that lays the golden eggs (their pay and perks).[67] My statistical analysis shows that this belief is grounded in reality. How was the belief formed? One possibility is that over time, as local bureaucrats experience consistent payoffs from profit-sharing practices, they converged upon an unwritten but common set of expectations, which they eventually took for granted. This is reinforced by county bureaucrats' informal comparison of their compensation with that of counterparts from other counties, with whom they regularly interact during study trips and higher-level meetings, and through office gossip. When they find that wealthier counties pay their staff members

---

[67] One analysis based in India also demonstrates the "golden goose" effect, but its focus is on "illicit future rents" – that is, bribe extraction – rather than fringe compensation (Niehaus and Sukhtankar 2013).

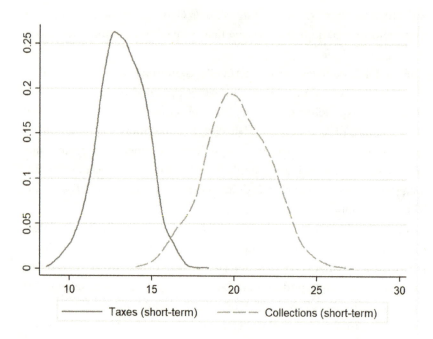

Figure 4.6 Increasing agency collections was more rewarding in the short term.

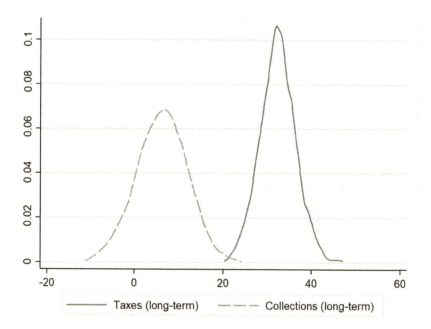

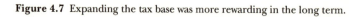

Figure 4.7 Expanding the tax base was more rewarding in the long term.

significantly more, it persuasively demonstrates that growing businesses and tax income is the best way to secure generous compensation, as one bureaucrat expressed:[68]

> Our compensation is only about half that of bureaucrats in adjacent County Y. Our formal salary is the same, but the difference lies in subsidies and allowances, which is paid according to local tax revenues. County Y offers their staff a transportation subsidy and extra bonuses for achieving targets, but not our county. Why the big difference among the counties? Our county is poor!

Additionally, leaders periodically and explicitly remind staff members of their personal stake in supporting local economic development. For example, at a staff meeting in a city of Fujian province that I studied, the deputy mayor intoned: "Do not forget the fact that taxes paid by our enterprises are closely and personally connected to your benefit. Taxes collected go toward paying your allowances. So serve our enterprises well!"[69] Over time, as this city's economy took off and the tax base grew, it stopped relying on fees and fines as a supplemental source of income for its local agencies.

NATIONAL ADMINISTRATIVE REFORMS

While carrots are important, they work only when combined with the appropriate sticks – mechanisms of control and punishments at both the national and local levels. In Chapter 3, I described the sweeping procedural reforms that Premier Zhu Rongji rolled out in 1998 to create a modern public administration that would complement a modern market economy. These budgetary and fiscal reforms increased state capacity to monitor and control financial transactions at lower tiers of government and among individual departments. Recall that many of the problems associated with agency-level corruption in the 1980s and 1990s, such as departmental slush funds (*xiaojinku*), arbitrary extraction of fees, fines, and levies (*sanluan*), and extortion (*tanpai*), resulted from excessive decentralization of bureaucratic self-financing and self-remunerating. All

---

[68] Interview B2008-136.   [69] Interview B2013-324.

public organizations engaged in these practices, but, in the early decades, there was little centralized monitoring or enforcement of penalties.

In the 2000s, the procedures by which agencies collected and spent revenue underwent a quiet revolution, which becomes apparent when we disaggregate the life cycle of fee collection. Prior to the 2000s, fees and fines were simply "collected and spent" (*zuoshou zuozhi*). For example, an inspector who accused a producer of violating regulations could demand a fine on the spot. He could then pocket a bribe, deliver the fine in cash to departmental coffers, or do both. Before the 2000s, it was almost impossible to track these numerous transactions. As a result, embezzlement and misappropriation were rampant (see Chapter 3). As one Ministry of Finance (MOF) official said, "We caught wrong-doers many times. But there were always more of them. It became clear to us that the system had gone wrong. So the system had to change."[70]

One major reform spearheaded by the MOF in 2001 was the creation of the Treasury Single Account (TSA), which was first piloted at the central level and then extended to subnational governments. The treasury system governs the structure of bank accounts in the entire public sector, and deposits and disburses public funds. Previously, public bank accounts were highly fragmented across levels of administration, regions, and departments. Before 2001, the default practice was that individual public units would set up "transitory accounts" at their own discretion. Because these accounts proliferated and were not linked to one another, even the MOF could not know how much other ministries collected and spent. Moreover, any transfer of funds had to pass through multiple layers and hands. As a senior official at the MOF related, in one instance, it took almost 10 months for the unit of another Ministry to receive its budgeted funds. Even within the central government, it took at least a month for funds to reach intended recipients.[71] Such extreme fragmentation not only hindered the execution of budgetary plans, but also enabled the diversion and misuse of public funds at all levels.

Reform of the treasury system began with the establishment of Treasury Disbursement Centers (TDCs) throughout the country, which process claims and make payments to vendors. The MOF outlawed

---

[70] Interview B2006-7.   [71] Interview B2006-3.

transitory accounts and consolidated all existing accounts into a single network so that they can be easily traced. To be sure, some agencies still violate these rules, but doing so is now clearly illegal.

After consolidating the network of accounts, the MOF required public units to make payments to employees and vendors through TDCs so that all expenditure could be centrally monitored. By 2006, the MOF was able to track every revenue and expenditure item in over 20,000 central-level public organizations at any point in time. As one MOF official remarked, "If someone in the bureaucracy goes to dinner with official funds, we know exactly where they dined and what they ate."[72] In recent years, the spread of digital payments has further enhanced fiscal transparency within the bureaucracy.

The introduction of cashless payments of fees and fines also aided the centralization of public accounts.[73] Instead of collecting payments in cash, regulatory officers are now required to issue a "non-tax revenue collection certificate." Like official receipts, these certificates are issued by the provincial governments and each one carries a bar-code so that payments can be traced.[74] To pay fees, citizens take the payment certificate to a bank at any administrative services center, where they receive an official receipt. The bank then directly deposits the fee into a centralized treasury system. Monitoring cameras deter staff members at administrative services centers from collecting petty bribes.[75]

As I argued in Chapter 3, these capacity-building measures only check non-transactional malfeasance; they do not prevent bribery. Officials may still receive kickbacks for procurement deals that are legally processed through the TDCs. Nor can these reforms withstand political pressures from corrupt powerful leaders who can override the system or collude with subordinated auditors to embezzle funds on a grand scale, as seen in the case of Chen Liangyu, the former provincial Party chief of Shanghai.

Still, there is no doubt that the post-1998 reforms have increased fiscal transparency, especially among street-level bureaucrats. In short, these institutional reforms have heightened the risks of getting caught for

---

[72] Interview B2006-7.

[73] This parallels recent attempts by Indian Prime Minister Modi to fight corruption through demonetization.

[74] Interview B2010-196; B2011-226; B2011-227; B2011-228.   [75] Interview B2011-237.

stealing. Unsurprisingly, cases of embezzlement and the misuse of public funds have precipitously fallen since 2000, as shown in Chapter 3.

ADDITIONAL LOCAL MEASURES. On top of nationally mandated administrative reforms, some local governments devised their own measures for curtailing the extortion and harassment of businesses by local agencies. This is especially common among poor localities, which rely heavily on individual departments to make up for their budgetary shortfalls by collecting fees and fines.

Some local governments established specialized monitoring agencies that review and approve requests from other departments to conduct inspections and collect payments from local businesses. In one county in Hunan province, the Office for Enhancing the Business Environment performed such a function. Chiefs of other agencies who conducted inspections without prior approval from this office could be reported to the county leadership and penalized.[76] This office was also put in charge of holding regular feedback sessions with companies and attending to their complaints about harassment.

In the poorest locales, where bureaucratic predation was most widespread, the local leadership issued a blanket order to prohibit inspections and fee collection from businesses on certain days of each month. In Hubei province, this was known as "leave businesses alone days" (*qiye anjingri*). As a county-level disciplinary officer described, "The purpose is to give our enterprises a peaceful environment to operate. Otherwise, they can't take it if they are inspected every day. Sometimes county-level officials conduct inspections, followed by city-level regulators. They can't do business this way." In addition, the prohibitions were built into the cadre-evaluation system, such that bureau chiefs would be held accountable for violations made by their staff members.[77]

Relying on individual agencies to partially self-finance is meant to be a crutch, not a permanent solution. In the wealthiest locations I studied, such as in Shanghai, districts and counties have become sufficiently wealthy to pay their civil servants entirely through formal tax income. As a result, these locales do not need draconian control

---

[76] Interview REG 2012–012; REG 2012–015. [77] Interview B2013-334; REG 2012–023.

measures to curtail bureaucratic extraction. Nor do they require strong incentives for self-financing through informal refund procedures. But these cases are more the exception than the norm. Because most local governments are still financially constrained,[78] their objective is not to eradicate the collection of supplemental income, but rather to regulate it.

WHY STANDARD REFORMS FAIL. More broadly, this chapter sheds light on why replicating "best practices" in developing countries frequently fails. Standard public sector reforms, adopted by international agencies such as the World Bank and national governments,[79] aim to slash redundant staff and raise formal wages to deter corruption. A number of African countries also tried to pay salaries according to performance by importing Strategic Performance Management (SPM) models from industrialized OECD countries and the private sector.

Although such reforms seem right in principle, they rarely work in practice. For example, in 2007, the Nigerian government increased wages by 15 percent across the board. The result was "a huge financial burden on public services with little in the way of positive outputs,"[80] African scholar Oluwu concludes. Similarly, Uganda tried to pay civil servants a living wage but gave up due to unsustainable costs.[81] Meanwhile, attempts to import pay-for-performance models from the first world soon fell apart because evaluating "performance" in patronage-dominant contexts proved unrealistic. These examples illustrate "capability traps," which Andrews, Pritchett, and Woolcock define as "a dynamic in which governments constantly adopt 'reforms' to shore up legitimacy and ensure ongoing flows of external financing yet never actually improve."[82]

Why did seemingly straightforward, technical reforms fail? First, firing bureaucrats and public employees is always politically contentious. Second, raising formal wages across the board poses a huge burden to state budgets,

---

[78] Sub-provincial governments face intense budgetary pressures because of a vertical fiscal imbalance, meaning that tremendous fiscal responsibilities are placed upon them (World Bank and DRC of State Council 2013).

[79] Lindauer and Nunberg (1994).   [80] Olowu (2010).   [81] Olowu (2010, 642).

[82] Andrews *et al.* (2013).

and without robust monitoring and administrative capacity, it does not ensure less corruption or better performance.[83] Third, pay-for-performance models imported from wealthy industrialized economies are premised upon first-world conditions,[84] namely, that civil servants receive a secure living wage and that politics is separated from public administration. Where these conditions have been established, governments can set and enforce standards of performance, centered on citizens' rating of public services and accountability. The problem with much of the prescriptive literature in public administration is that Western models are marketed as universally applicable to developing states even though they are not.

The problems that plagued Nigeria and Uganda were also present in China. But instead of "skipping straight to Weber," China adapted pre-existing prebendal practices and pegged bureaucratic compensation to fiscal performance. This does not mean, however, that other developing countries should simply "copy" what China did – to do so would be to repeat the folly of mimicking best practices from the West.[85] What we should take away from China's experience, rather, are broad lessons and principles, of which I highlight three.

First, if policymakers expect bureaucracies to promote growth and deliver services, then they must think about giving rank-and-file public agents a personal stake in the outcomes of their efforts, a condition woefully absent in the developing world. Indeed, as Klitgaard remarked, "the problem of public sector incentives in developing countries seems not yet to have been noticed by scholars and aid agencies."[86] China's bureaucracy is unusual in its focus on *monetary* incentives, but non-monetary incentives such as organizational solidarity and a sense of purpose may be just as important.[87] That said, filling stomachs is an imperative; inspirational

---

[83] Becker and Stigler (1974); Di Tella and Schargrodsky (2003).

[84] On Strategic Performance Management, see Heinrich (2004); Lah and Perry (2008); Richard (2013). An earlier first-world model that diffused widely to developing countries is New Public Management, which drew management techniques from the private sector and was inspired by New Zealand's experience (Lane 2000).

[85] I thank Woolcock for stressing this point. He and his co-authors caution against trying to "look" like modern states without functioning like them (Pritchett and Woolcock 2004; Pritchett *et al.* 2013).

[86] Klitgaard (1988).

[87] Kaufman (1960); Woolcock and Narayan (2000); Tsai (2007b); Lee (2015); McDonnell (2017). Recent surveys of the Nigerian and Ghanaian civil service define and measure

messages alone cannot whip public workers into action. Public administrations in developing countries must therefore consider a *mixture* of non-monetary incentives and monetary incentives beyond formal pay.

Second, instead of skipping straight to Weber, policymakers should develop transitional strategies of administrative reform. Qian points out that in China "transitional institutions," such as dual-track pricing (part centrally planned, part market-based), worked, because "they improve economic efficiency on the one hand, and make the reform a win–win game and interest compatible for those in power on the other."[88] Qian's logic extends to the realm of administrative reform. As this chapter shows, the compensation structure in the reform-era bureaucracy is also "dual-track" – part fixed wages, part variable benefits. China did not become trapped in cycles of petty corruption because as local governments became wealthier, they compensated bureaucrats with increased tax revenue. China presents one example of *transitional administrative institutions*, but many other forms may exist or be improvised in other national contexts.

Third, the literature in public administration should acknowledge its first-world, Western-centeredness. Just as scholars of non-Western countries are routinely expected to justify the generalizability of their cases, scholars of public administration who study countries such as those in Western Europe and the United States should acknowledge the same caveat – their models are limited to first-world conditions.[89] For example, the vast literature on "public service motivation" assumes that civil servants need not worry about salary or subsistence, which is not the reality faced in countries like China and Uganda.[90]

"performance-based incentives" as career incentives (Rasul *et al.* 2017; Rasul and Rogger 2018), whereas my analysis focuses on fringe compensation.

[88] Qian (2003).

[89] For example, Wilson's classic is generically titled *Bureaucracy* (1989), even though it is focused on the American bureaucracy. Likewise, Rainey's (1997) textbook, hailed by reviewers as "the Encyclopedia Britannica of public management," is titled *Understanding and Managing Public Organizations*, even though it is specifically a book on Western or first-world public organizations. Can we imagine a study based on Chinese or African experiences being titled *Public Organizations*? When Western experiences are held up as the norm, non-Western experiences are assumed to be anomalous (Wong 1997; Centeno 2002; Hui 2005).

[90] Perry and Wise (1990); Perry (1996).

THE VALUE OF DISCOVERY BEFORE TESTING

Apart from its substantive findings, this chapter also illustrates a particular style of mixed-methods research – relying on in-depth fieldwork to *discover* practices that were hitherto undocumented or misrepresented in the literature (for example, how fringe compensation works in the Chinese bureaucracy), and then *testing* qualitative findings using statistical analyses (whether developmental behavior really benefits bureaucrats more than extractive behavior).[91] Political scientists have long debated the merits of qualitative research in opposition to quantitative research.[92] The classic textbook *Designing Social Inquiry*, by King, Keohane, and Verba (KKV), argues that both qualitative and quantitative research should abide by the same standards of logical inference.[93] While I completely agree that qualitative research must be conducted rigorously, I would argue that KKV's methodological paradigm misses two key points.

First, before we can proceed to test any causal argument, we must first discover an interesting problem and/or possible solutions. For example, in cancer studies, medical scientists must first have discovered the ailment of cancer, described its manifestations, and speculated about its possible causes, before future generations of scientists could test a particular cause of cancer using statistical data and regressions. Similarly, in the social sciences, *discovery* through observation and immersion is indispensable. Had I not spent time talking with local Chinese bureaucrats, I wouldn't have known how they were actually compensated, let alone have hypothesized the incentive logic behind their profit-sharing practices. In this instance, my hypotheses were inductively derived from "soaking and poking," to use Fenno's famous phrase, rather than deduced from abstract assumptions.[94] It is unfortunate, however, that such qualitative work is increasingly dismissed as mere "description" and perceived as inferior to statistical methods.[95] As one graduate student once asked me, "Why didn't you do research?" I did – discovery *is* research.

---

[91] On complementarities between qualitative and quantitative research, see George and Bennett (2005).
[92] Collier *et al.* (2003).   [93] King *et al.* (1994); for a critique, see Mahoney (2009).
[94] Fenno (1978).
[95] To "describe" means to narrate without providing any analytic value, but to discover is to find something interesting or important. Discoveries can be made either by observing patterns in numerical data or by immersion in real-world settings, or both.

Second, mainstream methodological norms, such as those advanced by KKV, presume first-world conditions, where the context and "rules of the game" are transparent and firmly established. But, in developing and transitional countries, how things really work on the ground is generally obscure because informal, unwritten practices prevail and quality data are lacking. Thus, unlike the study of first-world countries, that of the developing world demands far more on-the-ground investigation. Oftentimes, in these settings, what matters most and how it matters hasn't even been *discovered*, let alone understood and made ready for hypothesis testing. Those who study or try to "help" developing countries through the lens of first-world experiences often end up chasing the wrong questions or problems.[96]

This chapter illustrates that a simple qualitative discovery can transform theories and the way we collect numerical datasets. Through interviews, I found that fringe compensation in the Chinese bureaucracy isn't just "corruption" – it comprises about three-quarters of average compensation and performs an important incentive role. And such compensation exists across public administrations across developing countries. If this reality is taken into account, we can open up new theories and tests of public wage incentives. For example, Di Tella and Schargrodsky present an intriguing test of the relative effects of stronger audits and higher wages on corruption among public hospitals in Argentina. Their data on wages, however, were obtained through interviews that asked hospital staff for "their nominal wage," omitting fringe pay and benefits, which could be significant, as we saw in China.[97] The inclusion of intermediate categories – neither formal nor corrupt – can revise and expand our understanding of bureaucratic incentives.

CONCLUSION

How can poor and institutionally backward countries escape the trap of "corruption-causing-poverty-causing-corruption"? This chapter illustrated

---

[96] This is a common problem in international development, where well-meaning organizations deliver aid that local communities in third-world settings do not actually need or want (Ang 2018d; Coyne 2013).

[97] Di Tella and Schargrodsky (2003, 276).

that fringe compensation, which is neither formal salary nor illegal monies, can serve as a form of efficiency wages. To incentivize economic performance, Chinese local states evolved profit-sharing practices that linked the personal payoffs of tens of millions of bureaucrats both to their locality's tax income and to their agency's non-tax collections. However, in the long term, fostering economic growth is more beneficial for bureaucrats than extracting rents. This was common knowledge among the Chinese public agents I interviewed – and my statistical analysis of bureaucratic compensation patterns reflected their beliefs.

China's unorthodox experiences must not be seen as a template for copying, however. Their value lies in highlighting the need for deeply contextual research that uncovers realities in developing countries and tailors solutions to them. As Riggs pointed out decades ago, the study of developing countries calls for theories of governance and public administration that reflect their capability constraints.[98] Such research has been particularly lacking in the design of incentives and transitional administrative institutions.

Having unpacked the incentive structure of the bottom 99 percent of China's bureaucracy, the logical step is to move up the hierarchy. Chapter 5 will turn to the top one percent of political elites who rule over local jurisdictions. Profit-sharing for leaders follows a different logic: the more economically prosperous the locality, the more personal rents they can extract – not in the form of petty allowances or perks, but as massive graft.

---

[98] Riggs (1964). For a recent and influential extension of this perspective, see Andrews *et al.* (2017).

CHAPTER 5

Corrupt and Competent

E VER SINCE XI LAUNCHED HIS ANTI-CORRUPTION DRIVE
in 2012, scandals have occupied news headlines daily. Corrupt
officials are falling by the droves, revealing lurid details: piles of cash
stashed away in multiple properties, vacant mansions stocked with illicit
gifts (in one case, a gold boat, a gold wash basin, and a gold statute of
Mao),[1] ghost accounts in a mother's name, public offices for sale, hired
thugs, sex tapes, mistresses, even murder.

In *China's Crony Capitalism*, which draws on 260 corruption scandals
reported in the media, Pei paints a dire picture. According to him,
market reform under one-party rule has produced "a rapacious form of
crony capitalism," a gigantic apparatus of officials "who can with great
ease convert their public authority into illicit instruments," and a political
economy marked by "looting, debauchery, and utter lawlessness."[2]

But there are some things that the news doesn't cover. In reality, many
corrupt Chinese officials were once political stars, workaholics famed for
their ability to deliver results, who were genuinely appreciated by local
residents.[3] The best-known example is Bo Xilai, Chongqing's former Party
chief, who became a notorious symbol of corruption and Machiavellian

---

[1] Demetri Sevastopulo, "China's Goldfinger General Quizzed in Corruption Probe,"
Financial Times, 15 January 2014.

[2] Pei (2016), cited from pp. 2, 183, and 1. Bachman, Howson, and Sun offer a careful set of
reviews in *Asia Policy* in 2017.

[3] Indeed, even after Bo's disgrace, some Chongqing residents continued to express appreciation of his leadership, as one Weibo post wrote, "Bo gave us annual 15 percent growth.
Every day he gave 1.3 million rural children free eggs and milk. He gave rural residents
the same health insurance as urban residents. I will miss him." See "Party Ousts Chinese
Regional Chief," *The New York Times*, 15 March 2012.

intrigue. Before his fall, however, Bo was in the running for China's top leadership. His heavy-handed yet resolute style of leadership dramatically transformed the Southwestern backwater of Chongqing within five years, spurring its economy, distributing benefits to the poor, and reviving Maoist fervor all at once. At the height of his political career, Bo's "Chongqing model" seized national and even global attention.[4]

All over the country and at all levels of government, there are many other officials like Bo: ruthless and charming, at times fearsome, at times pitiful. To caricature all of them as sleazy crooks is to miss a core feature of China's political system: growth promotion and self-enrichment often go hand-in-hand.

This chapter serves three objectives. First, instead of repeating the salacious details of corruption scandals, I flesh out the entire career paths of two fallen officials: Bo Xilai (provincial party secretary of Chongqing) and Ji Jianye (city mayor of Nanjing). This exercise reveals that notoriously corrupt officials can be simultaneously growth-promoting. Second, consistently with Chapters 2 and 3, my accounts will show that corruption among Chinese political elites and local leaders primarily took the form of access money – elite exchanges of power and wealth – rather than theft or extortion. Third, I pinpoint the structural distortions and risks brought about by access money, even though this form of corruption can stimulate commerce and investment in the short term.

With case studies, my purpose is not to make generalizations, but rather to highlight mechanisms. I also hope to provide a counter-narrative to the deluge of corruption scandals churned out by the press and used in some studies as primary or even sole evidence. No doubt, corruption is endemic in China, but that's only one side of the story. For a full understanding, we must examine the two faces of Chinese officialdom.

BEFORE AND AFTER

Public esteem is capricious. When politicians are on the rise, the people and media are full of praise. But as soon as they fall, stars become pariahs

---

[4] Huang (2011); Mulvad (2015); Stromseth *et al.* (2017).

overnight. Before diving into the case studies, it is useful to compare Chinese media portrayals of Bo Xilai and Ji Jianye – the two protagonists of this chapter – *before* and *after* their fall from grace.

For this comparison, I conduct a word cloud analysis of media coverage in the *People's Daily* and *Xinhua,* two official press outlets. A word cloud is a method of visualizing word frequency in a corpus of texts, where the size of the words represents the frequency of mentions, and the most dominant words are placed at the center. Word clouds help to identify the focus or priorities of a given set of discourse. In this instance, they reveal how the two politicians were perceived and portrayed before and after they fell.[5]

First, consider Bo Xilai, who became the poster man of Chinese corruption in 2012. Figure 5.1 visualizes media coverage of Bo: the top half shows the most frequently used words a year prior to his fall and the bottom half presents the period after his fall.[6] Table 5.1 lists the top 10 words in each period. Before Bo fell, Chinese media coverage touted his accomplishments. "Development" (*fazhan*) was the most frequently used term. In addition to spotlighting his work on the "economy" (#3) specifically in Chongqing (#2), the media profiled non-economic parts of his portfolio: "society" (#6) and "culture" (#7). Reflecting his populist appeal, Bo was described in connection to "the people" (#9) and "masses" (#10). Other words that frequently appeared with him include "livelihoods," "poverty alleviation," "industries," "audit," "new zones," "speed up," and "participate." Altogether, the portrait emerges of a dynamic leader who got many things done at once.

After he fell in March 2012, however, public discourse of Bo turned sharply toward corruption and his political stand-off with the leadership, President Hu Jintao and Premier Wen Jiabao. The words "Chongqing," "economy," "culture," "citizens," and "masses" dropped off the top-10 list,

---

[5] After cleaning the data source by removing stop words (words that serve grammatical functions but have no substantive meaning), I count the occurrence of words in the pre-fall and post-fall clusters, divided by the total number of articles in each cluster. The maximum number of words is set at 250.

[6] In Bo's case, I analyze mentions in the *People's Daily,* drawn from the China National Knowledge Infrastructure (CNKI) electronic database. Bo officially fell on 15 March 2012. The period before his fall covered March 2011 to 15 March 2012, whereas the post-fall period covered 16 March 2012 to April 2013. In total 66 articles were analyzed.

TABLE 5.1 *Top 10 words describing Bo Xilai before and after his fall*

Rank of frequency	Word, before fall		Word, after fall	
1	发展	development	建设	construct
2	重庆	Chongqing	工作	work
3	经济	economy	腐败	corruption
4	工作	work	中央	central (authority)
5	建设	construct	发展	development
6	社会	society	干部	cadres
7	文化	culture	中国	China
8	全国	entire country	全国	entire country
9	人民	the people	胡锦涛	Hu Jintao
10	群众	masses	社会	society

Before fall

After fall

Figure 5.1 Media coverage of Bo Xilai before and after his fall.

being replaced by "corruption," "central authority," "cadres," "China," and "Hu Jintao." The replacement of "Chongqing" by "China" signaled that events surrounding Bo were no longer just local politics but a national crisis. Other prominent words include "inspect," "anti-corruption," "promote clean government," "resolute," and "strengthen," indicating that media coverage after the exposure of Bo's infractions focused on central authorities' attempts to place him in cuffs.

Whereas Bo was a Politburo member and provincial chief, Ji Jianye, former city mayor of Nanjing, was a sub-provincial official of lower (vice-ministerial) rank. Nevertheless, in Figure 5.2 and Table 5.2 we see a similarly sharp reversal of media coverage of Ji before and after his fall.[7] Prior to being investigated for corruption, Ji was famous in Jiangsu province and even nationally as a competent but heavy-handed leader. Before he fell, the top three words describing Ji in the media were "Nanjing," "development," and "city/urban." Like Bo, his accomplishments went beyond growing the economy and extended into provision of social welfare and public services, as indicated by these words on the top-10 list: "society" (#5), "services" (#7), "civic affairs" (#10). Other common terms project the image of ambitious, well-rounded leadership: "happiness," "globalize," "ecology," "investment," "employment," "pensions," "subway," and "technology."

But soon after Ji's investigation was announced, the media stopped mentioning his development-promoting leadership. Indeed, media mentions of Ji plummeted, as he wasn't a national celebrity-and-villain like Bo, who continued to attract attention until the end of his criminal trials. The few times that Ji was mentioned, his crimes and punishments dominated media coverage: "inspect" (#2), "power" (#4), "problem" (#7), and "corrupt" (#8). References to his achievements as mayor all but vanished.

To sum up, a simple text analysis shows that it is misleading to draw conclusions about the Chinese political system solely on the basis of media reports of corruption. Once officials fall from grace, stories of their crimes and vices eclipse their past contributions to development. As Bachman

---

[7] In Ji's case, I analyze mentions in the *People's Daily* and *Xinhua*, drawn from the CNKI electronic database. Ji's investigation was publicly announced on 16 October 2013. My analysis includes a total of 49 articles that covered the period of a year before and after his fall.

TABLE 5.2 *Top 10 words describing Ji Jianye before and after his fall*

Rank of frequency	Word, before fall		Word, after fall	
1	南京	Nanjing	干部	cadre
2	发展	development	监督	monitor
3	城市	city/urban	领导	leadership
4	建设	construct	权力	power
5	社会	society	工作	work
6	工作	work	中央	central (authority)
7	服务	services	问题	problem
8	产业	industries	腐败	corruption
9	经济	economy	建设	construct
10	民政	civic affairs	制度	institution

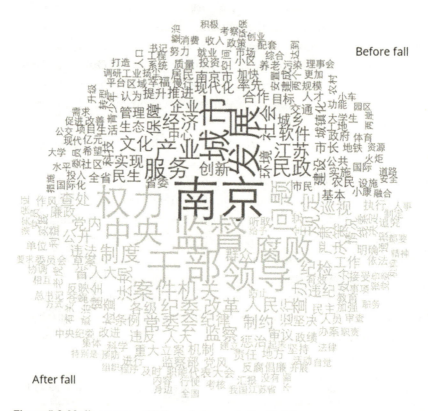

Before fall

After fall

Figure 5.2 Media coverage of Ji Jianye before and after his fall.

incisively asks in his review of *China's Crony Capitalism,* "Corruption may be endemic, but is it the whole story or even the most important part of the story?"[8] The word clouds in Figures 5.1 and 5.2 visualize my answer to Bachman's question: no – it's only the *bottom* half of the story.

BO XILAI: A FALLEN PRINCELING

Bo Xilai (Figure 5.3) was a princeling, the son of one of the Party's revered pioneers, Bo Yibo. In other words, he was a second-generation aristocrat in modern capitalist China. During the Cultural Revolution (1965–1975), Bo's family was purged and forced to live in miserable conditions. But when Deng took over the helm of the Party, he resuscitated Bo Yibo's career, enlisting him as Vice Premier to help steer the opening of markets and global trade.

As scion of a revolutionary clan, Bo Xilai catapulted through the political ranks. Table 5.3 lists the milestones in his career path. Unlike regular officials who typically climb their way up from bottom rungs, Bo

Figure 5.3 Bo Xilai is surrounded by reporters when arriving at the 11th National People's Congress in Beijing in 2010.

[8] Bachman (2017).

TABLE 5.3 *Milestones in Bo Xilai's career path*

Period	Location and office	Position
1982–1984	Central Party Committee, Secretariat and Research Office	Officer
1984–1987	Liaoning province, Jin County	County deputy Party secretary, then Party secretary
1987–1988	Liaoning province, Dalian City, Jinzhou District	District Party secretary
1988–1989	Liaoning province, Dalian City	Chief of publicity
1989–1992	Liaoning province, Dalian City	Deputy mayor
1992–1999	Liaoning province, Dalian City	Deputy Party secretary, mayor
1999–2000	Liaoning province, Dalian City	Provincial standing committee member, city Party secretary and mayor
2000–2004	Liaoning province	Deputy provincial Party secretary, governor
2002	Central/National	16th central committee member
2004–2007	Central/National	Minister of Commerce
2007	Central/National	17th central committee and 17th politburo member
2007–2012	Chongqing	Provincial Party secretary

was parachuted into Liaoning, a Northeastern province, as a county deputy Party secretary at the age of 36. Later, he was promoted to mayor of Dalian, a port city, before ascending to the next rung as Minister of Commerce in 2004. Shortly after, in 2007, Bo was inducted into the Politburo, an elite committee of national leaders, which signaled his potential to seek top posts in the next leadership contest. Yet, in the same year, he was transferred to Chongqing, a moderately poor municipality in the Southwest, where he would serve as provincial Party secretary until his dramatic fall in 2012.

Vaunted by the media as "tall, handsome, and charismatic,"[9] Bo was a natural publicist who frequently seized news headlines. The BBC once called him "the nearest thing China has to a Western-style politician."[10] Bo's ambition and charm, however, may have rattled the leadership in Beijing, who transferred him to Chongqing to remove him from the spotlight. But, instead of lying low, Bo stirred up even more attention and controversy.

[9] "Bo Xilai, the Insider Brought Down by His Tendency to Break Rules," *The Guardian*, 21 September 2013.
[10] "Bo Xilai Removed by China from Chongqing Leadership Post," *BBC News*, 12 March 2012.

BO'S BIG SPLASH. Chongqing is a municipality ranked administratively as a province, like Shanghai and Beijing, with a population of about 10 million, twice that of Singapore. But, unlike Shanghai, Chongqing had long been starved of economic growth because its landlocked geography prevented it from replicating the coastal development strategy of export-oriented industrialization. In the past decades, Chongqing ranked among the poorer provinces,[11] providing a vast supply of low-wage, rural migrant labor to coastal factories yet benefiting far less from global capitalism than the Eastern provinces. When Bo came to office in 2007, however, he rapidly – and forcefully – turned the situation around.

Within six years, Bo narrowed the economic gap between Chongqing and the national average. In 2007, Chongqing's GDP per capita was only 82 percent of China's average; by 2012, this figure was nearly on a par with the national average of 40,000 Yuan.[12] Prior to Bo's arrival, from 2000 to 2006, Chongqing's mean annual growth rate was 10.7 percent. Impressively, during the six years of his tenure, Chongqing pulled off a double-digit annual growth rate of 15.3 percent, even as the rest of the country suffered from the 2008 financial crisis, as Figure 5.4 shows. After he left, average growth fell back to 10 percent between 2012 and 2018.

In terms of provincial rank in GDP growth rate, the reversal was especially stark. In 2006, Chongqing ranked 26th out of 31 provinces in GDP growth. The year that Bo took office, it jumped to third in rank, reaching first in 2011. This high rank was sustained for several years after Bo's departure, until 2018, when Chongqing suddenly dropped to 28th place.

During Bo's tenure, Chongqing's government revenue more than tripled. Foreign direct investment (FDI) jumped more than 10 times to US$10.5 billion by 2012. The volume of external trade increased sevenfold, while domestic trade more than doubled. Rapid economic growth appeared to directly benefit Chongqing's residents: urban residential income grew 1.7 times and rural income doubled. The ratio of urban to rural income narrowed from 420 percent in 2007 to 340 percent by

---

[11] From 1998 to 2005, Chongqing's GDP per capita was ranked 18th out of 31 provinces, and it fell to 19th place in 2006. By 2012, the end of Bo's leadership, it had risen to 12th in rank.

[12] In 2007, Chongqing's GDP per capita was 16,728 Yuan, and in 2012, it rose to 39,236 Yuan. The source is the National Bureau of Statistics.

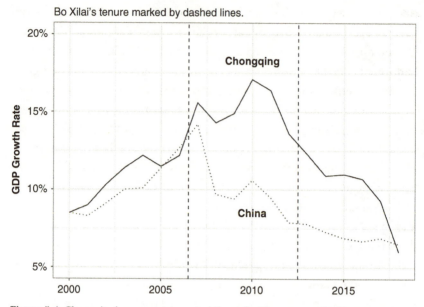

Bo Xilai's tenure marked by dashed lines.

Figure 5.4 Chongqing's economy surpassed the national average under Bo.

2012. Urbanization spread briskly too (Figure 5.5), with the share of urban residents growing from 48 to 57 percent during this period.[13]

How did Bo and his team pull off this economic turnaround? They adopted a highly statist approach, pumping in large amounts of state-financed infrastructure projects, strategically branding Chongqing as a low-wage industrial hub and a portal to the inland domestic market, and offering tax incentives and services to entice investors. Infrastructure projects were critical for overcoming geographic limitations and reducing transportation costs, for example, the construction of a new direct railway connecting Chongqing to Germany via Kazakhstan, Russia, and Poland cemented Chongqing's strategic position as the logistics magnet of inland China. To create a civil aviation hub, the municipal government established a network of four airports and increased the carrying capacity of Chongqing's international airport from 7 million to 25 million passengers a year by 2012.[14] This combination of infrastructure, business-friendly

---

[13] Calculated from *Chongqing Economic Statistics Yearbooks* and the *Chongqing 20th Anniversary Development Report*.

[14] David Lammie, "Pillar of the West," *US–China Business Review*, 1 January 2009.

Figure 5.5 During Bo's tenure, Chongqing saw a rapid construction boom.

policies, and low wages succeeded in attracting foreign investment, including multinationals like Ford, Hyundai, Foxconn, Acer, Sony, and Goodyear. In 2008 Hewlett-Packard opened a sprawling factory to produce desktop and notebook PCs. By 2013, one in four laptops in the world, or 55 million of them, were made in Chongqing.[15]

Bo's leadership delivered more than just economic growth. In his campaign branded "Five Chongqing," he set goals across five areas of social welfare: residential life, transportation, public safety, greening, and public health.[16] Impressively, as summarized in Table 5.4, Bo delivered concrete results across all of them. Not only did the economy and employment grow, but also the residents of Chongqing enjoyed more roads, direct flights, green spaces, health care providers, and access to

---

[15] "Chongqing: Land of Laptops," *China Daily*, 16 June 2014. The move of manufacturing facilities, both foreign and domestic, from the coastal provinces to Chongqing is part of a broader trend of domestic industrial transfer that began in the 2000s (Ang 2018b).

[16] "五个重庆：落实科学发展观的生动实践 [Five Chongqing: A Vivid Illustration of Scientific Development]," *Chongqing Ribao*, 6 February 2012. The website for "Five Chongqing," created by Xinhua's Chongqing Office, and now no longer available, is archived at this link: https://web.archive.org/web/20100812003230/http://www.cq.xinhuanet.com/2009/5.cq/ (accessed 16 March 2019).

TABLE 5.4 *Bo's deliverables across five areas of social welfare*

	2007	2008	2009	2010	2011	2012
Residential life						
Rebuilding dilapidated buildings (million square meters)	–	2.4	4.5	4.3	1.2	0.4
Low-income public housing (million square meters)	–	–	–	13	16.9	15.5
Transportation						
Length of roads per capita (km)	8	9	9	9	10	10
Number of direct domestic flights	65	69	73	82	98	120
Number of direct international flights	58	61	64	74	85	83
Greening						
Green spaces (square km)	66	66	78	97	118	124
Spending on environmental protection (billion Yuan)	3.8	5.3	5.0	6.9	10	12.8
Public safety						
Traffic accidents per 10,000 cars	9	8	6	4	3	3
Spending on public safety (billion Yuan)	5.5	6.5	7.5	9.8	13.3	14.1
Public health						
Number of health providers	6,292	6,266	6,512	6,898	17,660	17,961
Trained medical personnel per 10,000 residents	26	27	30	33	36	39
Percentage of rural areas with access to tap water	73	76	81	88	90	90

Source: *Chongqing Economic Statistics Yearbooks.*

running water. Particularly noteworthy are Bo's pro-poor policies, including the construction of 45 million square meters of public housing for low-income residents within three years. His team also introduced policy innovations, the most famous of which was allowing farmers to sell their land-use rights on the market, landmarked by the establishment of China's first rural land exchange agency in 2008.[17]

Chongqing's development model was heavily driven by investment and construction. Between 2007 and 2012, the municipality's total fixed asset investment expanded three-fold, reaching 87 percent of GDP in 2010, compared with 68 percent in 2007 and only 41 percent in 2001.[18] Although other provinces also increased investment, Chongqing's

---

[17] Cai (2014). See also "Chongqing Sets Stage for China's National Land Reforms," *Nikkei Asian Review*, 9 January 2014.

[18] Calculated from *Chongqing Economic Statistics Yearbooks*.

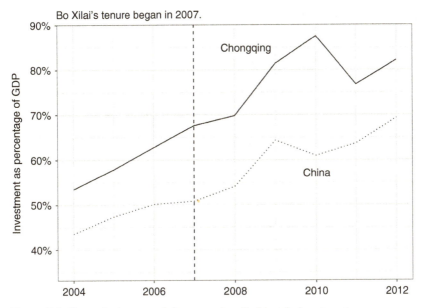

Figure 5.6 Chongqing's economic boom was heavily driven by investment.

investment to GDP ratio was consistently higher than the national average (see Figure 5.6).

But a construction spree doesn't come free. Chongqing's infrastructure projects were financed partly by government spending and even more by loans, typically using land as collateral. During Bo's six-year tenure, outstanding bank loans tripled to a total of 1.6 trillion Yuan by 2012. Simultaneously, land proceeds grew five-fold, rising from 52 percent of budgetary revenue in 2006 to 77 percent in 2012. Chongqing's rising debt was especially evident in its debt-to-GDP ratio, which was 105 percent in 2002, then dramatically spurted from 110 percent in 2008 to 136 percent in 2009. After Bo's expulsion in 2012, this ratio continued to grow, peaking at 146 percent in 2018 (Figure 5.7). Comparable statistics for the whole country, which are available only from 2013 onward, indicate a clear trend of rising debt across China and a narrowing gap between Chongqing and the rest.[19]

---

[19] Debt statistics are from *China Finance Yearbooks*, under "outstanding loans in domestic and foreign currencies," and GDP statistics are from *China Statistical Yearbooks* and *Chongqing Statistical Yearbooks*.

Bo Xilai's tenure marked by dashed lines.

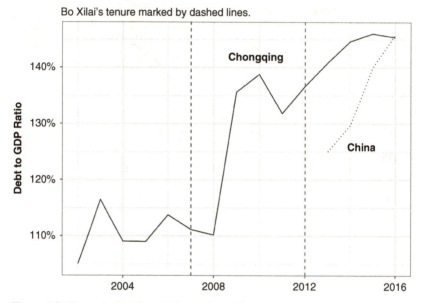

Figure 5.7 Chongqing's debt-to-GDP ratio kept rising.

More controversial than Bo's economic and social welfare policies was his dual campaign to "celebrate red and smash black" (*changhong dahei*) – that is, to revive mass singing of Mao-era patriotic songs and fight organized crime. Although hardcore Maoists and members of the so-called "new left" enthusiastically embraced his policies, others worried that Bo was rekindling Maoist nostalgia to win popularity. His crackdown on crime brazenly flouted the legal process, exacting beatings, torture, and forced confessions on thugs and innocent victims alike, including private businessmen deemed to be in cahoots with Bo's political rivals.[20]

The Chongqing model's heavy reliance on government-built infrastructure and debt raised concerns about economic sustainability and financial risks. An economic downturn – such as the one that is happening now across China – could undermine the city's ability to pay its debts and spark a downward spiral, as several observers warned.[21] Indeed, by

---

[20] Sharon Lafraniere and Jonathan Ansfield, "Bo Xilai's Crackdown Adds to Scandal," *New York Times*, 26 March 2012.

[21] Zoey Zhang, "What Chongqing's Declining Growth Tells us about China's Slowdown," *China Briefing*, 14 March 2019; Sidney Leng, "Chongqing Battles Unemployment," *South China Morning Post*, 15 February 2019.

2018, Chongqing's GDP growth had fallen to its lowest since 2000 (see Figure 5.4). Bo's favoritism toward state investment and attacks on private entrepreneurs had weakened the private sector, which now hobbles the city's ability to rebound.[22]

Compare Bo's approach in Chongqing with classic models of state-directed development. In the 1970s to 1990s, analysts characterized the East Asian economies such as South Korea and Taiwan as "developmental states," where national governments accelerated industrial catch-up through extensive state planning and investment.[23] More recent literature has called for social developmental states that promote social welfare on top of economic growth.[24] By these criteria, Chongqing under Bo may be described as a local variant of social developmental states – but on steroids and armed with a sledgehammer. Not only did the charismatic princeling turn around the economic fortunes of a landlocked municipality, but also he delivered social welfare and policy innovations, branding himself as a trailblazing populist, or, as Cheng Li puts it, "a guy who gets things done."[25]

THE BIGGEST SCANDAL. Nobody could have predicted that Bo's ascendant career would eventually end in what *The New York Times* dubs "the biggest scandal facing China's leadership in a generation."[26] One fateful day, 6 February 2012, Wang Lijun, Chongqing's police chief and Bo's long-time henchman, fled to the US embassy in Chengdu, pleading for asylum. Before a group of startled American diplomats, he frantically explained that he possessed incriminating evidence about Bo's intrigue and his wife's murder of a British businessman.[27] Soon after, Wang was taken away by national security authorities to Beijing.

---

[22] In 2018, the private sector accounted for less than half of Chongqing's economy, lower than the national average. See "In Chongqing, a Painful Economic Transition Is on Full Display," *South China Morning Post,* 18 January 2019.

[23] Amsden (1989); Wade (1990); Evans (1995); Johnson (1995); Kohli (2004); Haggard (2018).

[24] Sen (1999); Evans and Heller (2013); Singh (2013).

[25] Quoted in *New York Times,* 26 March 2012.

[26] Steven Myers and Mark Landler, "Frenzied Hours for U.S. on Fate of a Chinese Insider," *New York Times,* 17 April 2012.

[27] Malcolm Moore, "Bo Xilai Tells the Moment His Life Fell Apart," *Telegraph,* 24 August 2013.

From there, the edifice of Bo's power began to crumble, fast. On 14 March, Premier Wen Jiabao rebuked him publicly, stating that the Chongqing leadership "must reflect seriously and learn from the Wang Lijun incident." The next day, Bo was formally stripped of his position and seized by investigators. Party leaders issued a statement that denounced him for "grave violations of party discipline." In August, the Party held a public trial, which lasted five days. Although Bo remained defiant, he was sentenced to life imprisonment on charges of bribery, abuse of power, and embezzlement. His wife was given a suspended death sentence for murder and Wang Lijun was sentenced to 15 years in prison.[28]

GRAVE VIOLATIONS. Bo's show trial gave the Chinese public a rare peek into the secretive world of state–business collusion and lavish consumption among super elites. According to the court's indictment, Bo accepted a total of 22 million Yuan in bribes over the course of his career. Prosecutors traced Bo's history of bribe-taking back to his early days as Dalian's mayor and city Party secretary. During this time, he allegedly took 11 million Yuan in bribes from Tang Xiaolin, general manager of Dalian International Group, in exchange for helping him purchase a land parcel and obtain preferential quotas to import cars. At his trial, Bo flatly denied these charges, calling Tang a "crazy dog" who "sold his soul."

But Bo could not dismiss his connections with a second businessman, Xu Ming, founder and chairman of the conglomerate Dalian Shide Group. Court records indicate that, between 2001 and 2012, Xu plied Bo's wife and son with numerous gifts and received lucrative privileges in exchange, including construction projects contracted by Dalian's government and favorable regulations from the Ministry of Commerce while Bo was Minister. Bo's son, Bo Guagua, attended expensive private schools in England from the age of 12.[29] Even before his father's fall, Bo junior's fondness for flamboyant parties, sports cars, and equestrian sports had raised questions about how his parents could afford such luxury on their

---

[28] "薄熙来受贿、贪污、滥用职权案庭审纪实 [Court indictment of Bo Xilai's bribery, embezzlement, and abuse of power]," *Jiancha Ribao* [*Procuratorate Daily*], 28 August 2013.

[29] Andrew Jacobs and Dan Levin, "Son's Parties and Privilege Aggravate Fall of Chinese Elite Family," *The New York Times*, 16 April 2012.

modest official salary. In court, Xu testified that he had paid for the family's extravagant purchases, including a $3.2 million villa in France, private jet trips to Africa, luxury bikes, and credit card bills, totaling 21 million Yuan in value. While Bo denied knowledge of these gifts, he could not deny his cozy relations with Xu.

Bo was also charged with abuse of power. Court proceedings revealed that Bo's wife, Gu Kailai, poisoned British businessman Neil Heywood over an alleged financial dispute. When Bo was Dalian's mayor, Heywood cozied up to the family, offering his services as fixer and intermediary. Through his connections, he placed Bo Guagua in the prestigious Harrow School in England, making him the first Chinese to enroll.[30] In 2012, Heywood died mysteriously in a hotel in Chongqing, which the government hushed up as a case of over-intoxication. When police chief Wang Lijun began to suspect that Gu had murdered him, Bo furiously tried to cover up his wife's crime, prompting Wang to flee for his life. Summing up the entire drama, an editor at *Wall Street Journal* quipped, "It's like a Hollywood movie."[31]

Ultimately, Bo was found guilty of all charges, notwithstanding his feisty defense. But, although Bo undoubtedly broke laws and exploited his power for material gain, the formal charges against him should not be taken at face value. Beijing had to strike a delicate balance between ruining Bo's reputation and extinguishing lingering support for him while still maintaining the Party's legitimacy. It's worth noting that the sum of Bo's bribery – 22 million Yuan – though large for ordinary people, is nowhere near as massive as what one imagines a nationally ranked leader could fetch. Indeed, many lesser officials have taken far larger bribes.[32] Equally perplexing is that Bo was not charged with any corrupt action during his tenure as Chongqing's provincial party secretary, when he wielded far greater power than in his earlier position as a city leader of Dalian. This could be because the leadership did not want to sully the

---

[30] *Ibid.*

[31] Li Yuan, Managing Editor at the *Wall Street Journal*, quoted in video "Bo Xilai: Inside the Scandal" (2012).

[32] For example, a deputy director at the National Reform and Development Commission's Coal Department was charged for taking 200 million Yuan in bribes – in cash rather than gifts. His predecessor, who was also seized for corruption, took 36 million Yuan in bribes. Both exceed the official sum of Bo's bribery. See "Corrupt Coal Official Had 200 Million Yuan in Cash Stacked at Home," *South China Morning Post*, 31 October 2014.

Party's image by revealing the full extent of his corrupt takings.[33] Or maybe Bo lusted more for power than for money.

JI JIANYE: MAYOR BULLDOZER

As a princeling and nationally ranked leader, Bo Xilai's status may be exceptional. But among lower-rank officials, there are many similar figures, who are neither complete villains nor heroes. Ji Jianye (Figure 5.8), whose name means "to build," is an especially illustrative case.

Born into a poor family, Ji worked his way up a 39-year career in his native province of Jiangsu, a wealthy industrial powerhouse adjacent to Shanghai (see Table 5.5). Unlike Bo, who was parachuted into high office, Ji started at the bottom rung of the bureaucracy as a publicity officer in Shazhou County, then Suzhou City, and later as a newspaper editor. It was not until 1990, 16 years into his civil service career, that he

Figure 5.8 In this screenshot, Ji Jianye stands trial at a court for taking bribes.

[33] An independent Chinese paper based in the United States alleged that the law firm of Bo's wife was involved in "legal advising of almost all the large foreign investment projects in Dalian." See "薄熙内定三宗大罪 [Three Internally Decided Indictments of Bo]," *Mingjing News*, No. 27, May 2012.

TABLE 5.5 *Milestones in Ji Jianye's career path*

Period	Location and office	Position
1975–1976	Jiangsu Province, Shazhou County, Department of Publicity	Officer
1976–1981	Jiangsu Province, Suzhou City, Department of Publicity	Officer
1981–1986	Jiangsu Province, Suzhou City, Department of Publicity	Deputy division head, in charge of publicity education materials
1986–1990	Jiangsu Province, *Suzhou Daily* (newspaper)	Deputy editor
1990–1996	Jiangsu Province, Wu County	Deputy county Party secretary
1996–1997	Jiangsu Province, Kunshan City	Deputy city Party secretary, deputy mayor
1997–2000	Jiangsu Province, Kunshan City	Deputy city Party secretary, mayor
2000–2001	Jiangsu Province, Kunshan City	City Party secretary
2001–2002	Jiangsu Province, Yangzhou City	Deputy city Party secretary, interim mayor
2002–2004	Jiangsu Province, Yangzhou City	Deputy city Party secretary, mayor
2004–2005	Jiangsu Province, Yangzhou City	City Party secretary
2005–2009	Jiangsu Province, Yangzhou City	City Party secretary; chairman of the city people's congress
2009–2010	Jiangsu Province, Nanjing City	Deputy city Party secretary, interim mayor
2010–2013	Jiangsu Province, Nanjing City	Deputy city Party secretary, mayor

took his first leadership post as deputy Party secretary in Wu County. Afterward, he was laterally transferred within Jiangsu to govern the cities of Kunshan, Yangzhou, and Nanjing. In 2013, while serving as Mayor of Nanjing, Ji was seized for corruption, making him the 10th vice-ministerial-level official to fall in Xi's crackdown on corruption.

FROM KUNSHAN TO YANGZHOU. Over the course of his career, Ji built a reputation for competence, resolve, and authoritarianism. In Kunshan, he oversaw the establishment of the city's first special economic zone for export processing in 2000, which attracted more than 20 tech companies that invested over US$1 billion in the first year of operation alone. This zone also became one of the first cities in China to allow wholly foreign-owned enterprises.[34]

In 2002, Ji was transferred to Yangzhou, located in the central part of Jiangsu, which is less industrialized and prosperous than Kunshan.

---

[34] "与时俱进看昆山 [Going with the Times in Kunshan]," *People's Daily*, 14 November 2002.

According to local media, within three months of taking office, Ji "turned the whole of Yangzhou into a massive construction site."[35] He refurbished 130 streets, rezoned and reconstructed areas around the city's river, and undertook a city-wide greening campaign, which "laid the foundation for Yangzhou's urban map until this day," *Caixin* reports. His sweeping demolition schemes earned him the nickname Mayor Bulldozer. Local residents even coined a rhyme to capture his style of development: "To demolish, he stamps his feet; to topple, he points."[36]

In fact, Ji did more than bulldoze. Branding Yangzhou as "a famous city blending ancient culture and modern civilization," he also invested heavily in the restoration of historic sites. The leader did so not because he was a conservationist, but because he saw a commercial opportunity in preserving history. In 2006, Yangzhou won the United Nations Habitat Award. From then on, tourism flourished (Figure 5.9). The number of visitors rose by one-third between 2007 and 2009, the year Ji left

Figure 5.9 Ji Jianye strategically branded Yangzhou as a blend of ancient city and modern civilization.

---

[35] "始于城建，终于城建 – '季拆拆' 城建史 [The Construction History of Li the Bulldozer]," *Nanfang Weekend*, 24 October 2013.

[36] "季建业升迁路 [Ji Jianye's Promotion Path]," *Caixin*, 25 October 2013.

Yangzhou. This boom persisted after his departure, and, by 2012, Yangzhou had nearly twice the number of tourists it had welcomed in 2007.[37]

Yet Ji's real forte was industrial policy. In 2002, long before other parts of the country thought about industrial upgrading, Ji proposed a plan to promote a cluster of three new industries in Yangzhou: energy, lighting, and construction materials. Taking lessons from his experience in industrial planning in Kunshan, he strategized, "Attracting investment requires selectivity and complementarities. We must create a complete industrial supply chain." To achieve this vision, Ji persuaded the China Science Academy and Nanjing University to establish research centers for industrial upgrading. In 2005, Yangzhou's GDP surpassed the average in Jiangsu Province for the first time.

According to *Nanfang Weekend*, a Guangdong-based newspaper known for investigative journalism and piercing commentary, "In Yangzhou, most people agree that Ji is the leader who has made the greatest contributions to the city since 1949."[38] Not only was Ji fiercely pro-growth, but also he had strategic vision and demonstrated localized, adaptive governance. Ji once said, "We cannot blindly replicate the Southern Jiangsu model of development and copy Kunshan. Instead, we must forge a development path compatible with our conditions [in Yangzhou] and select industries suitable for us."[39]

HITTING A SNAG IN NANJING. But when Ji moved to Nanjing in 2009, his habit of bulldozing through decisions without public consultation hit a snag. As the capital city of several previous dynasties and the Republican government, Nanjing prided itself on its historical and cultural heritage. Dear to the heart of its residents are the numerous plane (*wutong*) trees that line the city's streets, offering shade during searing summers. Cui Manli, a best-selling author and native of Nanjing, expressed impassionedly, "When you see these gigantic trees, you know

---

[37] Source: CEIC Data, based on figures from China Statistical Office, www.ceicdata.com/zh-hans/china (accessed 25 November 2019).
[38] *Nanfang Weekend*, 24 October 2013. [39] *Caixin*, 25 October 2013.

that this is history, civilization, the passing of time, a source of great pride."[40]

Mayor Bulldozer had little taste for sentimentality, however. Repeating his past campaigns, he launched into a massive infrastructural overhaul, replacing roads in three major routes, demolishing old buildings in 1,400 streets, undertaking an 18 billion Yuan scheme to separate rainwater from wastewater, and constructing new subway lines all at once. Within a year, his "Operation Iron Wrist," as the local press dubbed it,[41] razed an astonishing 10 million square meters of unlicensed buildings, equivalent to 66 Forbidden Cities, making it the largest scale of demolition in Nanjing's history. Quoting Ji, *China Daily* (the Party's English-language newspaper) reported, "[Ji] reiterated that no compromise will be made ... no compensation will be given to owners of houses with limited property rights."[42]

For Nanjing's residents, the government's announcement that more than 1,000 *wutong* trees would be uprooted to make way for a new subway was the last straw. Organizing spontaneously through social media, hundreds gathered at a library in formal protest against the decision. Stunned by this public outrage, city officials promised to spare some of the trees. The chastened mayor underestimated Nanjing citizens' emotional attachment to trees.[43]

GRAFT EXPOSED. Ultimately, however, Ji's undoing came not from public protests but from his own corrupt dealings. In October 2013, disciplinary authorities seized him in connection with parallel probes of several businessmen close to him. A few months later, in 2014, Ji was prosecuted on charges of "using public office to help others advance personal gain, accepting massive wealth personally and through family members, and moral corruption."[44] A year later, Ji pleaded guilty to taking bribes and was sentenced to 15 years in prison.

---

[40] "南京市民对梧桐树有深厚感情 [Cui Manli: Nanjing Resident's Emotional Attachment to Plane Trees]," *Phoenix TV*, 19 March 2011.

[41] *Caixin*, 25 October 2013.

[42] Cang Wei and Song Wenwei, "Nanjing Announced Cleanup Program Ahead of Games," *China Daily*, 14 August 2012.

[43] "地铁与大树争路 '砍' 与 '移' 争锋 [The Battle between Subway and Giant Trees]," *Nanfang Weekend*, 18 March 2011.

[44] "南京原市长季建业被开除党 [Former Nanjing Mayor Ji Jianye Stripped of Party Membership]," *Caixin*, 30 January 2014.

According to court records, Ji was indicted on seven counts of corruption, adding up to 11 million Yuan over the course of his career.[45] The largest sum of his bribes came from private businessman and long-time crony Xu Dongming, who gave his political patron nearly 8 million Yuan in bribes to secure government procurement contracts. Second in line was Zhu Tianxiao, a real estate developer, who channeled 2.4 million Yuan in gifts and bribes through Ji's wife, daughter, and brother, including cash, artwork, a luxury car, and a discount of 540,000 Yuan on a condominium unit.[46] The remaining five of his official charges were conspicuously trivial sums, as little as 45,000 Yuan in cash and gift cards from another real estate developer, Zhou Kexing, from Hong Kong.

Like Bo, his real takings may be understated. If we believe the court's indictments, 11 million Yuan in bribes over Ji's entire career is minuscule compared with the earnings produced under his charge. For example, in Kunshan, the economic zone that he oversaw brought in on average US$10 million ($83 million Yuan) in FDI *every day*, which is equivalent to 20 percent the amount of FDI that Cambodia attracted in one year.[47] Chinese reports beyond the official press suggest other streams of rents. Ji's trusted middle-person, a hotel manager named Zhu Mei, a "god-daughter" of the leader's mother, periodically arranged for deal-buyers to offer bribes in exchange for various favors. In Nanjing, Ji rarely worked in the government building, as he used a premium hotel suite as his office, though it was unclear who paid for it.[48] Court indictments also did not mention his string of mistresses, several of whom worked under him and were promoted after their affair, including Yangzhou's head of the environmental protection bureau and deputy chief of the city's planning commission.[49]

[45] "季建业判决书要点公布 [Key Points of Ji Jianye's Indictment]," *People's Daily*, 7 April 2015.

[46] "季建业的家族腐败之路 [Corruption among Ji's Family Members]," *China Youth Daily*, 17 January 2015.

[47] "FDI in Brief: Cambodia," UNCTAD (accessed 4 May 2019). The *People's Daily* called it a "miracle." See *People's Daily*, 14 November 2002.

[48] "南京落马的季建业和时候苏南政商震荡 [The Shakeup in Southern Jiangsu Following Ji's Fall]," *The Paper*, 18 December 2014.

[49] *Ibid.*

SLUDGING THE WHEELS

What we should take away from Bo's and Ji's sagas is not merely feelings of shock and disgust, but rather insights into the Chinese political system. One clear commonality between Bo and Ji is that their corruption primarily took the form of access money – elite exchanges of power and wealth – rather than extortion or embezzlement.[50] Such corruption went far beyond "greasing the wheels," which implies paying bribes to overcome delays or red-tape. Rather, the more appropriate analogy should be "sludging the wheels," as corrupt capitalists derived windfall deals from their political patrons.

In Bo's case, virtually all his bribes were supplied by a mogul named Xu Ming, a Chinese version of the robber barons of America's Gilded Age. A native of Dalian, Xu graduated from college in 1990, when China was on the verge of transitioning to an accelerated phase of market opening (Chapter 3). Xu cleverly capitalized on the lack of clear property rights at the time. In 1992, he convinced county government officials in Dalian to establish Shide Private Limited through a state-owned subsidiary where he worked. Then in 1999, all of the shares from Shide were mysteriously transferred from the county government to Xu, his brother, and two other associates, giving Xu control of his privatized company.[51] When Bo arrived in Dalian, Xu immediately ingratiated himself with the new leader and his family, and soon became the princeling's favorite associate.

In exchange for his loyal clientage and connections to Bo, Xu received access to lucrative business opportunities and massive loans from state banks, as *Caixin* reports:[52]

---

[50] Although Bo was charged for embezzlement, the amount of 500,000 Yuan was paltry compared with his bribes. Most likely, the charge was added to diminish Bo's image before the Chinese public by labeling him as a thief. According to court indictments, when Bo was city Party secretary of Dalian, the manager of a state construction project offered to transfer 500,000 Yuan from the project's balance to Gu's private account. In court, she claimed to have informed Bo of this transfer, which Bo denied.

[51] This self-enriching strategy, common in the late 1990s as China underwent rapid privatization, is known as "asset stripping" (Pei 2006; Wedeman 2012). Although it was an act of corruption, it spawned the first wave of shrewd, politically connected private-sector bosses like Xu Ming (Ang 2016, Chapters 5 and 6).

[52] *Caixin*, 6 December 2015.

Xu's first pot of gold came from construction projects in Dalian ... According to Xu's press interviews, his company [Shide] won a bid to construct the Victory Plaza [a large shopping and entertainment mall]. Xu further urged the government to use the soil and sand dug out from the construction of Victory Plaza to reclaim Xinhai Bay and construct Xinhai Square, thereby killing two birds with one stone. Xu Ming's construction methods were innovative, and it earned him 30 million Yuan. In the years after, Xu Ming continued to build up Shide ... expanding into construction materials, cultural and sports industries, finance, real estate, ultimately turning his company into a massive conglomerate.

As Bo moved up the political ladder, Xu's wealth rose with him. Xinhai Square is one of Bo's signature projects. Converted from a gigantic dumping site, it is the world's largest city square, larger than New York City's Times Square. Xu profited handsomely from constructing the square and simultaneously helped Bo score a political victory. In 2005, Xu reached the height of his fortunes: Forbes named him the eighth-richest person in China.

But Xu could not escape the so-called "Forbes curse" – that tycoons on the list eventually fall into trouble. When Bo fell, Xu was detained with him and eventually sentenced to prison. Just months before his scheduled release, Xu mysteriously died. He Weifang, a professor at Peking University, summed up this robber baron's life in 12 Chinese characters on Weibo: "A flamboyant life, a bizarre sentence, a mysterious death."[53]

Similarly, Ji the mayor used his position to award lucrative contracts and deals to a trusted "circle of friends," who colluded for over two decades. Among them were Zhu Xinliang, Director of Golden Mantis Conglomerate, also known as the "richest man in Suzhou," and Xu Dongming, a shareholder of Golden Mantis and Ji's former subordinate in the Kunshan city government. Golden Mantis, a privately owned listed company, became a primary conduit through which rents were generated and shared within this circle.

During his tenure as leader of Yangzhou, Ji ensured that Golden Mantis received an abundant stream of government procurement

---

[53] This message, posted on Weibo on 7 December 2012, has been deleted, but it was reported in a Chinese website, China Human Rights Journal (*Zhongguo renquan shuang zhoukan*), http://biweeklyarchive.hrichina.org/repost/30869.html (accessed 16 March 2019).

projects. The company first entered Yangzhou in 2002 as an advertisement company. As soon as Ji was appointed interim mayor, Golden Mantis won a hefty contract to supply 10 years' worth of bus advertisements for the city. According to a Chinese report, Ji "personally greeted the bus company," meaning he hinted to whom the contract should be awarded. But later on, as his power grew, Ji dispensed with subtleties and directly awarded construction projects to Golden Mantis without any bidding process, in brazen violation of procurement rules.[54]

In 2003, Golden Mantis made its initial public offering (IPO) on the stock market, and shortly after, its share price rose more than 10-fold. Zhu and Xu "shared the fragrance" (Suzhou dialect for sharing the spoils) by funneling 0.2 percent of their company's shares to the mayor through his wife's shell company,[55] valued at approximately 9.9 million Yuan, far exceeding the value of his cash bribes. The politician entrusted his equity with Xu, his crony and financial manager, who used it to extend loans on the market, generating interest payments that were handed to Ji's wife.

To sum it up, Chinese politicians and capitalists share a relationship of "mutual prosperity," as *Beijing News* describes in Ji's context:[56]

> The businessmen "trailed behind" Ji throughout his political career. Their projects stretched from Yangzhou to Nanjing. All the contracts they secured bore tracks of Ji's manipulation and participation. Ji's wife and chauffeur grabbed many construction projects for themselves, particularly in greening and landscaping. From Yangzhou to Nanjing, as Ji bulldozed and built, his political fortunes soared.

But when entrepreneurs hitch their fates to those of their political patrons, it comes with danger – they perish together. Xi's anti-corruption campaign brought down the whole gang.

---

[54] "金螳螂捕钱，季建业在后 [Ji Jianye Backs Golden Mantis' Profit-Making]," *Xinjingbao*, 24 October 2013.

[55] "张蕾：公诉季建业 [Zhang Lei: Prosecuting Ji Jianye]," CCTV-13 News Documentary, 12 April 2014.

[56] "多名地产商因季建业落马被查 [Developers Investigated Along with Fallen Official Ji Jianye]," *Xinjingbao*, 21 November 2013.

THE INDIRECT HARM OF ACCESS MONEY

What were the effects of Bo's and Ji's style of corruption on the economy? Access money functions like the steroids of capitalism – it stimulates growth but distorts by misallocating resources, breeding systemic risks, and exacerbating inequality. As my qualitative accounts show, corruption in the manner of access money is not a tax but rather an *investment*. This calls for a revision of the conventional focus in the political economy literature on corruption as only a "tax" on business.[57] Clearly, the capitalists who extended graft to Bo and Ji all got terrific deals, including this list of perks.

- **Major construction contracts**: Xu Ming's construction of the Xinhai Square and Victory Plaza, both part of Bo's development plan in Dalian, were his "first pot of gold," earning him 30 million Yuan that financed a rapid expansion of his business into a conglomerate.[58]
- **Monopoly privileges**: When Ji was in charge of Yangzhou, his client Golden Mantis monopolized renovation projects in the city's residences, hotels, and hospitals.[59] Within only six years of his tenure, the company's profits multiplied 15-fold,[60] catapulting it into being the first Chinese listed company specializing in renovation.
- **Access to credit**: Shortly after Xu Ming had famously acquired Dalian's soccer team to ingratiate himself with Bo, who was an avid soccer fan, he received his first major loan from the China Construction Bank. Loans extended to his company subsequently ballooned to as much as 1.6 billion Yuan.[61]
- **Access to land**: Developers are required to bid for land, which is scarce and in high demand. As Nanjing's Mayor, Ji helped Dehao Corporation acquire two of six land parcels available at the time, even though the company had been established only shortly before the bid.[62]

---

[57] Shleifer and Vishny (1993); Bardhan (1997); Gray and Kaufman (1998); Wei (2000); Fisman and Svensson (2007).

[58] "大连实德原董事长徐明病死狱中 [Former Chairman of Dalian Shide Dies in Prison, Principal Briber of Bo Xilai]," *Caixin*, 6 December 2015.

[59] *The Paper* (Chinese), 18 December 2014.   [60] *Xinjingbao* (Chinese), 24 October 2013.

[61] Yu Ning and Wen Qiu, "Dalian Businessman Who Built an Empire Vanishes," *Caixin*, 9 April 2012

[62] *China Youth Report* (Chinese), 17 January 2015.

- **Regulatory exemptions**: In Yangzhou, Ji helped Zhu Tiaoxiao, another real estate magnate, to skip approval processes and to flout land use and construction restrictions, and even aided his company's demolition work, which frequently entailed state coercion and thuggery.[63]

Evidently, when corruption takes the dominant form of access money, it can enrich some private companies and even hoist them onto stock markets and Forbes' list of billionaires. It also stimulates construction and investment, all of which translates into GDP growth.

Yet this does not mean that access money is "good" for the economy – on the contrary, its harm is indirect but deep. Such corruption channels excessive investment into real estate, a sector offering unmatched windfalls for the politically connected. In China all land is state-controlled, meaning that it can be leased through a bidding process but not sold. Even though Beijing limits the amount of land for lease and restricts local governments from changing designated land use categories (agriculture, industry, or commerce), local authorities can still find numerous ways of manipulating land sales and use for private gain.[64] Powerful officials can help developers acquire valuable land parcels at bargain prices, which they can either turn into pricey properties or resell for colossal profit. Therefore, real estate is described in Chinese as a "super rents" (*baoli*) sector.

One long-term structural risk is that Chinese investors face distorted incentives to abandon productive economic activities for real estate investment, a trend termed *qishixiangxu*.[65] Since market opening, manufacturing has been the foundation of China's "real economy" (*shiti jingji*) – meaning the production of essential goods and services – which drove massive job and wealth creation. But, facing rising labor costs and trade frictions with the United States, manufacturing's appeal has drastically weakened. The rush of investment toward real estate exposes the economy to speculative bubbles and over-construction, as is evident from the hordes of empty apartments across China. One study estimates that about 22 percent of Chinese urban housing is unoccupied

---

[63] *Ibid.*   [64] See Ang (2016, Chapter 3).
[65] One way corruption harms is by diverting actors away from productive activities (Krueger 1974; Bhagwati 1982).

even though the units are sold, which amounts to over 50 million homes.[66] This situation is dangerous, as an article in *Bloomberg* explains: "The nightmare scenario for policy makers is that owners of unoccupied dwellings rush to sell if cracks start appearing in the property market, causing prices to spiral."[67] Adding to the risky brew are rising local government debts, which have financed infrastructure projects such as the ones Bo and Ji commissioned.

A capitalist machine fueled by access money also exacerbates inequality, both within society and between politically connected and non-connected firms. Xu Ming's staggering loans from state banks stand in marked contrast to private companies that are denied credit and forced to borrow at usurious rates from informal "shadow banking" institutions.[68] Cronies can easily secure government contracts and race ahead of their competitors. In society, over-investment in real estate and soaring prices have put urban housing out of reach for many regular citizens, inspiring the drama series "Humble Dwellings" (*Woju*), whose plot was so realistic that censorship authorities banned its broadcast.[69] The super-rich, meanwhile, snap up strings of luxury apartments, waiting to resell them at higher prices. The tragic consequence is that the majority of Chinese people who need homes can't afford them while the minority who own homes don't live in them.

Last but not least, access money generates strong vested interests which block economic reforms and distort the allocation of resources. Local governments have few incentives to provide affordable public housing, as propping up demand for private residential properties produces rents. (Bo Xilai's low-income housing scheme in Chongqing is exceptional, as his ambition was to win popular support for a seat in Beijing.) Investment continues to pour into some money-losing industries because "these firms' involvement in large numbers of construction projects, no-bid contracts, and related party transactions creates ample

---

[66] This study is the China Household Finance Survey, conducted by Gan Li of Chengdu's Southwestern University of Finance and Economics. See "A Fifth of China's Homes Are Empty," *Bloomberg*, 8 November 2018. Consumers purchase multiple properties for investment, as they see real estate offering the highest returns.

[67] *Ibid.*   [68] Ehlers *et al.* (2018).

[69] See "Narrow Dwellings: A TV Series That Slipped through SARFT's Guidelines," *Danwei*, 11 December 2009.

opportunities for leaders at all levels to obtain private benefits," Rawski writes. Similarly, Walder argues that top political elites who control key sectors of the economy, from finance, to electricity, to oil, have "enormous vested interests in a status quo from which their families have greatly benefited in recent decades," forcing Xi to use the anti-corruption campaign to break them up (more details are given in Chapter 6).[70]

To sum it up, it is imperative to think beyond the simplistic binary of whether corruption is "good" or "bad" for economic growth. As my analysis shows, while some forms of corruption are unambiguously harmful or taxing – corruption with theft and speed money – access money can stimulate growth yet produce serious side effects. Although its risks and distortions affect all Chinese citizens, the impact is impossible to quantify.

HOW CHINESE CRONY CAPITALISM REALLY WORKS

My analysis revises our understanding of how crony capitalism really works in China. Pei portrays the system as one "in which capitalists gain valuable rents from politicians," leading to "the decay of the CCP." I fully agree with the problems that Pei sees in crony capitalism, particularly "the enrichment of a small minority and high levels of inequality."[71] Yet his portrayal ignores the other side of the coin: corrupt officials are often also competent and development-promoting. Thus Pei falls completely silent on *why* crony capitalism, if it is so corrosive, has accompanied four decades of economic boom.

I highlight four takeaways from my analysis. First, Chinese politicians are corrupt, but they also promote economic development and even deliver social welfare. Indeed, from the portraits of Bo and Ji, we learn that the strategies for growth promotion among the most competent leaders have advanced far beyond merely bulldozing and building empty "ghost cities." Rather, both Bo and Ji strategically positioned and branded their locales. Bo and his lieutenants effectively forged the brand

[70] Rawski (2017), cited in Lardy (2019, 77); Walder (2018, 30).
[71] Pei (2016, 7, 22, 267).

"Chongqing model," leveraging Chongqing's advantage as a gateway into central China. Ji knew that Yangzhou could not compete in export manufacturing with Kunshan (a city he had previously governed), so instead he branded Yangzhou as a heritage site. To accomplish this, he refurbished the historic Guyun Canal that runs through the city, thereby attracting both tourists and developers of luxury properties. As a former newspaper editor, Ji was also shrewd at harnessing the media to his advantage. In Yangzhou, he organized a marathon by city leaders along the refurbished canal, which was broadcast on TV. Through this publicity stunt, he showed off the impressive landscape and won the support of local residents.[72] A sole focus on his later scandals would obscure these development strategies.

Second, the more Chinese politicians promote development, the more rents they can generate for their clients and themselves. This constitutes a system of elite *profit-sharing*, which parallels but is different from profit-sharing among rank-and-file bureaucrats (Chapter 4), whose performance is rewarded through fringe compensation. For political elites, their rewards come in the form of massive bribes and even company shares. In Ji's case, he literally shared the profits of Golden Mantis by holding the company's stock. By successfully revamping Yangzhou into a modern city with historic appeal, he raised not simply economic growth but rather the value of land and real estate – thereby vastly increasing the stock of rents. This "profit-sharing" style of corruption distinguishes it from Pei's repeated emphasis on "looting," which sometimes occurs in China but is not the dominant or preferred style of corruption (also see Chapter 2).

Third, cronyism is not just for personal enrichment but also helps ambitious politicians get things done. Xu Ming's relationship with Bo Xilai is a case in point. Bo accepted Xu as his favorite not simply because he gave bribes (as numerous capitalists would queue up to do the same), I surmise, but because Xu was competent and proved he could deliver. In constructing Xinhai Square and Victory Plaza, both Bo's pet projects, Xu cleverly used discarded sand from one site to construct the other site, a method that even *Caixin* commended as

---

[72] *Caixin*, 25 October 2013.

"innovative."[73] For political elites whose formal pay is abysmally low (Chapter 4), wealthy cronies not only finance their personal wealth and lavish consumption but also help them achieve development targets, which is necessary for career advancement. Crony capitalists donate to public works,[74] mobilize their business networks to participate in and execute state-led schemes, and help politicians deliver their signature projects, which improve both a city's physical image and the leader's personal track record. Thus understood, Bell's praise of the Chinese political system as a meritocracy that selects officials by "ability and virtue" misses a crucial reality: it is difficult for politicians to perform without political patrons and corporate clients.[75]

Fourth, Chinese crony capitalism is competitive. As a princeling, Bo was exceptional in the power and influence he wielded. Other leaders, however, must demonstrate ambition and ability to draw capitalist cronies, who otherwise will not want to hitch themselves to weaklings or losers. One example is Hengyang city Party secretary Tong Mingqian (see Appendix: Chapter 5), who was perceived as timid and mediocre; "even county leaders don't take him seriously," local media reported. Businessmen were known to barge into his office, demanding responses, rather than to curry his favor.

Another manifestation of competition lies in local governments' provision of "preferential policies" (*youhui zhengce*), including tax and fee exemptions, worker training, subsidies, and so forth, for attracting investors. They are similar to incentive packages that state and city governments in the United States offer to entice companies, except that in China they tend to be tainted with graft.[76] As numerous locales all vie for businesses, local governments enter into a "vicious competition" to offer ever better deals. As one Chinese article reports, "Before enterprises decide on their investment destination, they will visit multiple sites, using one local government's deal to extract better deals from

---

[73] *Caixin*, 6 December 2015.   [74] Lin *et al.* (2015); Jia *et al.* (Forthcoming).

[75] Bell (2016); Eric Li, "A Tale of Two Political Systems," TED Talk, posted 1 July 2013.

[76] Louise Story, "As Companies Seek Tax Deals, Governments Pay High Price," *The New York Times*, 1 December 2012.

other local governments."[77] Preferential policies used to be publicized by local governments on their websites, in brochures, and at investment recruitment events, but, since the launch of Xi's anti-corruption campaign, the topic has become taboo because of its association with corruption and special deals extended by leaders to selected investors. As one official cautioned in an interview, "Nowadays, don't ever mention 'preferential policies.' In the past, you could use the term, but now you can't ... It will get people into trouble."[78] In sum, despite the absence of electoral contests, Chinese political elites compete intensely both for economic growth and for corporate clientele for themselves.

CONCLUSION

Chinese crony capitalism is a story of impressive growth accompanied by financial risks and sharp inequality. Officials who are *both* competent and corrupt, exemplified by Bo and Ji, are the protagonists behind China's paradox of prosperity and corruption.[79] By detailing their portraits, we can avoid gross simplifications and begin to grasp the contradictions built into China's political economy. Importantly, this chapter showed that growth promotion and graft do not merely coexist – rather they feed off each other.

For students of corruption, it is high time to challenge the simplistic belief that all corruption deters investment and growth. In China access money spurs politically connected capitalists to feverishly invest and build, while enabling politicians to achieve their development targets and ascend career ladders. Yet, functioning like steroids, this corruption also produces serious but indirect harm. Its effects on the economy are likely to be punctuated (building up to an eruption) rather than linear (hampering annual growth).

---

[77] "地方优惠政策整治风暴 [Controversy of Local Preferential Policies]," *Shidai Zhoubao*, 18 December 2014.

[78] The interviewee added, "Nowadays, with regard to land, everything must be done according to regulations and the allotted quota. Previously, we could refund taxes and give benefits to some enterprises [as an incentive], but now this cannot be done, too" (B2013-325).

[79] In Appendix: Chapter 5, I examine other categories of officials apart from Bo's and Ji's type.

The leadership under President Xi is painfully aware that it must deal with the festering ills of crony capitalism over the past decades. Will Xi succeed in curbing corruption and bring about a Chinese-style Progressive Era? Or will his campaign produce unintended new problems? I turn to these questions in the next chapter.

CHAPTER 6

All the King's Men

SINCE COMING TO POWER, PRESIDENT XI JINPING HAS MADE fighting corruption a cornerstone of his administration. His anti-corruption drive is the most vigorous in the Party's history. To date, a staggering 1.5 million officials have been disciplined.[1] Could Xi's determination to stamp out corruption stifle the economy? In the prior decades, Chinese officials made a headlong dash for rapid growth using any means necessary. Now many worry that anti-corruption measures will douse bureaucratic entrepreneurism and risk-taking, qualities displayed by the pro-development leaders featured in Chapter 5.

One indirect way of inferring the development implications of Xi's anti-corruption campaign is to examine which factors predict the fall of local leaders.[2] In the lingo of Chinese politics, to "fall from the horse" (*luoma*) means to be investigated for corruption. This chapter turns from case studies of individual leaders (Chapter 5) to a statistical analysis of 331 city-level Party secretaries – the first-in-command of city governments – who were in office in 2011, a year before Xi's war on corruption began. This cohort of leaders has borne the brunt of Xi's unusually intense crackdown ever since its inception.

Are local leaders who deliver impressive economic results and who feature frequently in the media more or less likely to fall? What happens

---

[1] "China's Effective Campaign Sets Model for Global Anticorruption Cause," *Xinhua*, 11 March 2018.

[2] We cannot assess whether anti-corruption measures hurt growth simply by running a regression of the campaign's effects on growth rates. That is because Xi's campaign was rolled out across the whole country simultaneously, which means we cannot isolate the effects of anti-corruption measures on economic growth by comparing regions that underwent anti-corruption drives and those that did not.

when patrons tumble? Or is the crackdown like a mass raid, where large numbers of officials are shot down in no predictable way?

My analysis finds that patronage, not performance, predicts the likelihood of downfall.[3] Performance neither exposes nor shields city leaders from investigations. When patrons take a hit, however, the risk of fall for their clients rises steeply. Apart from patronage, the likelihood of downfall also reflects the temporal trends of the campaign: it intensified quickly after 2012, rose to a crescendo in 2014, and then tapered off afterward.

Yet, unlike usual policy campaigns, Xi's anti-corruption drive has abated but not stopped. Chinese officials today face an environment of intense scrutiny, making this a "new normal" in the bureaucracy rather than a temporary blip. As Xi's campaign extends beyond fighting graft into ideological control and conformity with the Party line, bureaucratic paralysis has intensified.

XI'S CRUSADE AGAINST CORRUPTION

On 15 November 2012, Xi Jinping delivered his first speech before the Politburo, the elite body of the CCP. Ominously, his debut came on the heels of a dramatic face-off among the Party's national elites that concluded with the dismissal of Bo Xilai (see Chapter 5), former party chief of Chongqing and Xi's political rival for the top seat. Bo was subsequently charged with "grave violations of Party discipline." Mincing no words, Xi warned that corruption had festered to a point of crisis and would "doom the party and the nation" if left untreated.

Campaigns against corruption are not new in reform-era China. Five such campaigns have taken place since market opening, between 1982 and 1995, making Xi's the sixth.[4] Up until 1995, anti-corruption activity was conducted through "campaign-style mass mobilizations."[5] Since then, the Party has shifted its methods from episodic crackdowns to systematic capacity-building measures, as I detailed in Chapter 3.[6]

---

[3] This finding applies only to the period I analyze, which is 2012–2017. Determinants of downfall can change considerably over time.

[4] Manion (2016).   [5] Quade (2007).

[6] Quade (2007); Ko and Weng (2012); Ang (2016).

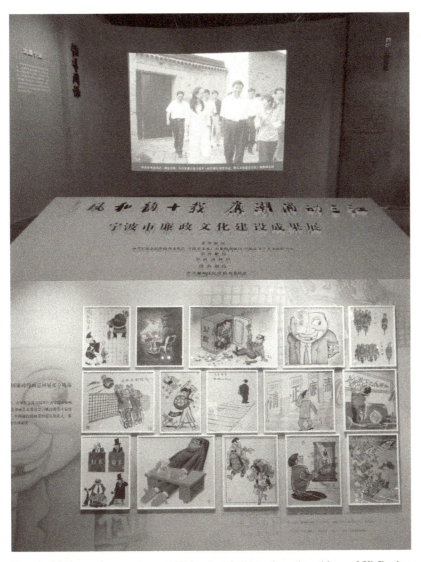

Figure 6.1 An anti-corruption exhibition in Zhejiang, featuring videos of Xi Jinping, artwork, and posters.

Xi's campaign (Figure 6.1) is unlike previous campaigns in five remarkable ways. First, it's unusually long and is still proceeding. As Manion points out, normally, campaigns are "a burst of intensive enforcement" – meaning dramatic but short – as the intense mobilization of resources and manpower can be sustained only for a limited time, much like election campaigns in the United States. Yet this one, already in its sixth year, shows no sign of stopping, making it "not a campaign at all but the new normal in China."[7]

Second, a staggering number of officials have fallen into the dragnet. According to the latest official statistics, between 2012 and 2017, disciplinary authorities received a total of 12 million tips and reports from the public, followed up on 2.7 million leads, investigated 1.5 million cases, and disciplined 1.5 million individuals, including more than 8,900 *ting*-level (equivalent to city Party secretaries) and 63,000 *chu*-level (equivalent to county Party secretaries) officials. Criminal charges were pressed against 58,000 offenders.[8] Among the 1.5 million cases, disciplinary actions ranged from Party censure (warning letters and pep talks), to removal of Party membership, demotion, dismissal, and even criminal penalties, including, in the most serious cases, the death penalty.[9] In 2018 alone, more than half a million Party cadres were penalized for corruption, including 68 officials at the Central Organization Department, the Party organ that makes appointment decisions at the highest level.[10]

Third, Xi vows to purge corrupt officials of both high and low ranks, or, in his famous phrase, "tigers and flies." This includes some "mega-tigers" – officials at the highest, national rank.[11] In 2015, the Central Discipline Inspection Commission released a list of 99 officials at the vice-ministerial level who had fallen. The most towering figure in the list is Zhou Yongkang, who until 2012 was one of China's nine national leaders (a member of the Politburo Standing Committee) and the Minister in charge of China's formidable public security apparatus. Other mega-tigers who fell include Ling Jihua (former aide to President Hu Jintao), Guo Boxiong (Vice Chairman of the Central Military Commission), and Sun Zhengcai (Politburo member and provincial Party secretary who succeeded Bo Xilai

---

[7] Manion (2016).

[8] "Work Report of the 18th Central Discipline Inspection Commission," 29 October 2017, www.ccdi.gov.cn/xxgk/hyzl/201710/t20171031_114178.html (accessed 3 March 2019).

[9] One study finds that the death penalty was meted out in 3 percent of corruption cases from 1993 to 2010 (Zhu 2015).

[10] Zhao Runhua, "Half a Million Party Members Penalized for Corruption in 2018," *Caixin*, 21 February 2019.

[11] Manion (2016).

in Chongqing). A host of provincial leaders, who will later on feature in my data analysis, also fell.

A fourth feature is that the campaign has extended beyond Party and state organs into the military, state-owned enterprises, financial organizations, and, more recently, the state media and universities. In finance, the latest target to fall is Lai Xiaomin, a former chairman of Huarong Asset Management, one of China's largest state lenders, that was created by central authorities in 1999 to clean up bad debts. Lai was apprehended with "three metric tons of cash hidden at home, a 300 million Yuan bank account in the name of his mother and a history of trading favors for sex," *Caixin* reported.[12] At China Central Television (CCTV), several producers were probed for taking bribes from companies in exchange for not exposing their misconduct on television.[13] Corruption also appears to have infected China's higher education system, where violations include misuse of funds, rigging promotions, bribery, and selling degrees. In recent years, the government has nabbed a string of top university administrators.[14]

Last but not least, in addition to arresting a litany of officials, the current anti-corruption drive aims to straighten bureaucratic norms. A month after Xi's maiden speech to the Politburo, the Party issued a list of eight regulations to curb "extravagance and undesirable work practices" (Figure 6.2). The rules are comprehensive, including reducing the number of meetings, restricting overseas visits, and even forbidding leaders from "publishing anything by themselves or issuing congratulatory letters in their own name."[15] This norm-correcting exercise was accompanied by an extensive organizational restructuring of various agencies involved in disciplinary work, culminating in the creation of a consolidated superagency in 2018: the National Supervisory Commission.

In short, Xi has taken the battle on graft to a whole new level, creating the longest, widest-ranging, and most penetrative anti-corruption

---

[12] Dong Jing, Wu Hongyuran, and Charlotte Yang, "Fallen Chief of Bad Assets Had Tons of Cash, Literally," *Caixin*, 16 October 2018.

[13] "3 CCTV Employees Detained in Probe," *China Daily*, 18 June 2014.

[14] Yang (2015). See also "China Arrests University Official in New Graft Crackdown," *Reuters*, 25 December, 2013.

[15] "Eight-point Austerity Rules," *China Daily*, 28 October 2016.

Figure 6.2 Poster on the "eight-point regulations," including restrictions against gambling, Internet surfing, banqueting, and drinking at work.

campaign in the post-Mao era. Indeed, Xi has invented a paradoxical policy tool: a *sustained* campaign.

WHAT INFLUENCES WHO FALLS?

Both performance and patronage shape political careers in China.[16] During Xi's crackdown on corruption, which is a more significant predictor of political survival?

PERFORMANCE. It is common knowledge that China's promotion system rewards economic performance, particularly the ability to generate GDP and tax revenue growth.[17] If this is true, then we should expect that high economic performers are less likely to fall, given that they deliver results and contribute to the Party's legitimacy.

But performance might also cut in the opposite direction. As we saw in Chapter 5, aggressive growth promoters take more risks and shoulder more personal responsibility for innovative development strategies and policies. Vibrant economic and investment activities also create opportunities for large-scale graft. Furthermore, ambitious leaders like Bo not only deliver growth but proactively court media coverage. Cultivating a high profile may garner unwanted attention and incur enemies, thereby hastening a politician's fall.[18]

With regard to performance, my statistical analysis will examine two questions.

- Are leaders who deliver high economic performance more or less likely to fall?
- Are leaders who have a high media profile more or less likely to fall?

PATRONAGE. A second prominent factor is patronage. Dyadic patron–client relations, or "factionalism," is an enduring feature of Chinese elite

---

[16] Li and Walder (2001); Li and Zhou (2005); Landry (2008); Jia *et al.* (2015); Zuo (2015).

[17] Li and Zhou (2005); Lü and Landry (2014); Huang (2015).

[18] A recent study finds that political elites with more frequent media appearances receive fewer votes from Party Congresses (equivalent to legislature), indicating less peer popularity (Lu and Ma 2018).

politics.[19] As Nathan describes, "The hierarchy and established communications and authority flow of the existing organization provides a kind of trellis upon which the complex faction is able to extend its own informal, personal loyalties and relations."[20] Mega-tigers cultivate an expansive, multi-level network of underlings, protégés, and associates throughout the hierarchy, who collude to generate and share rents from power. When a mega-tiger falls, one would expect his gang to topple with him.

Many commentators believe that the current crackdown is nothing more than an instrument for Xi to purge enemies and install loyalists. For instance, Kevin Rudd, an Australian former politician, dubs the campaign a "masterclass in political warfare."[21] An op-ed in *The New York Times* by Chinese commentator Murong Xuecun calls it a "Stalinist purge."[22] Such claims should and can be statistically examined.

If the anti-corruption campaign were simply "political warfare" or a "purge," then the political status of a city leader's patron should matter greatly. I define a patron as the particular provincial Party secretary who appointed a city Party secretary to office (more details are given in the data section). Specifically, if a city leader's patron is a member of the 18th Politburo (2012–2017), we would expect their clients to be protected. But should a Politburo member fall, we would expect to see all or many of his appointees to fall with him (for background, see Box 6.1). The only member of the 18th Politburo who fell was Sun Zhengcai, who was investigated in 2017 on charges of bribery and rumors of conspiring against Xi.[23]

To summarize, my analysis will explore three questions about patronage.

- Are city leaders more likely to fall when their provincial-level patrons fall?

---

[19] Nathan (1973); Shih (2008). Clientelism is a defining feature of Chinese politics even at the lowest village level (Oi 1985).

[20] Nathan (1973).

[21] "Can Xi Jinping Make Use of the Power He Has Accumulated," *The Economist*, 31 March 2018.

[22] Murong Xuecun, "Xi's Selective Punishment," *The New York Times*, 16 January 2015.

[23] Scott Neuman, "Sun Zhengcai, Once a Rising Star, Gets Life Sentence," *National Public Radio*, 8 May 2018.

Box 6.1 China's Committee of National Leaders

The Politburo Standing Committee (PSC) is the most powerful body of national leaders that rule China. Once every five years, the Party leadership would announce the seven to nine members who make up this collective leadership. The 18th PSC (2012–2017) had seven members: Xi Jinping, Li Keqiang (Premier), Zhang Dejiang, Yu Zhengsheng, Liu Yunshan, Wang Qishan (who headed the anti-corruption agency), and Zhang Gaoli. The top post within this committee is that of the General Party Secretary, also the nation's President – which is currently occupied by Xi Jinping.

The PSC is a subset of the Politburo, a larger committee of about 15–25 national leaders that is dubbed "the command headquarters of the Party."[24] Politburo members simultaneously hold other positions, serving as ministers, provincial Party secretaries, and military chiefs. They meet regularly to decide national policies for the country.

In theory, some 2,000 delegates of the National People's Congress, China legislative body, elect the Central Committee (about 200 members), who in turn elect the Politburo, from which the PSC members are chosen. But in reality, as Lieberthal observes, "The opposite is true – the smallest committee is the most important structure."

After Deng Xiaoping took over the reins of power, following Mao's death, he instituted a norm of collective leadership, embodied at the highest level in the PSC. To prevent any one leader from usurping power for himself, as Mao did, he also abolished the posts of Chairman and Vice-Chairmen of the CCP in 1982.[25] Today, however, many worry that Xi has been steadily recentralizing personal power, and, by ending constitutional term limits in 2017, placed himself in office for life.[26]

---

[24] Lieberthal (1995).   [25] Lieberthal (1995).   [26] Economy (2018).

- Are city leaders whose patrons are members of the Politburo and/or Politburo Standing Committee (PSC) consistently protected from fall?
- Did Sun Zhengcai's fall make his clients more likely to fall?

TIMING. There is also a third factor: timing. One distinctive feature of the Chinese political system is campaign-style policy implementation, a legacy of the CCP's revolutionary origins, which, in Perry's words, is by nature "convulsive."[27] In contrast to rule-based, routine policy implementation in technocratic bureaucracies, campaigns involve mass mobilization, where the top commander orients the resources and attention of the entire bureaucracy and even society toward a particular goal. An advantage of this approach, as one official told me, is that "we can get things done fast, especially great things."[28] But the extreme intensity of efforts also means that campaigns are usually brief, rising to a feverish peak and then quickly extinguishing. The likelihood of removal from office may simply reflect this generic campaign rhythm. To examine the effects of temporal trends, in addition to performance and patronage, I will conduct an event history analysis.

DATA AND MEASURES

For this analysis, I examine subnational political outcomes for officials during the anti-corruption campaign. This cohort covers 331 officials who were Party secretaries of city-level jurisdictions in 2011 throughout China (except in the province-level cities of Beijing, Shanghai, Tianjin, and Chongqing). Party secretaries are the first-in-command at every level of government; they not only exercise supreme authority on political matters such as appointments, but also have the final say on economic and social policies. My data follows these officials even as they are promoted, transferred, or investigated for corruption, creating a panel structure from 2012 to 2017.

An analysis at the city level sheds light on the impact of anti-corruption on local governance and development in ways that are likely to directly

[27] Perry (2011).   [28] Interview B2013-323.

affect the lives of residents. In China's five-tiered hierarchy (center, province, city, county, township), the city is the level of government right below the provinces. One city leader explains the respective roles of different levels of government as follows:[29]

> The work of a city Party secretary is at once macro and micro, abstract and concrete. Leaders in the townships [the lowest level] don't have much authority to solve problems. But cities do possess macro planning powers. Provinces are even more macro. As for the central government, it's completely macro, concerned with setting strategic direction for the entire country. Policy implementation occurs most concretely at the county level.

As this quote suggests, the first stop in examining local development is the city. An analysis at this level lays the groundwork for analyses at the lower (county and township) levels.

In particular, I focus on the 331 city Party secretaries who were in office in 2011, as they have experienced Xi's crackdown since its inception in 2012. Given that the current anti-corruption campaign is the most forceful ever conducted by the Party, this may be the most distressed cohort of city leaders in Chinese reform history.

Tables A6.1 and A6.2 in the Appendix summarize the variables in my study. The dependent variable (outcome of interest) is the "fall" of an official, defined as the initiation of any investigation into alleged corruption (rather than a conviction, which may occur years later). Whether or not an official is convicted, investigations end careers. This variable is constructed on the basis of media reports and official reports on the websites of the Procuratorate and Central Committee for Discipline Inspection (CCDI).

MEASURING PERFORMANCE. I measure the performance of city Party secretaries using percentage growth in the city's share of provincial GDP in 2012 over the previous year. (In the regression, I also included other measures of economic performance, such as annual growth in GDP and tax revenue per capita, but omitted them in the

---

[29] Interview B2012-291.

final analysis as they did not change the results.) I believe that *growth in share of provincial GDP* is a better measure of economic performance than the standard measure of GDP growth because, from the perspective of higher-level superiors, assessments are likely to be made in comparison with peers: whether a city leader delivers a higher share of economic growth to the province is more significant and memorable than absolute GDP growth.[30] I also include *media mentions* in 2011,[31] a measure of the frequency of references in a cluster of Chinese national and local newspapers, normalized by the number of papers in the province.

These measures of performance are no doubt imperfect. As my case studies in Chapter 5 show, the performance of highly competent leaders includes but goes beyond economic growth. Developmental leaders like Bo Xilai and Ji Jianye also make their mark on social development by providing public goods, infrastructure, and welfare services. But instead of exhaustively including every social indicator, I highlight economic performance, as this is still the top deliverable of every leader. I also use media mentions as a proximate measure of public prominence and the ability to deliver newsworthy social outcomes.

MEASURING PATRONAGE. To measure the effects of patronage, I employ a stricter definition of patronage than the conventional literature does. Typically, patronage is measured by a client's (in this case, a city leader's) proximate connections to leaders at the next higher level of government, such as whether they came from the same province or town, attended the same universities, or previously worked in the same unit.[32] This loose definition creates the variation that is required for regression analysis but it fails to accurately capture patronage. For example, if a high-level official comes from the same hometown as many lower-level officials, they will all be coded as sharing a patron–client relationship,

[30] According to Lü and Landry (2014), leaders' performance should be evaluated in comparison with their peer group within a province.

[31] I measure *media mentions* before the anti-corruption campaign began, as an indication of leaders' preexisting prominence, because the campaign and possible indictments that followed could affect their subsequent coverage in the media.

[32] Shih (2008); Shih *et al.* (2012); Jia *et al.* (2015); Zeng and Yang (2017).

even though some are not in fact dependent upon the higher-level official.

In authoritarian regimes, power lies in one's ability to appoint favored candidates or protégés at lower-level positions – this is what defines patronage. Party secretaries control appointments.[33] Given this feature of China's political system, I define "patron" as the provincial Party secretary who was in office when a city Party secretary was appointed to a given city. Even if the provincial Party secretary did not personally choose the city Party secretary, he or she at least did not veto the appointment. For example, Chen Chuanping was party secretary of Taiyuan city, Shanxi province, in 2011. He was first appointed to Taiyuan in 2010, when Yuan Chunqing was provincial party secretary of Shanxi. In my dataset, Yuan Chunqing is identified as his patron. Since 2012, 84 percent of the city leaders were transferred to other locations and thus may be coded as having more than one patron between 2012 and 2017. When any one of their patrons falls in a given year, the variable *patron fall* is coded as 1.

In addition to *patron fall*, I also coded whether a city leader is a former appointee of a member of the 18th PSC, or of the Politburo, or a client of Sun Zhengcai (the Politburo member who fell in 2017). These measures allow us to examine whether the national political status of patrons affects the likelihood of their clients' political survival.

OTHER VARIABLES. I include each city's GDP per capita in 2011 as a measure of economic wealth. To capture institutional quality, I draw on the National Economic Research Institute (NERI) Marketization Index, a set of province-level indicators that measure the quality of market-supporting institutions.[34] My analysis includes the NERI index on "state-market relations" and "rule of law," as these two factors are most relevant to corruption. In provinces where state–market relations are healthy and the rule of law is strong, I expect less corruption, and city leaders should therefore be less susceptible to investigations.

---

[33] In theory, decisions about the appointment of key personnel (for example, city leaders) should be collectively made by members of the Party Committee and the Organization Department at the higher level of government (for example, the province), but, in practice, party secretaries hold tremendous sway over this matter.

[34] Fan and Wang (2000).

I also coded a variety of characteristics of the city leaders: whether they are localists (served in the same province throughout their careers), in addition to gender, ethnicity, age, and age of joining the CCP. Finally, I code whether the city leaders were transferred between 2012 and 2017. These are later omitted from the final regression and do not affect the results.

WHO STAYS AND WHO FALLS?

A description of this cohort of 331 city Party secretaries is illuminating as we know little about the patterns of political survival and fall at the sub-provincial level despite intense media coverage of the anti-corruption campaign. The first striking feature is that the number of falls follows an inverted V-shape pattern, as illustrated in Figure 6.3: it started at two in 2012, rose sharply to 18 in 2014, and then declined. In 2017, eight city Party secretaries fell, higher than in 2012 and 2013. By 2017, a total of 54 officials, or 16 percent of the original cohort, had fallen. Taking into account the shrinking size of the cohort each year, Figure 6.3 (right box) visualizes the hazard rate, an estimation of the likelihood of fall using

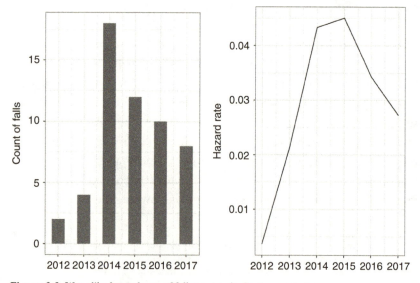

Figure 6.3 Wave-like hazard rate of fall among city Party secretaries.

TABLE 6.1 *High turnover rate among city Party secretaries*

	Transferred = 1		Transferred = 0		Cumulative falls	Cumulative transfers
Year	Fall	Did not fall	Fall	Did not fall		
2012	1	72	1	257	2	73
2013	3	201	1	124	6	204
2014	9	211	9	96	24	220
2015	10	242	2	53	36	252
2016	8	266	2	19	46	274
2017	8	271	0	6	54	279

only the number of falls in a given year's remaining cohort. Just as in the simple counts of falls, the estimated hazard rate rose sharply from 2012 to 2014, peaked in 2015, and tapered off afterward. In short, the crackdown became less intense but did not end.

A second feature that stands out is the high turnover rate among the city Party secretaries (Table 6.1). This is consistent with earlier studies that find average tenure lengths shortening over the years.[35] Constitutional rules stipulate that local Party secretaries and chief executives should be appointed for a term of five years, up to a maximum of two terms,[36] but in practice, local leaders rarely stay in one office beyond five years. Among the cohort of 331 Party secretaries, only six secretaries (2 percent) remained "intact" in their original office – that is, they were neither transferred nor investigated – by 2017.[37] Within a six-year period, 279 (84 percent) were transferred to other localities or positions, and 54 of them (16 percent) fell. The intensity of Xi's anti-corruption drive has evidently created a volatile and stressful environment for sub-provincial leaders.

Third, geographic patterns of fall are noteworthy, as summarized in Table 6.2.[38] The largest number of falls (20) is found in the central

---

[35] Landry (2008); Guo (2009). [36] B2011-236; B2011-241.

[37] "Transfer" includes leaders who were transferred to other cities or higher-level offices, leaders who retired, and those who were transferred to unspecific posts. The vast majority of them fall in the first category.

[38] Table 6.2 describes the geographic distribution of fallen leaders by the province within which they were based in 2011. Of the 54 leaders who fell, only one, Gu Chunli, was transferred to a different province, from Liaoning to Jilin.

TABLE 6.2 *Geographic distribution of falls by region and province*

Region	Total falls in region	Province	Falls in province (2012–2017)
Eastern/	7	Jiangsu	3
Coastal		Zhejiang	1
		Guangdong	1
		Fujian	1
		Shandong	1
Central	20	Shanxi	6
		Anhui	3
		Jiangxi	2
		Henan	3
		Hubei	2
		Hunan	4
Western	15	Ningxia	1
		Gansu	2
		Shaanxi	1
		Inner Mongolia	2
		Guangxi	2
		Sichuan	4
		Guizhou	1
		Yunnan	2
Northeastern	12	Heilongjiang	5
		Liaoning	4
		Jilin	3

region. Shanxi, a major mining province, topped the charts with a total of six fallen city Party secretaries from 2012 to 2017. Second in rank is the Western region, with 15 fallen leaders, followed by the Northeast region at 12, and the coastal – and most prosperous – region at seven falls. With the notable exception of Jiangsu province (three falls), city leaders in the 2011 cohort tended to fall in less prosperous provinces, particularly in mining and heavy industrial rustbelts.

Finally, a look at the individual characteristics of the fallen. Among the 54 city Party secretaries who fell, 52 are men; 52 are Han Chinese; their ages in 2011 range between 46 and 59 years old; 47 are localists; 40 were transferred between 2011 and the time they fell; two had patrons in the PSC; 14 had patrons in the Politburo. In the fallen category, 20 percent experienced a patron's fall, compared with 14 percent among the remaining 277 officials who did not fall. Among the fallen, the median value of their city's growth in share of provincial GDP is 0.86

percent and the median of media mentions is 9.98, compared with 1.22 percent and 9.13, respectively, in the opposite group. Notably, 22 of the 54 fallen leaders (40 percent) were promoted prior to or in the year they fell, which reiterates my point in Chapter 5: competence and corruption go together in the Chinese political system.

While these descriptive statistics give a rough sense of the characteristics of leaders who fall, they do not identify which of these features are statistically significant predictors of fall, nor do they account for the effects of time. Thus, in the next section, I proceed to a statistical analysis of my data.

AN EVENT HISTORY ANALYSIS

Event history analysis (EHA) is a dynamic model that estimates the probability, or hazard rate, of a particular event occurring at particular times. In my case, this event is a "fall" – whether a Party secretary is investigated for corruption. Hazard rates cannot be directly observed; instead, they are estimated using the results of the regression. What can be observed is the binary variable of "fall," measured as either 1 (yes) or 0 (no).

EHA allows us to compare hazard rates over time, rather than as a composite estimate. Because of its dynamic qualities, EHA is widely used by sociologists and historical institutionalists to study temporally sensitive phenomena such as class mobility, migration, founding of organizations, and policy evolutions.[39]

Yet, in China studies, the bulk of analyses of career patterns, promotion, and corruption investigations do not employ EHA models. Instead, the norm is to use standard logistic regressions, where, as two methodologists describe, "temporal dependence [is treated] more as a statistical nuisance that needs to be 'controlled for,' rather than as something substantively interesting."[40] In examining an evolving anti-corruption campaign, the effects of time should be taken seriously.

---

[39] For example, see Baydar *et al.* (1990); Crowley and Skocpol (2001); Walder and Hu (2009).

[40] Carter and Signorino (2010).

More specifically, my analysis uses a discrete-time hazard model, a variant of EHA. Although Cox proportional-hazard models are the most frequent choice for temporal analysis in the social sciences, these models assume a continuous notion and measurement of time (for example, if the occurrence of investigations is tracked by hour or day). This assumption doesn't apply in my case, the dependent variable and the associated covariates are aggregated as year-person observations, such that information about when during the year a Party secretary was investigated for corruption is not relevant for my analysis. Discrete-time models also make it easier to deal with time-varying (rather than fixed) covariates and to test relationships that violate the proportional-hazards assumption.

Following Carter and Signorino, I include splines (that is, t, t^2, t^3), rather than time dummies in my analysis, as this renders temporal dependence "much easier to implement and to interpret."[41] Using splines allows us to plot and interpret the hazard, as I do below. I begin my discussion by examining the logistic regression results shown in Table 6.3, in which Models 2 to 5 include splines and Model 4 includes province-level fixed effects.

Across all five models in Table 6.3, it is clear that only *patron fall* registers a substantial and statistically significant association with the fall of city Party secretaries, which is robust even with the addition of economic variables, NERI institutional indices, specific patron characteristics, and temporal effects. Economic performance (as measured by growth in share of provincial GDP) and media mentions do not show a statistically significant effect, which indicates that high performers are neither more nor less likely to fall during the campaign. The cities' level of wealth also does not predict the likelihood of fall.

The non-significant results of the NERI indices deserve some attention. Perhaps the single greatest difficulty of studying corruption is that we do not know which official is really corrupt, even after an investigation. It is possible that those who are arrested are not the most corrupt, or

---

[41] Carter and Signorino (2010). This approach also has the advantage of dealing straightforwardly with problems shown in Cox models, which may require unrealistic assumptions about proportionality of hazards.

TABLE 6.3 *Determinants of downfall among city Party secretaries*

	Dependent variable: fall				
	(1)	(2)	(3)	(4)	(5)
Patron fall	1.144***	1.079***	0.815**	3.368***	0.982**
	(0.374)	(0.401)	(0.404)	(1.071)	(0.389)
Growth in share of provincial	2.968	3.210	3.177	6.301	3.037
GDP (2012)	(4.202)	(4.210)	(4.108)	(4.859)	(4.209)
Media mentions (2011)	0.003	0.002	0.000	0.005	0.002
	(0.016)	(0.017)	(0.017)	(0.023)	(0.016)
Prefecture GDP per capita	0.000	0.000	0.000	0.000	0.000
(2011)	(0.000)	(0.000)	(0.000)	(0.000)	(0.000)
NERI government–market		−0.020			
relations (2012)		(0.135)			
NERI rule of law (2012)		0.154			
		(0.105)			
Client of 18th Politburo member			−0.543		
			(0.377)		
Client of 18th PSC member			0.123		
			(0.750)		
Client of Sun Zhengcai			0.795		
			(0.805)		
time, time^2, and time^3		✓	✓	✓	✓
Province fixed effects				✓	
Observations	1,586	1,586	1,586	1,586	1,586
Log likelihood	−211.018	−203.869	−203.346	−181.280	−204.621
Akaike information criterion	432.036	426.138	428.693	420.559	425.241

Note: * p < 0.1; ** p < 0.05; *** p < 0.01.

that the truly corrupt are not apprehended. But we may reasonably infer that in provinces where the rule of law is strong and where the state is smaller and less interventionist,[42] there should be less corruption. That both NERI indices are non-significant suggests that the actual prevalence of corruption does not hugely influence the likelihood of fall; instead, patronage is the overwhelming determinant.

Turning to patronage, Figure 6.4 plots the hazard rate based on Model 5 in Table 6.3, where the effects of patronage are statistically significant at the 90 percent confidence interval. The plot on the left shows the hazard rate for city leaders whose patron did not fall, and that

[42] The NERI state–market relation is a composite measure of three dimensions: (1) strength of market mechanisms relative to state planning, (2) reduction of state intervention in the market, and (3) size of the state administration and public sector.

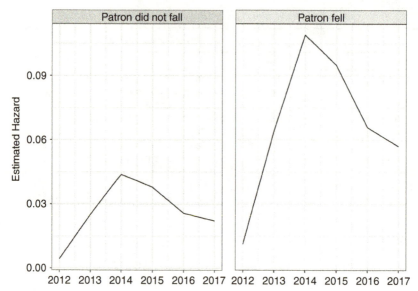

Figure 6.4 Effects of patron's fall on city leaders' likelihood of fall.

on the right represents the opposite group. The results indicate that the strong effects of *patron fall* intersect with the temporal rhythm of campaign-style enforcement. Both groups exhibit a wave-like pattern: the hazard rate peaked in 2014 and declined afterward, but, by 2017, had stabilized at levels above 2012. The difference is that city leaders whose patron fell were much more likely to fall than those whose patron survived. In 2012, the former group was only slightly more susceptible than the latter, but in 2013, the gap between the two jumped dramatically by more than two-fold. This large difference persisted until 2017.

One might question whether *patron fall* might be capturing province-level idiosyncrasies; for example, in the earlier descriptive section, we see that provinces reliant on mining and heavy industries had a higher number of falls. But this does not appear to be the case. Adding province fixed effects in Model 4 actually increases the substantive effects of *patron fall* by a large magnitude and does not decrease its statistical significance.

Although *patron fall* posts a robust large effect, city leaders' ties to national leaders do not consistently predict their political outcome, as Model 3 indicates. Clients who were appointed by the current PSC and Politburo members are not consistently protected; some survived, but some fell. Among the 54 fallen city Party secretaries, two had patrons in the PSC (including Premier Li Keqiang and Yu Zhengsheng) and 14 had patrons in the Politburo. Nor is being a client of Sun Zhengcai a statistically significant predictor of downfall; among his seven former appointees, only two fell. Given the relatively small number of city leaders with patrons in the Politburo or ties to Sun Zhengcai, these results must be interpreted with caution. But they do not support popular claims that Xi's anti-corruption campaign is merely "political warfare" among national leaders.

If I were to explain the results of the regression to city Party secretaries, my response would be: good news, bad news, neutral news. The good news is that the peak of the crackdown is over; the bad news is that it hasn't stopped. The neutral news is that delivering economic growth and having a high media profile is neither good nor bad, but if a city leader's patron falls, his clients should be nervous. Finally, having a patron in the Politburo doesn't necessarily inoculate one from investigations, so even with strong backing at the highest national level, local officials must constantly watch their backs.

FALLING ACROSS THE COUNTRY

My analysis zooms in on a special cohort of city Party secretaries who experienced the entire anti-corruption drive. Future studies may expand to cover all nationally and provincially appointed leaders. For this purpose, it is useful to explore patterns of investigations across the country. Drawing on the CCDI website, Figure 6.5 shows the number of investigated cases from 2013 to early 2018, divided by rank.[43]

Altogether, 256 investigations involved centrally appointed officials, such as provincial Party secretaries and ministers – represented by the darker bars in Figure 6.5 – an unprecedented number of fallen mega-tigers. Notably, there isn't a single discernable peak, although fewer officials fell in the latter half of the period examined. Instead, at the national level, we see a string of periodic crackdowns.

---

[43] Statistics for Figure 6.5 were scraped from the CCDI website. There could have been corruption investigations that were not reported on the website, so this is not necessarily a full sample.

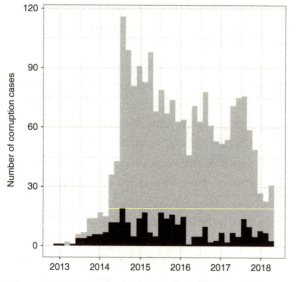

Figure 6.5 Falls of national and local officials since 2013.

Turning to provincially appointed officials, including city-level Party secretaries, mayors, and directors in ministries and large state-owned enterprises, my dataset captures a total of 1,724 corruption cases. Among this group, we see a wave-like campaign rhythm that peaked in 2014, which is consistent with patterns in the smaller cohort I analyzed. In 2013, there were 27 investigations. By the next year, the number had exploded to 385. The 76 cases in the peak month of August was more than all the cases in 2013 combined. Although the trajectory points downward after August, at least 20 officials fell each month from June 2014 to September 2017, with periodic bursts of investigations in the middle of 2016, middle of 2017, and early 2018. The past six years must have been unusually high-stress ones for local leaders.

WILL ANTI-CORRUPTION MEASURES DAMPEN GROWTH?

To assess whether anti-corruption measures will dampen China's growth, we must distinguish between immediate and long-term effects. In the short term, when opportunistic capitalists can no longer rely upon their patrons to override rules and extend privileges, they do less business, which leads to lower growth.[44] The unusually harsh scrutiny also makes government officials nervous and risk-averse, which means they would rather do nothing and avoid blame than sign off on initiatives. For example, in 2015, local officials dragged their feet on implementing 45 billion Yuan worth of investment projects, despite approval from the National Development Reform Commission (NDRC).[45] This is peculiar in an economy known for overzealous investment. Finally, fearful of being implicated in the crackdown on officials, wealthy private entrepreneurs are fleeing abroad, provoking worries about capital flight that is estimated to have approached US$425 billion in 2014.[46] But, arguably, these are painful but necessary adjustments that accompany the Party's determination to root out cronyism, which, if successful, should eventually bring about a healthier economy and a more disciplined administration, as economist Yao Yang argued.[47]

Yet Xi's anti-corruption drive may not reap the expected long-term benefits and could even worsen future prospects for two reasons. First, his campaign has gone beyond hunting down corrupt officials and is fast evolving into a tool for tightening political control. Xi insisted that officials demonstrate loyalty and adhere strictly to Party ideology, as he declared at a speech to the CCDI in 2019, "We must resolutely safeguard the authority of the central Party and the central leadership, ensure that the entire party marches in step and acts in unison."[48] In line with this speech, the central disciplinary authorities have expanded the scope of the campaign from policing corruption to monitoring policy implementation and ensuring correct political thinking,[49] as *Xinhua* declares:[50]

---

[44] Chen and Zhong (2017). Lin *et al.* (2016) add that the chilling effect of anti-corruption depends on firms' prior relationships with the state.

[45] "China Stimulus Push Stalls as Local Officials Avoid Anti-corruption Spotlight," *Reuters*, 15 November 2015.

[46] Li Yuan, "China's Entrepreneurs Are Wary of Its Future," *The New York Times*, 23 February 2019; Gunter (2017).

[47] Yao Yang, "Graft or Growth in China," *Project Syndicate*, 4 May 2015.

[48] "习近平在十九届中央纪委三次全会上发表重要讲话 [Xi Jinping's Important Speech to the 19th Central Disciplinary Committee]," 11 January 2019, www.ccdi.gov.cn/toutiao/201901/t20190111_186902.html (accessed 4 March 2019).

[49] "Report of the 7th Inspection Committee to the NDRC" [in Chinese], CCDI Website, 30 January 2019 (no longer accessible). See Andrew Gilholm, "Xi Jinping's New Watchdog," *Foreign Affairs*, 6 March 2018.

[50] "CPC Meeting Reviews Work Rules of Rural Organizations, Disciplinary Inspection Agencies," *Xinhua*, 26 November 2018.

> The CCDI and National Supervisory Commission (NSC) should take the lead in enhancing the Party's political building, and closely follow the CPC Central Committee with Comrade Xi Jinping at the core in terms of thinking, political orientation and actions ... The CCDI and NSC are also required to have the courage to "show their sword and fight" on major issues of principle.

While this message may be intended to empower disciplinary authorities, for Chinese bureaucrats, the subtext is clear: conform to the right "thinking" and don't argue. In effect, this extinguishes free speech within the bureaucracy, and, as we learnt from the Mao era, when honest feedback and debate was suppressed, disastrous outcomes ensued.[51] This is why in his monumental speech in 1978 that launched reform and opening, the first point that Deng made was to "think independently and dare to speak out."

Second, Xi has been simultaneously straitjacketing the bureaucracy and clamping down on social and political freedoms. If Xi seeks to transform bureaucrats from bold but corruption-prone, as seen in prior decades, to being strictly disciplined, then their entrepreneurial, risk-taking functions must be transferred to the private sector and civil society through progressive political liberalization. As Max Weber pointed out, in Western history, the emergence of legal-rational bureaucracy was accompanied by the rise of liberal market economies because the two were complementary. Since coming to office, however, Xi's policies have stifled freedom both within the Party-state and in society.

Put differently, the supreme leader's exhortation of his officials to be both daring and disciplined is not realistic.[52] This is why we see the emergence of a new problem – inaction and paralysis[53] – also known as

---

[51] At the Lushan conference, Mao openly rebuked and removed a senior leader, Peng Dehuai, for criticizing his policies. This led officials to fear speaking out, which set the stage for disastrous policies and the world's largest man-made famine during the Great Leap Forward (Yang 2012).

[52] The hit drama series *In the Name of the People* showcases the Party's ideal official: Party Secretary Li Dakang. Li is portrayed as a leader who tirelessly dedicates his life to economic development, even at the cost of making serious policy mistakes and neglecting his marriage, and never succumbing to corruption.

[53] The problem of bureaucratic paralysis due to a proliferation of targets is not new (Zhao 2013; Ang 2016; Zhang 2017), but it has been exacerbated by the anti-corruption campaign.

"lazy governance" (*lanzheng*). Laziness appears so widespread that the State Council issued warnings against it (Figure 6.6) by shaming individual offenders for dereliction of duty, delaying decisions, and leaving funds unused.[54] Xi also appears concerned about the backlash against the anti-corruption drive and mounting demands on the bureaucracy. The solution? The Central Party Secretariat declared 2019 the "Alleviate the Burden of Grassroots Cadres Year," by issuing more directives that order higher-level officials not to burden subordinates with conflicting, burdensome mandates.[55] Under Xi, the irony is that every top-down solution (harsh crackdowns) generates a new problem (inaction) that the regime tries to solve with more top-down solutions (punish inaction).

CONCLUSION

This chapter explored the implications of aggressive anti-corruption measures on China's future development. I offer four takeaways. First, Xi's war on graft takes the form of a sustained campaign, which is paradoxical, as campaigns are supposed to be intense but brief. My data shows that, although the crackdown reached its peak in 2014, it is still ongoing.

Second, the turnover rate for local leaders is remarkably high. Of the 331 Party secretaries in my dataset, 16 percent fell, and only six remained in their original office (that is, neither fell nor were transferred) six years later. Amid the unusually harsh scrutiny and steady drumbeat of fallen officials, local leaders must contend with an extremely volatile and stressful environment. Such conditions have a chilling effect.

Third, my analysis finds that performance does not protect local officials from downfall; if anything, their careers – indeed, their very

---

[54] "庸政懒政怠政问责了！这16个典型案例被国办通报 [Lazy Governance Will Be Held Accountable! 16 Textbook Cases]," China.gov.cn, 16 June 2017, www.gov.cn/xinwen/2017-06/16/content_5203106.htm (accessed 3 March 2019). Inaction was also prominent enough to claim prime-time space in *In the Name of the People*, which dedicated one episode to Party Secretary Li Dakang's furious rebuking of lazy officials.

[55] By 2009, township leaders were being evaluated according to more than 100 targets (Ang 2016, 118–22), and this number is still growing. Hence, the popular idea that creating a new target for every new priority will induce policy compliance is simplistic. See "解决形式主义突出问题为基层减负 [Solving the Problem of Grassroots Burden]," *The People's Daily*, 12 March 2019.

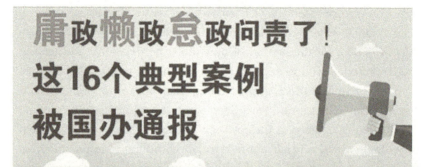

庸政懒政怠政问责了！
这16个典型案例
被国办通报

　　为贯彻落实党中央、国务院关于加强督促检查、严肃责任追究的决策部署，根据李克强总理关于严厉整肃庸政懒政怠政行为的重要指示批示精神，2017年2月至5月，国务院办公厅会同监察部等有关部门，对国务院第三次大督查、审计署跟踪审计及部门专项督查发现的突出问题，组织开展了核查问责，依法依规对117个问题涉及的1089人进行问责和处理。

　　6月15日，国务院办公厅正式对外通报了16个"庸政懒政怠政"督查问责典型案例。

重点问责哪些问题？

- 中央预算内投资项目进展迟缓
- 财政资金闲置沉淀
- 涉企乱收费
- 落实"放管服"改革政策不到位
- 公租房大量空置
- 医保基金管理使用不到位
- 套取挪用侵占保障性住房资金
- 挪用套取侵占扶贫资金

Figure 6.6 Screenshot from the website of the Chinese central government, warning against "lazy governance."

survival – are more closely tied to the rise and fall of their patrons, making the political system more personalist, rather than accountable to rules.[56] Yet it is too simplistic to dismiss Xi's anti-corruption campaign as merely a purge among national elites. Not all the appointees of the PSC and Politburo members are shielded from fall; nor did all the appointees of Sun Zhengcai topple with him.

Fourth, observers should look beyond the immediate effects of anti-corruption drives on growth,[57] and instead, pay attention to a deeper, long-term problem: the misalignment of Xi's economic and bureaucratic preferences. His administration's strong leaning toward a state-dominant economy – which calls for proactive, risk-taking officials – is in conflict with the paralyzing effects of his draconian crackdown. No doubt, to survive, the Party must fight corruption and discipline government officials, but achieving this objective would require simultaneous economic and social liberalization.

---

[56] Provincial institutional quality, which may be interpreted as a proxy for actual levels of corruption, also fails to predict the hazard rate.

[57] See "Robber Barons Beware," *The Economist*, 22 October 2015; Katy Barnato, "How China's Anticorruption Drive Is Hurting Growth," *CNBC*, 4 December 2015.

CHAPTER 7

Rethinking Nine Big Questions

MR. FU WON A FABULOUS DEAL. STUFFING SUITCASES FULL OF company shares, he lavished bribes upon influential officials in exchange for subsidizing his railway projects with cheap loans and land grants. The policymakers in charge of infrastructure and budgets were not only Fu's pals, but his indirect business associates: their family members ran businesses in the steel industry, which would benefit from a construction boom. As ties between capitalists and politicians grew closer, the deals got better. The government subsequently doubled land grants and loans to Fu's venture, while turning a blind eye to his inflated costs and risk of losses. Fu even convinced national leaders to change geological definitions so that he could profit from the higher value of land grants in mountainous areas. Through craftiness and connections, he successfully "moved mountains" to the tune of a staggering fortune.

Stories like this seem to expose the gravity of corruption in China: businessmen colluding with officials to exploit development projects for personal enrichment, cronyism seeping into central and local levels of government, and abundant graft. Economic expansion alongside such corruption has mystified observers, leading some to insist since the 1990s that the economy and regime will soon collapse.[1]

But, in fact, Mr. Fu is not Chinese – he's American.[2] In Chinese, Mr. Leland Stanford's last name translates into Si Tan Fu. A corporate

---

[1] "Red Alert," *The Economist*, 22 October 1998; Pei (1999; 2006); Chang (2001).
[2] This opening story is based on Brands (2010); see also White (2011).

titan and philanthropist, he founded a university at the height of America's Gilded Age in the late nineteenth century, which today ranks among the best in the world.

The Gilded Age was an era of crony capitalism, but these were also years of extraordinary growth and transformation. Millions of Americans moved from fields to factories, standards of living rose to unprecedented levels for large swathes of the population, new industries sprouted, capital markets expanded, railways opened up long-distance commerce, and super-magnates – such as Stanford, J. P. Morgan, and John D. Rockefeller – emerged triumphant. In this century, the United States overtook the United Kingdom to become the factory of the world, even as corruption flourished.

Today, China is passing through something similar – but not identical – to America's Gilded Age. Reformers under Deng held together a delicate political union and rebuilt from the debris of Mao's disastrous rule, just as American leaders reconstructed the nation after the devastation of the Civil War. China's market reform lifted 850 million people out of poverty yet produced stark inequality, as America also experienced in the nineteenth century. And, like in the United States, the corruption that prevails in China is of a particular type – access money – the purchase of privileges by capitalists from those in power. Yet, despite these parallels, the two nations' political systems could not be more different: China is an autocracy whereas America is a democracy.

This book demystified the Chinese paradox of growth with corruption by unbundling corruption and by placing China in comparative-historical perspective. In this concluding chapter, I recap my key arguments, revisit the comparison of the Chinese and American Gilded Ages in depth, and discuss the implications of this book for nine big questions about corruption and China's political economy.

WHY CHINA PROSPERED WITH CORRUPTION

The assumption that corruption always hurts economic growth is oversimplistic. Its effect on capitalist activities depends on the *type* of corruption. By unbundling corruption, I reveal four explanations for why China prospered amid corruption.

ACCESS MONEY DOMINATES. To be sure, China has all forms of corruption, but the dominant type today is access money. Rather than merely assert this claim on the basis of subjective judgement or anecdotes,[3] my study presents a range of evidence to demonstrate and compare corruption structures, both across countries (Chapter 2) and within China (Chapter 3). Given that access money dominates in China, it's no surprise that corruption has gone hand in hand with rapid growth. Functioning like the steroids of capitalism, this type of corruption spurs investment and transactions in the short term, but it also generates risks and misallocates resources toward super-profitable, speculative sectors (Chapter 5). On top of that, access money exacerbates inequality by enriching a club of corrupt officials and politically connected capitalists. These are all clear echoes of nineteenth-century America.

CHINA'S POLITICAL SYSTEM OPERATES ON A PROFIT-SHARING MODEL. Why does access money, rather than other forms of corruption, dominate? Put differently, how did China evolve a more growth-friendly structure of corruption? China's political system operates on a profit-sharing model. Among political elites, their career and financial rewards – graft in exchange for deals – are linked to economic prosperity. Hence, rather than "grab" from businesses through extortion, local leaders are typically eager to extend "helping" hands to favored investors by offering special deals, cheap land, regulatory exemptions, and other perks (Chapter 5). State–business relations in China are not "extractive," as Acemoglu and Robinson assert, but rather transactional.[4]

What about the millions of Chinese street-level bureaucrats who are poorly paid and lack the power to benefit from deal-making? As Chapter 4 explains, they also operate in a profit-sharing mode – through compensation practices. Even though formal public wages are standardized at "capitulation" (below subsistence) rates, the fringe benefits and pay of public

---

[3] For example, see Sun (1999); Rock and Bonnett (2004); Johnston (2008); Wedeman (2012).

[4] Acemoglu and Robinson (2006, 32).

employees are pegged to the financial performance of local governments and the agencies within them. In this way, their fringe compensation acts as an efficiency wage, incentivizing low-level bureaucrats to generate revenue and to avoid extortion and theft.

CAPACITY-BUILDING REFORMS HAVE CURTAILED DAMAGING FORMS OF CORRUPTION. Yet no profit-sharing arrangement could work without state monitoring and punishment of those who engage in growth-damaging forms of corruption. Aiming to create a modern bureaucracy suited to a globalized market economy, the central government has advanced a host of capacity-building reforms since 1998 (Chapter 3). Local leaders were on board with these reforms as they constrained theft and predatory practices among their subordinates. Indeed, some devised and added their own control measures on top of centrally mandated reforms (Chapter 4). The consequent pattern since 2000 is that, while grand bribery exploded, embezzlement, misuse of public funds, petty bribery, and extortive practices visibly declined (Chapter 3). Simply put, to channel corruption away from its most destructive forms, incentives and penalties must go hand in hand; neither is sufficient on its own.

REGIONAL COMPETITION CHECKS PREDATORY CORRUPTION, SPURS ON DEVELOPMENTAL EFFORTS, AND RATCHETS UP DEALS Although there is no electoral contestation, intense regional competition takes place within China's politically centralized autocracy. To stand out from competitors, apart from curbing "grabbing hands," the most able leaders such as Bo Xilai and Ji Jianye go much further by positioning and branding their locales, experimenting with policies, and fostering niches (Chapter 5), strategies that enhance the overall commercial appeal of their locales. Simultaneously, they also offer privileged access for selected capitalists, whose bribes sponsor their personal consumption and wealth accumulation. To win political patrons and corporate clients, leaders must demonstrate competence and career potential (Chapter 5 and Appendix: Chapter 5). In short, in China, both development and corruption are competitive.

TWO GILDED AGES

American cities present us with a puzzle. Between 1880 and 1930 the cities were notorious for corruption. Corruption generally undermines government performance and cripples economic growth, but American cities prospered.[5]

Once we unbundle corruption and recognize that access money is growth-enhancing yet distorting, China's combination of corruption and growth is not a paradox. Nor is it exceptional – Menes' description of the United States from the Gilded Age to the Progressive Era, quoted above, seems to apply just as aptly to China today.[6] But how alike are the two cases?

COMPARATIVE-HISTORICAL DATA. Although there is no data on unbundled corruption available over extended periods in the United States and China, we can nevertheless explore overall levels of corruption reported in the media. The data I employ for comparison are newspaper reports of corruption in the United States for a 70-year period from the 1870s to the 1940s, and in China, for a seven-year period from 1999 to 2016. As shown in Table 7.1, in these two separate time periods, the United States and China are at equivalent levels of GDP per capita. In other words, between 1999 and 2016, China's economy traveled a distance comparable to what its American counterpart achieved from the beginning of the Gilded Age to World War II. Immediately, one difference jumps out: China's economic transformation is 10 times more compressed.[7]

Following Glaeser and Goldin,[8] I take media coverage of corruption as a proxy for overall levels of corruption. Granted, this is an imperfect measure, but it is the best available indicator for comparing long historical periods, and media mentions reflect the significance of corruption in public discourse. In the case of the United States, I search for articles in

[5] Menes (2006, 63).

[6] Post-liberalization India is another emerging economy that resembles the American Gilded Age, being similar yet not identical. See Walton (Forthcoming) for a fascinating comparative analysis.

[7] Sociologists apply the term "compressed modernization" (Beck and Lau 2005; Han and Shim 2010).

[8] Glaeser and Goldin (2006).

TABLE 7.1 *China and the United States at equivalent levels of income*[a]

GDP per capita (US$)	Year in China	Year in the United States
3,500	1999	1873
3,925	2000	1879
4,185	2001	1880
4,575	2002	1881
4,910	2003	1887
5,365	2004	1890
5,755	2005	1898
6,555	2006	1903
7,230	2007	1918
7,845	2008	1923
8,500	2009	1936
9,070	2010	1937
9,325	2011	1939
10,065	2012	1940
11,465	2013	1941
12,125	2014	1942
12,530	2015	1942
12,960	2016	1942

[a] Figures on GDP per capita are from the Penn World Tables, www.measuringworth.com/datasets/usgdp (accessed 10 December 2019).

a bundle of newspapers that contain the word "corruption" and then adjust this figure by the total number of articles in a given year.[9] In the case of China, I repeat the same procedure using the *People's Daily*, which is the official press (see Appendix: Chapter 7).

A prior study by Ramirez compared mentions of corruption in the United States and China in an identical bundle of US newspapers, which is problematic as American media will likely report a lot more on corruption at home than in China.[10] For a more rigorous comparison, I compare mentions of corruption in indigenous news sources. Therefore, when interpreting the results that follow, note that the levels of corruption in the United States and China are not directly comparable

---

[9] This takes into account the size of the economy, based on the assumption that larger economies with more commercial activities produce more news reports.

[10] Ramirez (2014).

(unlike in Ramirez, as he uses the same media source); instead, my goal is to compare longitudinal trends in each case.[11]

FROM GILDED TO PROGRESSIVE. Figure 7.1 shows the corruption trends in China and the United States at comparable levels of economic development. In the US context, the timing of the Gilded Age (1870–1900) and Progressive Era (1890–1920) is well established in the historical literature. On the other hand, when did China's Gilded Age begin and end? This has not been established by historians, as it is a recent event. Judging from Figure 7.1, we may extrapolate two different timelines for the Chinese equivalent of the Gilded Age and the Progressive Era.

The simpler method is to identify comparable periods using GDP per capita. Following this method, the Gilded Age and Progressive Era in the United States stretched over an approximately 50-year period from the 1870s to the 1920s, while the corresponding period in China is extremely short, from 1999 to 2011, a 12-year period that encompasses the Jiang–Zhu and Hu–Wen administrations. Yet, judging by Xi's declaration of a corruption crisis in 2012, China clearly hasn't graduated from the Progressive Era – indeed, it appears to have only recently entered it.

A better measure, therefore, should take into account the defining political–economic transformations of the eras: the Gilded Age featured rapid economic take-off, rampant corruption, and sharp inequalities, whereas the Progressive Era was distinguished by a host of administrative and political reforms to correct the excesses of the preceding period. From this structural perspective, the 35-year period from market opening in 1978 to 2012 may be characterized as China's Gilded Age.

Demarcating the Chinese Progressive Era is a lot trickier and open to interpretation. As I documented in Chapter 3, in 1998, the Jiang–Zhu administration rolled out a sweeping program of administrative reforms to curtail petty corruption and fiscal malfeasance. If this period of reform is considered a Progressive Era, it would overlap with China's Gilded Age

---

[11] Furthermore, the measure in China captures the Party-state's attention to corruption, which both shapes and reflects public opinion, whereas the coverage of corruption in the United States was independent.

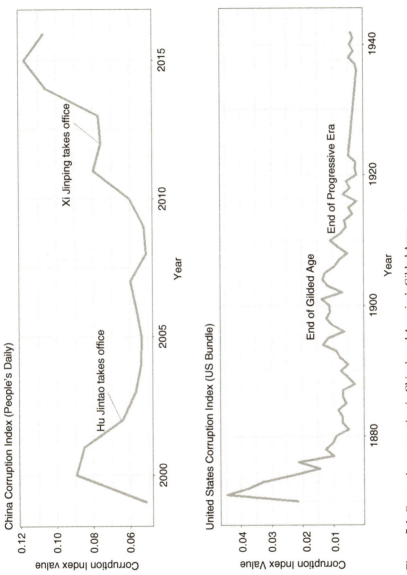

Figure 7.1 Comparing corruption in China's and America's Gilded Ages.

(1978–2012). More than a decade later, in 2012, Xi launched the most sweeping anti-corruption campaign in the Party's history, focusing on arresting numerous corrupt officials, though it also has some norm-correcting features. This may be considered a second stage of progressivism. In either case, it's reasonable to conclude that China in 2019 – now a superpower and middle-income economy – has entered the Progressive Era.

With that in mind, let's first take a look at corruption trends in the United States from the 1870s to 1940. The overall pattern is clear: corruption peaked at the beginning of the Gilded Age but rapidly declined and stabilized afterward. The height of corruption was the 1870s, centered on the scandal-ridden Grant administration. The most notorious scandal involved Crédit Mobilier, a railway company whose owners gave influential congressmen company shares in exchange for approval of federal subsidies and disregard of the company's financial risks. But, following this peak, corruption reports fell sharply. The twentieth century ushered in the Progressive Era, during which corruption reports picked up again marginally, a reflection of the financial crisis of 1893 and the spread of muck-raking journalism. By the end of this period, the incidence of corruption reports had dwindled, and it remained flat through World War I.

China's corruption trends are less straightforward. If we identify comparable periods simply using GDP per capita, then China from 1998 to 2010 would display patterns similar to America's Gilded Age through the Progressive Era: a sharp rise in corruption at the beginning, followed by a steady decline. But if we take 1978–2011 to be China's Gilded Age (my dataset does not include years prior to 1999) and 2012 as the beginning of a Progressive Era, then it appears that, unlike the US historical experience, China does not display a steady decline of corruption reports after an initial peak. Instead, it saw two spikes: first in 1998, when the Jiang–Zhu government launched administrative reforms nationwide, then again in 2015, when the number of fallen officials peaked (Chapter 6).

Compared with the United States, another distinction in China is that coverage of corruption is highly sensitive to leaders' policies. Figure 7.2 shows the amount of corruption reports in China from 1990 to 2016, covering three administrations (Jiang–Zhu, Hu–Wen, and Xi–Li) using

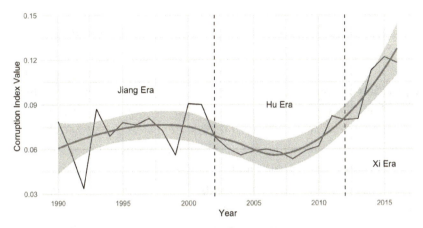

Figure 7.2 Corruption reports in China from 1990 to 2016.

a smoothed curve that can better represent trends. The amount of corruption reports fluctuated within a narrow band from the Jiang–Zhu era to the Hu–Wen era, dipping to its lowest point during the latter. This, however, does not mean that the amount of corruption was actually low; rather, as Walder describes, it was a period of "drift and delay under an amorphous collective leadership that has let structural problems like corruption fester" (see also Chapter 3).[12] Xi's personal campaign against graft pushed media reports on corruption to unprecedented heights.

MODIFYING EARLIER COMPARISONS. Although my analysis is not the first to draw parallels between America's and China's Gilded Ages, it modifies the conclusions of earlier studies. In *Double Paradox*, Wedeman argues that post-Mao China is similar to America's Gilded Age because both saw the coexistence of localized corruption and rapid economic growth, both underwent structural transformations, and the spread of corruption motivated anti-corruption efforts.[13] However, while Wedeman is right in pointing out these similarities, he lacks data for systematically comparing the two cases and therefore misses some key differences.

My data highlights a divergence in longitudinal trends between the two Gilded Ages. The United States followed a clear evolutionary

---

[12] Walder (2018, 32).   [13] Wedeman (2012, 190–91).

sequence: corruption was most rampant during the Gilded Age, which prompted political and administrative reforms during the Progressive Era,[14] such that, by 1940, corruption no longer dominated news head-lines. In China, on the other hand, the sequence is less clear-cut. Anti-corruption measures through administrative reforms began in 1998, preceding Xi's sweeping crackdown in 2012 by more than a decade. At present, corruption reports are at their highest level since 1999.

In addition, determining the start and end points of China's Gilded Age is tricky even when comparative data on corruption reports is avail-able. Ramirez's analysis employed only US news reports and used GDP per capita to identify comparable periods in nineteenth-century America and post-1978 China. On the basis of this method, he concluded that "while corruption in China is an issue that merits attention, it is not at alarmingly high levels, compared to the US historical experience."[15] My analysis, however, questions his choice of data and his demarcation of "comparable stages" by GDP per capita alone. Employing a revised meth-odology, I arrived at a different set of observations: corruption in China's Gilded Age did not appear to be less serious than its American counter-part. In addition, we should take into account that corruption reports in authoritarian China are primarily influenced by top leaders' policies rather than by independent journalism.

FROM THUGS AND THIEVES TO INFLUENCE PEDDLERS. My comparative-historical exercise prompts a rethinking of Huntington's "life cycle" theory of corruption,[16] which argues that corruption rises steeply during stages of modernization and then decreases as countries grow richer and acquire state capabilities. This evolutionary pattern appears to manifest itself in eighteenth-century Britain, in the nine-teenth-century United States, and, according to Ramirez, in China in the 2000s as well.[17] Yet this argument considers only the decline of illegal corruption, such as bribery, as captured by media reports in Figure 7.1. Crucially, it overlooks the qualitative evolution of corruption toward

[14] Glaeser and Goldin (2006); Menes (2006).   [15] Ramirez (2014, 76).
[16] Huntington (1968), cited in Ramirez (2014).
[17] See also Brewer (1988); Theobald (1990); Ramirez (2014).

legalized exchanges – access money – as countries grow richer and more sophisticated.

Although present-day first-world economies are not overrun by thugs and thieves, they do have corruption. As Whyte observes in the context of the United Kingdom, "We are not Afghanistan or Russia," but "it is the pursuit of institutional interests that characterizes British corruption."[18] Similarly, the historian White underscores continuities in the money politics of the nineteenth-century Gilded Age and the 2008 financial crisis: "As in the nineteenth century, highly leveraged corporations, marketing dubious securities that were more inventive than comprehensible even to their creators, precipitated massive losses, receivership, government rescues, and severe economic downturns. The present seems so nineteenth century."[19] One striking difference, however, is that whereas influence peddling entailed bribes during the Gilded Age, no bribes were exchanged and few individuals were indictable in the present day.

How did access money in the United States become institutionalized and legal? The Progressive Era laid a foundation for this process by clearly demarcating certain forms of corruption – including bribery and embezzlement – as illegal and morally unacceptable. Progressives dismantled the spoils system and gradually instituted a professional and adequately paid civil service that no longer relied upon petty bribes and fees for income.[20] They also passed laws that broke up powerful monopolies, banned corporate contributions to political campaigns, and required the disclosure of campaign finance. Rules-based budgeting and accounting, meanwhile, replaced arbitrary collection and spending of public monies.

Yet this did not spell the end of corruption. To circumvent campaign finance restrictions, lobbyists and interest groups formed political action committees. As the twentieth century went on, campaign contributions soared. Lobbyists found creative ways to purchase influence without cash bribes. As Jack Abramoff, an infamous K-street lobbyist, reveals, these strategies include plying politicians with plush vacations and tickets to expensive sports games, free flow of food and alcohol at designated

---

[18] Whyte (2015, 3–4).   [19] White (2011, Kindle 547).   [20] Parrillo (2013).

restaurants, and, most effective of all, enticing staffers with lucrative positions in the private sector. In an interview on *60 Minutes*, Abramoff baldly stated, "We owned them [members of Congress]. What does that mean? Every request of our client, everything that we want, they are going to do. Not only that, they're going to think of things we can't think of to do."[21]

Over time, the expanding menu of legal access money rendered bribery unnecessary and indeed undesirable. Moving into the twenty-first century, money politics metastasized in an increasingly complex financial system, obfuscated by technicalities and contorted leveraging schemes that few can decipher. Meanwhile, financial institutions aggressively lobby for lax regulations that enable their risk-taking behavior. According to the United States Financial Crisis Inquiry Commission, "From 1999 to 2008, the financial sector expended $2.7 billion in reported federal lobbying expenses; individuals and political action committees in the sector made more than $1 billion in campaign contributions."[22] Regulatory capture in a supersized black box led up indirectly but eventually to the 2008 financial crisis.[23] Indeed, lenders who lobbied engaged in more risk-taking, faced higher delinquency rates, and were more likely to be bailed out, as one study finds.[24]

Comparing China's trajectory with the West, the two appear similar in their evolution of corruption toward access money. Yet China's style of access money still remains crude and personal, whereas it became sophisticated and institutionalized in Western politics (see Chapter 2). In addition, to curb crony capitalism, Xi deploys a top-down disciplinary apparatus to hunt down individual corrupt politicians and capitalists, while rejecting democratic checks.[25] The American Progressive Era, on the other hand, successfully mitigated illegal forms of corruption

---

[21] See "Jack Abramoff: The Lobbyist's Playbook," *60 Minutes*, 6 November 2011.

[22] *The Financial Crisis Inquiry Report: Final Report of the National Commission on the Causes of the Financial and Economic Crisis in the United States.* Washington, DC: Financial Crisis Inquiry Commission, 2011, p. xviii, https://lccn.loc.gov/2011381760 (accessed 29 November 2019).

[23] Although there were multiple causes behind the 2008 financial crisis, regulatory capture and influence peddling was undeniably among them (Baker 2010; Igan *et al.* 2011; Fisman and Golden 2017, 45–46).

[24] Igan *et al.* (2011, 34).   [25] Stromseth *et al.* (2017).

through democratic means: investigative journalism, electoral competition, secret ballots, and transparency policies.

Will China under the CCP one day evolve an institutional, legal style of access money, as seen in Washington's K-Street? I do not think so. Institutional corruption is a perversion of formal political representation, which lies at the heart of democracy. The First Amendment of the US Constitution enshrines "the right of the people ... to petition the government for a redress of grievances." In Lessig's words, this right becomes corrupted when political institutions are "systematically responsive to the wrong influence."[26] Given Xi's centralization of power in both the Party leadership and himself, elite corruption in China will remain highly personal and dyadic. Indeed, as Chapter 6 finds, under his anti-corruption campaign, patronage has become more central to the rise and fall of Chinese politicians than before, exceeding the importance of performance.

WHAT'S DIFFERENT ABOUT THIS BOOK?

There is a wealth of excellent literature on corruption, including on typologies of corruption, elite rent-seeking, and micro studies of petty corruption and bribery. Although my book builds on this rich foundation, it is distinct from prior studies in at least four main ways.

First, I challenge an implicit assumption in seminal theories of political economy that rich nations are non-corrupt and became successful by erecting "good" institutions early on in their development process. As Acemoglu and Robinson famously argued, economic prosperity requires "non-extractive" and "inclusive" institutions, which they illustrated with England's introduction of parliamentary institutions after the Glorious Revolution of 1688. Likewise, North, Wallis, and Weingast stated that in order for societies to transition from "limited" to "open access order," certain doorstep conditions, including the rule of law, must be in place.[27] A common implication of these theories is that corruption impedes growth, as corruption is an "extractive" activity that both threatens private property rights and undermines the rule of law.

---

[26] Lessig (2018, Kindle 237). [27] North *et al.* (2009); Acemoglu and Robinson (2012).

This influential literature forms an intellectual basis for conventional wisdom about the growth-dampening effects of corruption. It inspired the push for "good governance" – with control of corruption being a key aspect – among international development agencies such as the World Bank. In *The Quest for Good Governance,* Mungiu-Pippidi posited the core challenge of anti-corruption as changing social norms from "particularism to one of ethical universalism," with universalism meaning "equal treatment applies to everyone."[28] The assumption is that OECD countries have reached the end state of "good governance," a view that global metrics, which rank these countries at the top, affirm.

My book suggests that rich nations are not all free of corruption, nor does equal treatment in fact apply to everyone, even though clientelism, kinship-based patronage, embezzlement, and extortion have successfully been abolished. Corruption among the modern is of a different type – access money – which is usually legal, institutionalized, and hard to measure. Furthermore, the process of arriving at this outcome is not "first, get institutions right" and then all good things will follow. Rather, as some historians remind us, the emergence and spread of democracy, the rule of law, and meritocracy in Western societies coincided with rampant deal-making at home and the extraction of resources from colonies abroad.[29] The rise of the West was by no means just the result of good institutions and "a culture of innovation" – undeniably, it went hand in hand with corruption, exploitation, and inequality. An honest evaluation of Western history,[30] warts and all, helps us better understand the process of economic and political modernization in developing countries today. Corruption does not necessarily disappear with affluence and modern institutions; rather, it evolves toward impersonal exchanges and sophistication. Post-communist China underwent a similar process of structural transformation on a tightly compressed time scale, and it is still ongoing.

Second, my book demonstrated the *mechanisms* of profit-sharing in the Chinese political system, rather than merely asserting the existence of this system. The idea of political elites having a share in economic growth

---

[28] Mungiu-Pippidi (2015, 14).   [29] Pomeranz (2000); White (2011); Khan (2012).
[30] Chang (2002).

is expressed in many prior studies, beginning with Olson's famous analogy of the "stationary bandit."[31] Khan's framework on "political settlements" and that of Pritchett, Sen and Werker on "deals space" spells out the variety of elite deals on rents-sharing that either foster or block economic development.[32] Similarly, the literature on the "East Asian Paradox" argues that East Asian economies flourished despite corruption because their corruption took the form of "stable and mutually beneficial exchanges of government promotional privileges for bribes and kickbacks." Sun's labeling of Chinese corruption as "profit-sharing" also falls under this rubric.[33] Although this literature maintains that "stable exchanges" and "profit-sharing" can be growth-enhancing, it does not explain how such arrangements arise or work. How do numerous parties, apart from a handful of top elites, "share" the gains of growth?

My book fills the crucial gaps on *how*, not only among political elites but also among non-elite actors in the bureaucracy. Several scholars earlier pointed out that the reformist leadership laid the foundation for capitalist growth by allowing party apparatchiks to benefit from promoting it. For elite officials, this benefit came in the form of enhanced career prospects, as well as bribes and kickbacks they can personally collect from aiding favored companies in an economy that is thriving overall (see the case of Ji Jianye in Chapter 5). But that is not all: my study reveals that profit-sharing also operates among rank-and-file bureaucrats through compensation practices. Cumulatively, these institutions made the reform-era Chinese bureaucracy distinctly profit-oriented, which spurred on revenue-generating activities along with corruption.

Third, I provided an integrated account of corruption at both macro and micro levels. With only some exceptions, the analyses of elite rent-sharing and bureaucratic capacity building tend to proceed on separate tracks. Those who study rents and cronyism focus exclusively on political elites for a good reason: unless the most powerful state actors agree to share rents and restrain themselves from looting, they will not make welfare-enhancing policies. The literature on "state capability," on the other hand, features street-level bureaucrats and strategies that enable

---

[31] Olson (2000).   [32] Khan (2010); Pritchett *et al.* (2018).   [33] Sun (2004).

them to deliver public services and enforce rules.[34] Yet neither perspective on its own is sufficient. Good policies will not be implemented effectively if the public administration is underpaid, bloated, and corrupt, and competent bureaucrats cannot make a transformative difference if leaders at the helm fail to get their act together.

My framework on unbundling corruption considers both elites and non-elites, transactional and non-transactional corruption, which I apply to the analysis of an important case – China. At the macro level, I traced the Chinese leadership's decision to open markets and to restructure the economy and governance at critical turning points (Chapter 3), which changed state-business relations as the economy grew (Chapter 5). The second half of my story turned to the dry, technical work of building administrative capacity and creating bureaucratic incentives, which served to reduce petty corruption and theft (Chapters 3 and 4). This integrated perspective should and can be applied to analyzing development and corruption in any country.

Fourth, my book rejects simplistic conclusions about corruption being either "good" or "bad" for growth. It maintains that all corruption is harmful, but that the harms of different forms of corruption manifest themselves in different ways. Access money is like steroids, a growth-enhancing drug that comes with serious side effects. Cross-national correlations are not able to capture the accumulative risks that result from crony capitalism and regulatory capture. Observers were therefore stunned when the financial boom in East Asia and that in the United States crashed in 1997 and 2008, respectively. In assessing the economic effects of corruption, we must look beyond annual GDP figures and qualitatively examine its indirect distortionary consequences. My account warns about the dangers linked to corruption in China's near future, as well as its potential mutations (see the next section).

FOUR BIG QUESTIONS ON CHINA

Having explained China's paradox and placed it in comparative-historical perspective with America's experience in the nineteenth

---

[34] Andrews *et al.* (2013; 2017).

century, I now move on to revisit four big questions on Chinese political economy, on the basis of findings in this book.

POPULAR ACCOUNTS PAINT A CONFLICTING PICTURE OF CHINA, AS EITHER A CONFUCIAN-STYLE MERITOCRACY OR A FESTERING REGIME THAT WILL SOON CRUMBLE: WHO IS RIGHT?

Accounts of the Chinese political system are sharply divided. One camp, represented by Eric Li and Daniel Bell, portrays China as a Confucian-style meritocracy where officials are selected top-down "in accordance with ability and virtue," rather than by elections.[35] They argue that Chinese meritocracy presents a superior alternative to democracy. Making strong recommendations for action, Bell states, "the Chinese government can play a more active role promoting its model abroad," though he later claims to defend only "an ideal."[36] On the other end are naysayers, including Minxin Pei and Gordon Chang, who have insisted for decades that the regime is decaying and on the verge of collapse.[37]

This book shows that neither view is correct. As Chapter 5 detailed, corruption and competence can coexist – and even mutually reinforce – in China's political system.[38] Chapter 6 provided another supporting sign: in my dataset of city Party secretaries, 40 percent of the leaders who were netted for corruption had been promoted prior to or in the year they fell.

Champions of Chinese meritocracy admit the existence of patronage and corruption, "but merit remains the fundamental driver," Li maintains.[39] In fact, my book shows that corruption is not an occasional glitch; it is endemic to the system. The ruling Party controls valuable resources such as land, finance, and procurement contracts, and

---

[35] Bell (2016, 6). For other critiques, see Yasheng Huang, "Why Democracy Still Wins," *TED Blog*, 1 July 2013; Andrew Nathan, "The Problem with the China Model," *Chinafile*, 5 November 2015.

[36] Bell (2016, xii, 10).   [37] Pei (1999; 2006; 2016); Chang (2001).

[38] A study by Lu and Lorentzen on Xi's anti-corruption campaign assumes that corrupt officials are incapable, and therefore by arresting the corrupt, the Party can raise the level of competence: "The Party needs a group of officials who can efficiently implement its policies and decrees. The current anti-corruption campaign of China embodies that need" (Lu and Lorentzen 2016, 25). This assumption, as my book shows, is incorrect.

[39] Eric Li, "A Tale of Two Political Systems," TED Talk, posted 1 July 2013.

individual leaders command immense personal power. This is why they are constantly inundated with requests for their intervention and favors, often accompanied by graft (Chapter 5).[40]

The meritocracy school also fails to address the problem of who guards the guardians. Li praises the Party's Organization Department, which appoints officials, as a "human resource engine that would be the envy of some of the most successful corporations." But this department, too, can be corrupted, and indeed is especially corruptible because it controls appointments and promotion. Lo and behold, in 2018, 68 officials at the Central Organization Department were punished for corruption.[41]

Naysayers, on the other hand, err in the opposite direction: they magnify stories of Chinese corruption but ignore vigorous growth-promotion efforts among corrupt officials (Chapter 5). The current slowing economy does not validate their predictions of collapse, which were made as early as the 1990s. Part of the slowdown results from the fact that most countries, not only China, experience slower growth as they reach middle income.[42] More importantly, assertions of decay provide no explanation for why China has sustained four decades of transformative development despite massive corruption.

While it is commonly assumed that patronage is in opposition to meritocracy, under the CCP, they go together. In most patronage-ridden systems, political patrons appoint unqualified clients into offices; Geddes' study of Latin American bureaucracies is a case in point.[43] Chinese political patrons, on the other hand, spot promising clients and nurture their competence over the course of their careers. As one Party school leader explained to me, "It is their patrons who strategically arrange positions for [officials at lower levels], giving them an opportunity to prove themselves." In other words, while we normally think of

---

[40] This is a consistent theme in Zhou Hao's documentaries, which show local leaders personally intervening in numerous affairs, down to trivial demands from individual petitioners (see Chapter 5 and Appendix: Chapter 5).

[41] Zhao Runhua, "Half a Million Party Members Penalized for Corruption in 2018," *Caixin*, 21 February 2019.

[42] Furthermore, there remains room for growth, as Lardy (2019) argues, if China continues with economic reform and reduces state dominance in the economy.

[43] Geddes (1994).

"merit" as intrinsic to individuals, in the Chinese political system, it is cultivated by political patrons. He added, "We are after all a top-down system, not elected by the people, so it is those on top who decide who gets to move along and ahead."[44]

In short, readers should be skeptical of any argument that either hails or bashes China. Paradoxes are the most consistent trait of the reform-era Chinese political economy. Understanding it requires that we underscore and grasp these paradoxes.

HOW HAS AUTHORITARIAN CAPITALISM SHAPED CHINESE CORRUPTION? "Xi Jinping's China seeks to be rich and communist," reads the headline of a Martin Wolf op-ed in *The Financial Times*.[45] The title is scintillating, but Wolf gets a fact wrong: China is not communist. Far from egalitarian, China has seen widening inequality, at a level exceeding even capitalist America.[46] In practice, Chinese political economy operates not according to Marx's exhortation of "each according to his needs" but rather by the principle of "each according to his ability and connections" (Chapters 4 and 5). From this perspective, China is better understood as a capitalist dictatorship disguised as communist.

When the CCP regime's concentration of power meets capitalist open markets, the result is a distinctive mix of competitive corruption and growth promotion. Access money easily dominates in China because authoritarian officials can make unilateral decisions and grant exclusive access to profit, in contrast to fragmented democracies such as India, where, as Bardhan aptly expressed, officials can "stop a file immediately," but they cannot "move a file faster" (Chapter 2). Unimpeded by opposition and consultation, Chinese officials also

---

[44] Interview B2007-08.

[45] Martin Wolf, "Xi Jinping's China Seeks to Be Rich and Communist," *Financial Times*, 9 April 2019.

[46] China features high income, urban–rural, and regional inequality. When Xi took office as President in 2012, China's Gini coefficient was 0.472, higher than the United States and Britain. The Household Finance Survey, conducted by Southwestern University of Finance and Economics, reported an even higher score of 0.61, placing China's income inequality nearly on a par with South Africa. See "Gini out of the Bottle," *The Economist*, 26 January 2013; "To Each, Not According to His Needs," *The Economist*, 15 December 2012.

command extraordinary capacity to "bulldoze" (Chapter 5). They make big changes fast, which can spur growth but also bring about costly blunders, even disasters.

For political economists, my account of a single yet important case – China – indicates that classifying entire countries as "inclusive or non-inclusive," "extractive or non-extractive," and "open or limited access" may be more confusing than clarifying when it fails to capture mixed realities.[47] Conventionally, China is automatically classified as "non-inclusive," "extractive," and "limited access" because it is a single-party autocracy. Yet, as my book shows, within this autocracy, there can still be plenty of decentralization, competition, and private sector participation, elements normally associated with democracies.[48]

WILL CORRUPTION IN CHINA LEAD TO REGIME COLLAPSE?

There is no doubt that China has a serious corruption problem – the Chinese President himself stated that it poses an existential threat to the Party. But Xi is most concerned with a certain type of corruption: grand transactional corruption enmeshed with patron–client relations among political elites, particularly powerful "red" families (of senior Party leaders), princelings like Bo Xilai, and vested interests among powerful sectors of the state-owned economy (for example, Zhou Yongkang's control of the oil sector).[49]

Such corruption is unlikely to topple the regime by directly slowing the economy or provoking mass protests. As I show throughout this book, even though Chinese officials engage in widespread collusion and deal-making, they do deliver social and economic development. Thus it is misleading to label the Chinese state overall as "extractive" or "predatory."[50] Evans defines predatory states as those that "extract large amounts of surplus and provide little in the way of collective goods,"[51]

---

[47] Acemoglu and Robinson (2008); North *et al.* (2009).

[48] Ang (2018a; 2018c). Also see "How the West (and Beijing) Got China Wrong," Lecture at Camden Conference, posted on YouTube in April 2019, www.youtube.com/watch?v=2_bNB4S_HTw&t=1374s (accessed 29 November 2019).

[49] Walder (2018).

[50] Pei (2006; 2016); Acemoglu and Robinson (2012); Wedeman (2012).

[51] Evans (1989, 562).

which he illustrates with the quintessential case of Zaire under Mobutu Sese Seko. China is not Zaire.

Nor is China similar to Egypt, where citizens took to the streets out of desperation and frustration with predatory corruption. Dickson's surveys of Chinese urban residents found that although many view corruption as widespread, considerably more think the situation has improved since Xi launched his anti-corruption campaign.[52] In addition, his survey found generally strong levels of political trust and support for the ruling government, despite complaints about corruption and other problems.

Rather, Chinese corruption undermines regime stability in other ways. Graft at the highest level intensifies factional rivalry and battles for political succession, as the Bo Xilai scandal displayed. As each fiefdom amasses astronomical rents, it grows ambitious and defiant of the top leadership. Walder compares the current dangers facing the CCP to the Guomindang in the 1930s and 1940s, which was torn apart from within, in Chiang Kai-Shek's words, by "a special class struggling for power and self-interests, alienating the masses."[53] Corruption may also trigger collapse in one particular scenario: when the structural risks linked to crony capitalism implode in a sudden meltdown, triggering cascading effects that lie beyond the leadership's control.[54] That is why Xi declared financial risks a matter of national security and made deleveraging a policy imperative.[55]

Notably, while many have been betting on China's collapse for years,[56] few ever question why the "regime" in the United States stayed resilient despite repeated crises linked to corruption over the course of US history, from the first great recession of 1839 to the crisis of 2008. Perhaps America is resilient because citizens can vote politicians or a political

---

[52] Dickson's survey was conducted in some 30 Chinese cities in 2010 and 2014. In 2014, 60 percent of the respondents perceived that the level of corruption had improved, compared with only 26 percent in 2010 (Dickson 2016).

[53] Walder (2018, 25).

[54] As discussed in Chapter 5, access money is connected with shadow banking, mounting debts among local governments and real estate conglomerates, and over-investment in speculative markets, which are all under particular duress in the ongoing economic downturn and trade war.

[55] Sherry Ju and Lucy Hornby, "Beijing Renews Warnings on Systemic Financial Risks," *Financial Times*, 25 February 2019.

[56] "The Land That Failed to Fail," *The New York Times*, 18 December 2018.

party out of office without losing faith in democracy.[57] The CCP, on the other hand, is inseparable from the administration and the economy. Hence, if massive failure occurs, the people may reject not just the Party's paramount leader but its entire authoritarian apparatus.

WILL XI'S ANTI-CORRUPTION CAMPAIGN SMOTHER GROWTH?

To his credit, Xi has boldly taken on the brewing crisis of corruption, while previous leaders have swept it under the rug. His anti-corruption campaign benefits China's long-term growth if it is able to rein in crony capitalism and create an even, transparent business environment. The problem is that the crackdown has gone beyond policing corruption and has expanded to emphasize conformity to the Party line and personal loyalty. Making matters worse, his demands for airtight discipline conflict with his calls for "daring" officials. Facing unusually harsh scrutiny and unrealistic expectations to "do it all," bureaucrats feel paralyzed, compromising their ability to adapt and innovate (Chapter 6).[58]

Although Xi's sustained campaign has placed officials in a state of high alert, it will not eradicate corruption in the form of access money unless his leadership tackles the root cause: the state's enormous power in the economy. So long as officials control valuable resources and their personal power is unchecked, there will be continuous demand for their favors. In this respect, Xi has worrisomely done the opposite: in the past few years, he has expanded the state sector and imposed more political control.[59]

A better question to ask, therefore, is not whether corruption will disappear but whether it could manifest itself in new forms and through new avenues. While access money was traditionally concentrated in land and real estate transactions (Chapter 5), in the near future, it could possibly migrate to technology and innovation sectors, which are powered by a formidable platform: government guiding funds (GGFs). As Wei *et al.* explain, a GGF is "a new form of industrial policy that aims to

---

[57] On "authoritarian resilience" in China, see Nathan's seminal article under that title (Nathan 2003).

[58] See the proliferation of cadre evaluation targets in Chapter 4 of Ang (2016); on adaptive governance, see Heilmann and Perry (2011); Oi and Goldstein (2018).

[59] Economy (2018); Lardy (2019).

use public funds as seed money to increase public and private investment in high-tech and emerging industries." Most GGFs hire venture capital and private equity firms, including foreign companies, to manage and invest the funds. By the end of 2017, the total target capital size of roughly 1,500 GGFs across China was a mind-boggling sum – RMB 9.5 trillion (US$1.4 trillion), roughly three times the US trade deficit with China in 2018.[60]

While GGFs present a novel financial instrument for industrial and innovation promotion, they may be susceptible to corruption, as it is unclear how funds are distributed, by and to whom, and for what goals. Furthermore, as investment in emerging sectors is inherently risky and prone to failure, it is difficult to hold fund managers accountable for their financial decisions. Some GGFs are also involved in overseas projects under the Belt and Road Initiative (BRI),[61] Xi's signature foreign policy, which has drawn global criticism for corruption.[62] This combination of mega transactions, complex financial instruments, and the lack of transparency and accountability may present fertile soil for an advanced mode of access money, despite Xi's crackdown.

FIVE BIG QUESTIONS ON CORRUPTION

Although centered on China's experience, my approach of unbundling corruption is relevant to all academics and practitioners working on corruption and governance. In this final section, I highlight what my book says on five key questions about corruption.

WHAT IS CORRUPTION? Corruption is commonly defined as the abuse of public office for private gain.[63] Most global indicators and

---

[60] The total invested capital is RMB 3.5 trillion (US$520 billion), which is still a staggering sum (Wei *et al.* 2019).

[61] One example is the Jiangsu Belt and Road Investment Fund (*Jiangsu yidaiyilu touzi jijin*), which was established in 2015 with 3 billion Yuan of assets under management. The Fund participated in the financing of Byton, an electric vehicle company, which has an extensive supply chain in BRI countries.

[62] For background on the BRI, see Yuen Yuen Ang, "Demystifying China's Belt and Road: The Struggle to Define China's Project of the Century," *Foreign Affairs*, 22 May 2019.

[63] World Bank (1997b); International Monetary Fund (2016); Transparency International (2016).

academic studies interpret this to mean *illegal* abuses of power, including bribery, embezzlement, and vote-buying, which are most prevalent in poor countries. Such a definition excludes "undue influence," defined by Issacharoff as "a distortion of political outcomes as the result of the undue influence of wealth,"[64] which exists in wealthy economies.[65]

In this book, however, the concept of "access money" encompasses legal actions aimed at buying influence, for example, revolving door practices, inviting politicians' family members to serve on corporate boards, and winning over staffers with promises of lucrative jobs. This broad scope may be controversial. As legal scholar Lessig acknowledges, the notion that "our Congress is corrupt as an institution, while none of the members of Congress is corrupt individually" is "hard ... for many to accept."[66] Some prefer "money politics" or "buying access" to describe systemic efforts at influencing policies to one's advantage – perhaps because corruption connotes backwardness. "To most Americans," as Glaeser and Goldin point out, "corruption is something that happens to less fortunate people in poor nations."[67] For others, calling out corruption in rich nations may appear to denigrate a "self-imagined national heritage ... [of] fairness and democracy," as Whyte observes.[68]

I see it differently: those who value democracy should be all the more vigilant about the potential perversion of formal political representation. The great challenge lies in pinning down money politics in the first world, which is often legal, institutional, and ambiguous. Consider lobbying in the United States: lobbyists are registered, campaign donations are mostly public,[69] and lobbying is legitimate and even necessary for the functioning of democratic representation. It is only "corrupt" when this influence is excessive, murky, or employed to advance narrow interests at the expense of society. In practice, however, with only a few exceptions,[70] it is impossible to determine when lobbying has crossed the line into

---

[64] For a review of definitions of corruption and why the definition matters, see Issacharoff (2010, 122); Nicholas (2017).

[65] Fisman and Golden (2017, 78–79).   [66] Lessig (2018, Kindle 237).

[67] Glaeser and Goldin (2006, 3).   [68] Whyte (2015, 1).

[69] Fisman and Golden (2017, 78–79).

[70] One exception is former lobbyist Abramoff, who was convicted of conspiracy, fraud, and tax evasion in an Indian casino lobbying scandal, where he charged his clients US$85 million in lobbying fees.

corruption, so all of it is accepted as normal. Bribery, on the other hand, gets everyone's attention because it is unambiguously corrupt.[71]

Failure to include access money in theories and measures of corruption reinforces the misleading perception that only poor countries are racked by corruption, whereas wealthy democracies are free of it, which contributes to apathy or complacency in the latter. When the perversion of formal institutions for the benefit of narrow interest groups is not recognized as corruption, it reduces public pressure for necessary reforms to address urgent problems: campaign finance, financial regulation, and climate action.

HOW SHOULD WE MEASURE CORRUPTION? Corruption is hard to measure; no single approach, therefore, can be "perfect." For cross-national comparisons, expert perception-based measures of corruption remain the most influential approach. In Chapter 2, I present a first step in measuring unbundled perceptions of corruption. Only by first systematically measuring different types of corruption across countries can we test whether certain forms of corruption are more damaging, and why. In particular, more efforts are needed to capture the elusive category of access money. While there are many country-specific studies on political connections, including in China,[72] cross-national measures in this area remain scarce.[73]

Specifically on measurements of bribery, my study highlights the need to distinguish between "speed" and "access" money – in other words, bribes paid for different purposes: the former to overcome harassment and delays and the latter to buy privileges. Firm-level surveys that include questions on bribes almost certainly capture only speed money,[74] as companies are unlikely to admit to buying influence, or even, if they were honest, may not see their influence-peddling actions as bribery.

---

[71] For example, the OECD Anti-bribery Convention, which has 36 signatories from OECD countries and eight from non-OECD countries, establishes "legally binding standards to criminalize bribery in international business." But the Organization also acknowledges that there are other forms of corruption beyond bribery (OECD 2008, 22, cited in Nichols 2017).

[72] Li *et al.* (2008); Ang and Jia (2014); Jia (2014; 2016); Wang (2015).

[73] One notable exception is Faccio (2006).

[74] Svensson (2003); see also the World Bank's Enterprise Survey.

This literature on speed money should be integrated with work on political connections for a full picture.

Apart from improving quantitative measures, scholars of corruption also need to rethink the way we classify the structures of corruption across countries qualitatively. Existing typologies of corruption assign entire countries to a single category on the basis of the analyst's personal judgement of where cases fit.[75] This approach is subjective, and, more significantly, it gives the false impression that each country has only one type of corruption. In fact, as I show through the visualization of my survey results in UCI (Chapter 2), all countries have a combination of multiple types of corruption but in varying degrees.

DOES CORRUPTION IMPEDE ECONOMIC GROWTH? According to conventional wisdom, corruption impedes economic growth, an assumption that seems consistent with casual observations and has strong backing in cross-national regression analyses.[76]

Yet the belief that corruption always impairs growth is flawed both in its conceptualization of "corruption" and of "economic growth." Cross-national indices do not unbundle corruption and routinely under-capture access money (Chapter 2).[77] And growth, typically measured as GDP per capita, is a woefully inadequate measure of the economic impact of corruption.

On the effects of access money, take the example in my opening anecdote: the construction of railways during America's Gilded Age. Money politics and lobbying induced politicians to grant enormous subsidies, ignore inflated cost and financial risks, and then step in to bail out the robber barons when a crisis erupted, always at the expense of the public. Corporate friendships with the government also licensed the abuse of construction workers, the forced removal of Native Americans,

---

[75] For example, Wedeman (1997); Kang (2002b); Johnston (2008); Wedeman (2012); Pritchett *et al.* (2018).

[76] Treisman (2007, 225).

[77] Statistical analyses on the differing impact of different types of corruption are few and far between. One study distinguishes between "red-tape" (a proxy for obstacles to business) and "corruption" (business transactions involving questionable payments). It finds that red-tape, but not corruption, adversely affects economic growth (Ehrlich and Lui 1999). But the authors' measures are coarse and patently outdated (1981–1992), reflecting the lack of cross-national measures on qualitatively different types of corruption.

and ecological damage.[78] Yet although these social costs may be staggering, "measuring them is near impossible," as Glaeser and Goldin state.[79] The result, as another economist, Jain, notes, is "a dearth of research on the link between corruption and the cost of misdirected public policies."[80]

In principle, we should measure what we value – yet in reality, we've valued what we can measure. Datasets that are easily downloaded and plugged into regressions have shaped concepts, theories, and policies more profoundly than we'd like to admit. Our understanding of corruption and capitalism can be immensely enhanced by developing unbundled measures of corruption and measures of economic impact that go beyond GDP.

Quantitative studies should also be integrated with historical-qualitative studies that examine the effects of corruption structures on economic development, and in particular, the political tactics for channeling such structures toward less growth-damaging forms. In *Without a Map*, Shleifer and Treisman show that some Russian reforms were successful when leaders "exchange more socially costly rents for less socially costly ones."[81] China's story is similarly one about the selective abolition of certain types of corruption that directly impair growth (Chapter 3), even as access money exploded.

HOW DOES CORRUPTION AFFECT INEQUALITY? Corruption impacts not just growth but especially inequality, both economic and political. The two types of inequality are inseparable, although the literature and popular discourse tend to focus only on income inequality.[82] The super-rich are not only far wealthier, they are also more powerful and can manipulate political and legal systems to their advantage, through means defined in this book as "access money."[83] No study of political inequality can be complete, therefore, without examining corruption.[84]

It is worth paying close attention to the Human Development Index (HDI), first developed and released by the United Nations Development Programme in 1990, which promises in 2019 to go "beyond income" and

---

[78] White (2011).   [79] Glaeser and Goldin (2006, 8).   [80] Jain (2001, 74).
[81] Shleifer and Treisman (2000, 10).   [82] Piketty (2018).   [83] Gilens (2012).
[84] One cross-national volume on political inequality considers democracy, class politics, and legislative representation of minorities, yet it contains virtually no mention of corruption (Dubrow 2015).

focus on "inequalities in other dimensions such as health, education, access to technologies, and exposure to shocks."[85] This expanded conception of inequality is crucial. My study suggests that future extensions of this measure should confront inequality in access to *political influence*, which is inextricably linked to corruption.

Such inequality takes varied forms across countries. In China, where the rule of law is weak compared with the West, it manifests itself as "political connections," ties that private entrepreneurs cultivate with individual elite officials for profit-making privileges. In advanced capitalist economies, with strong formal institutions and rule of law, unequal access to political influence is found in lobbying systems, through which big corporations and interest groups can legally exercise overwhelming influence on policymaking. Because unequal access to political influence profoundly shapes the making of laws and policies, it affects inequality in all other realms: income, access to public services, exposure to risks. To track this form of inequality, we need better measures of access money.

WHAT CAN BE DONE TO COMBAT CORRUPTION? The vast research on corruption has offered surprisingly few practical insights on fighting corruption. As Mark Pyman, former Commissioner of the Afghanistan Joint Independent Anti-corruption Monitoring Committee, laments, "Why is it that people working and researching in corruption seem only to enjoy showing how bad it all is? They seem to like nothing more than to 'admire the problem.'"[86] While I won't hazard a "solution," I will highlight a few implications of this study for anti-corruption efforts.

One-size-fits-all won't work in anti-corruption. My work on unbundling corruption underscores the need for tailoring solutions to the four categories (and sub-categories): petty theft, grand theft, speed money, and access money. This disaggregated approach is aligned with recent proposals for "micro," "sector-specific," and "project-specific" strategies that target corruption in particular contexts, rather than treating it as a homogeneous

---

[85] "2019 Human Development Report to Focus on Inequality," 21 March 2019, http://hdr
.undp.org/en/content/2019-human-development-report-focus-inequality (accessed 29 November 2019).

[86] Mark Pyman, "The Unhelpful Nature of Anti-corruption Research, as Seen by People Trying to Develop Solutions," *CDA Perspectives Blog*, 24 January 2017.

scourge.[87] My framework offers a balance between binary divisions, which are too coarse, and specific approaches, which are too diverse. This balance is essential for context-sensitive approaches to be widely applied in theory and in practice.

China's experience provides three key lessons for anti-corruption. First, in poor countries where public employees are paid below subsistence, preaching about first-world "best practices" and imposing "zero tolerance" laws on corruption are not realistic. Public sector reforms in poor-and-weak states should explore other varieties of "transitional administrative institutions" tailored to their national contexts, taking lessons from China but never blindly copying.[88]

Second, mitigating corruption with theft and petty bribery requires incentive-compatible, capacity-building reforms. While political economists tend to ignore technical policies,[89] technocrats often neglect the alignment of political incentives as a precondition for successfully implementing capacity-building reforms. Chinese politicians are committed to modernizing the administration and fighting growth-damaging corruption because they have a share in local prosperity and face tough competition from their peers. Without such incentives, reforming countries routinely adopt the formality of capacity-building reforms but fail to follow through.[90]

Third, combating access money calls for a different and deeper set of solutions. Although Xi's campaign has netted numerous corrupt officials, it sidesteps the root causes of access money: state control over the economy and leaders' personal power. Worse, Xi has clamped down on the press, the Internet, NGOs, lawyers, and civil society. His administration also cut back on local experiments in government transparency and consultative decision-making.[91] In an extremely large administration, top-down inspectors face sharp limits in detecting malfeasance – they need to enlist the aid of civil society.

---

[87] See Pyman's website, "Curbing Corruption," https://curbingcorruption.com/about/ (accessed 29 November 2019); OECD (2018).

[88] Ang (2016; 2017). See also Rodrik's (2007) argument to focus on institutional functions rather than forms.

[89] Instead, the focus of seminal political economy theories is on competition as a solution (Rose-Ackerman 1978; Shleifer and Vishny 1993; Ades and Di Tella 1999).

[90] Pritchett et al. (2013). [91] Stromseth et al. (2017, 2).

But citizens' ability to effectively monitor corruption is not automatic. It is conditional upon norms of civic responsibility, which are cultivated through practice and professional NGOs.[92] By smothering bottom-up initiatives, Xi is not only cutting off society's role in monitoring corruption but also crippling the formation of civic qualities. This sharply distinguishes China's path of anti-corruption since 2012 from the American Progressive Era.

A FINAL THOUGHT

Anthropologist Ruth Benedict, author of an enduringly insightful book on Japanese society, *The Chrysanthemum and the Sword*, wrote, "One of the handicaps of the twentieth century is that we still have the vaguest and most biased notions, not only of what makes Japan a nation of Japanese, but of what makes the United States a nation of Americans."[93] This handicap continues to persist in the twenty-first century, despite the ease of international travel and spread of information. At the height of Japan's rise in the 1980s, many Americans saw Japan as the principal "civilizational" threat from Asia. Today, China takes its place as perceived Enemy No. 1 – with far greater consequences for the world.

It seems that China and the United States are hurtling toward a new "cold war" shrouded in cultural terms. It is increasingly popular in Washington to frame the competition between the two superpowers as a "clash of civilizations."[94] Meanwhile, in Beijing, cultural arguments invoking Confucianism to justify authoritarianism are just as fashionable. But the insistence that China is exceptional and opposed to the West in every respect dooms understanding from the beginning. Understanding China requires that we consider both its differences from the West and their similarities. We should also revisit popular narratives that Western

---

[92] Ang (2014); also see Nichols and Robertson (2017). [93] Benedict (1974).

[94] Kiron Skinner, Director of Policy Planning at the State Department, said, "The Soviet Union and that competition, in a way it was a fight within the Western family. It's the first time that we will have a great power competitor [China] that is not Caucasian." Troublingly, her use of the term "Caucasian" – a racial category – frames China–US competition as a war between two races: Caucasian and non-Caucasian people. See "State Department Preparing for Clash of Civilizations with China," *Washington Examiner*, 30 April 2019.

societies hold about our own history. As Benedict's quote underscores, we cannot understand others without first understanding ourselves.

The pairing of rampant corruption and rapid growth in China finds its clearest parallel in America during the Gilded Age, but this history is often forgotten. Of course, in terms of political freedom, the role of the government in the economy, and each country's historical conditions, their differences are stark. Yet the two Gilded Ages share certain similarities: the rise of a nouveau riche, big businesses in bed with government, poverty amid plenty, and pushback against corruption and unbridled capitalism, to name a few.

Fundamentally, whether in China, the United States, or anywhere else, the study of corruption requires revising our basic concepts and theories. This book provided evidence for two core insights. First, while corruption is never good, not all forms of corruption are equally bad for the economy, nor do they cause the same kind of harm. Second, the rise of capitalism is accompanied not by the eradication of corruption, but rather by the evolution of the quality of corruption from thuggery and theft to influence peddling. To elevate our understanding of the relationship between corruption and capitalism, we must first unbundle corruption and then distinguish its effects on GDP from hard-to-measure social and economic costs. I've taken the first step and hope others will join in.

Appendix

Corruption and GDP Growth

It is commonly asserted that China is an "outlier" in achieving rapid growth despite corruption. One example is an article in *The Wall Street Journal* (WSJ), which used a scatterplot of CPI scores and average GDP growth rates to illustrate that "corruption normally goes hand in hand with low growth – but China doesn't fit that pattern."[1] In fact, the figure in the WSJ makes the opposite point: corruption goes hand in hand with *high* growth.

Figure A1.1 updates the aforementioned figure with recent data of CPI scores of all countries plotted against their average growth rates from 1995 to 2016. As we can clearly see, more corrupt countries have *higher* GDP growth. This is not surprising, as corrupt countries tend to be low-income countries, which usually experience faster growth. In Figure A1.1, China's corruption score falls below the regression line, which means that given its high growth rate, it was *less* corrupt than expected. The general correlation between corruption and poverty is measured by GDP per capita (see Chapter 1), not growth rates.

As argued in the introduction, China is not anomalous in having corruption with high growth rates; rather, what makes it an outlier is that it has achieved a 40-year period of sustained economic expansion on a nearly unparalleled scale, despite moderately high levels of perceived corruption.

This example illustrates the necessity of being precise about what we mean both by corruption (see Chapter 2) and by growth. In fact,

---

[1] Tom Orlik, "Eight Questions: Andrew Wedeman, China's Corruption Paradox," *The Wall Street Journal*, 26 March 2012.

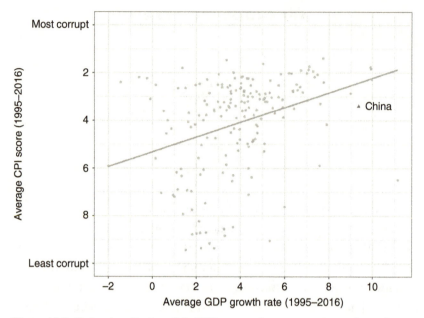

Figure A1.1 Updated replication of the WSJ's scatterplot on corruption and growth rate.

different measures of "growth" (GDP per capita, GDP growth rates, absolute GDP growth, and durability of high growth) correlate with corruption in dramatically different ways. In order to make sense of the Chinese paradox, we must first define the basic terms of our analysis.

UCI Survey Methodology

This appendix describes the survey design and implementation of the Unbundling Corruption Index (UCI) in more detail. The first step of the survey was to create a pool of potential respondents. After searching the literature and online resumes, and seeking recommendations by colleagues, I identified a group of individuals who have extensive experience in or broad knowledge of a country's political, economic, and social context. The survey is hosted on Qualtrics, a third-party online survey platform. Each member of the expert pool was sent a private link to participate. I informed the invitees that the survey is anonymous, meaning that no personally identifiable information was collected or stored through the platform or via the questionnaire.

Of the 372 invitations sent out, 135 surveys were started and 125 completed, yielding a response rate of 36% and a completion rate of 84%, which is within the normal range of surveys. The respondents are primarily academics with area expertise in a particular country (73), journalists (11), and business leaders or professionals with at least 10 years of experience (11). Others included development consultants and mid-to-senior-level civil servants. Among the respondents, 45% are natives of the countries that they evaluated.

In the final dataset (Table A2.1), only countries with at least four expert responses were included. The number of responses ranged from four to 20, as follows: Bangladesh (4), Brazil (6), China (20), Ghana (5), India (6), Indonesia (5), Japan (9), Nigeria (5), Russia (12), Singapore (7), South Africa (5), South Korea (9), Taiwan (5), Thailand (4), and the United States (20).

TABLE A2.1 *UCI scores and ranking for 15 countries*

UCI rank	Country	Petty theft (0–10)	Grand theft (0–10)	Speed money (0–10)	Access money (0–10)	UCI total score (0–40)
1	Bangladesh	7.9	7.0	8.7	8.2	31.8
2	Russia	7.5	7.2	8.6	7.7	30.9
3	Indonesia	7.8	7.1	7.5	8.2	30.5
4	Nigeria	7.6	8.2	7.4	7.3	30.4
5	India	7.6	5.4	8.0	7.0	27.9
6	China	6.9	6.1	6.6	7.6	27.2
7	Thailand	7.5	5.8	6.4	6.5	26.2
8	South Africa	6.6	6.1	5.9	7.0	25.5
9	Brazil	5.8	5.8	5.6	7.5	24.5
10	Ghana	6.5	4.1	7.1	5.8	23.4
11	United States	5.2	4.8	4.1	6.9	20.8
12	South Korea	4.4	4.1	3.5	6.1	18.0
13	Taiwan	4.3	3.7	3.8	5.1	16.8
14	Japan	3.6	3.0	3.3	4.9	14.7
15	Singapore	2.4	1.9	2.0	3.7	9.9
	AVERAGE	**6.1**	**5.3**	**5.9**	**6.6**	**23.9**

As discussed in Chapter 2, the UCI leverages stylized vignettes to capture perceptions of distinct categories of corruption. Altogether, our survey included 20 vignette-style questions, grouped into four categories: access money, speed money, grand theft, and petty theft. For each vignette, respondents rate the prevalence of each type of corruption on a five-level Likert-type scale, ranging from "extremely common" to "never occurs."

The greatest challenge of implementing this survey is getting experts to respond and having at least four respondents for each country. Understandably, experts and professionals are busy individuals, so it's not easy for them to find time to take an extended survey. One reader complained about the absence of European countries in my sample. The reason for this is that, despite repeated requests, I could not get enough experts from Europe to respond. Hence, I thank all the respondents who took time from their busy schedule to take the survey, and I hope that, in future iterations of the UCI, more experts from all over the world may be willing to share their time and expertise.

Definition of Three Main Corruption Terms

Below is a translation of the definitions of bribery, embezzlement, and misuse of public funds, as defined in the 1999 Regulations Regarding Cases Investigated by the Procuratorate (关于民检察院直接受理案侦查案件案标准的规定). See Tables A3.1 and A3.2 for data on bribery and embezzlement, respectively.

BRIBERY (贿赂)

Bribery includes crimes of accepting, receiving, and offering bribes, in the case both of individuals and of work units. For example, the crime of "receiving bribes" is defined as state officials using the privileges of their office to seek the property of others, or illegally accept the property of others, and to seek benefits on their behalf. "Using the privileges of office" indicates taking advantage of powers within the scope of individual work duties, the powers of supervision, undertakings, or handling of public affairs and the circumstances arising from those positions. Extorting the property of others, regardless of whether it is "seeking benefit for others" or not, can be treated as receiving bribes; illegally receiving the property of others must concurrently satisfy the condition of seeking benefits for others in order to be considered the crime of "receiving bribes," but whether or not the benefit sought for another party is appropriate and whether or not the benefit is realized does not affect the determination of the crime. [. . .] Those suspected of the following should have a case established against them: (1) An individual accepts a bribe of 5,000 Yuan or more; (2) An individual accepts a bribe of less than 5,000 Yuan, but it also involves one of the

TABLE A3.1 *Bribery by small vs. large cases and low vs. high rank*

Year	Number of cases	Number of individuals	Number of large-sum cases	Percentage of large-sum cases	Number of high-rank cases	Percentage of high-rank cases
1998	8,759	9,255	1,847	21	909	10
1999	8,192	8,606	2,552	31	983	11
2000	9,872	10,367	3,658	37	1,279	12
2001	10,347	10,785	4,248	41	1,378	13
2002	10,725	11,165	4,871	45	1,391	12
2003	10,553	10,922	5,424	51	1,378	13
2004	10,572	11,266	5,690	54	1,545	14
2005	10,446	11,225	3,610	58	1,527	14
2006	11,702	12,525	7,033	60	1,598	13
2007	12,226	13,191	8,045	66	1,650	13
2008	12,471	13,528	8,805	71	1,684	12
2009	12,897	14,253	9,875	77	1,755	12
2010	13,796	15,422	10,586	77	1,810	12
2011	13,915	15,685	10,927	79	1,682	11
2012	14,946	16,919	12,326	82	1,746	10
2013	15,940	18,101	13,395	84	1,867	10
2014	19,523	21,889	17,270	88	2,814	13
2015	19,402	21,427	17,435	90	3,145	15

TABLE A3.2 *Embezzlement by small vs. large cases and low vs. high rank*

Year	Number of cases	Number of individuals	Number of large-sum cases	Percentage of large-sum cases	Number of high-rank cases	Percentage of high-rank cases
1998	12,909	15,199	3,657	28	456	3
1999	14,372	16,737	5,173	36	570	3
2000	16,765	19,428	6,736	40	683	4
2001	16,362	18,718	6,932	42	696	4
2002	15,785	17,953	7,199	46	732	4
2003	14,161	16,162	7,191	51	632	4
2004	13,308	16,119	6,810	51	691	4
2005	11,792	15,005	6,133	52	591	4
2006	10,337	13,406	5,592	54	529	4
2007	9,956	13,529	5,866	59	462	3
2008	9,605	13,613	5,913	62	465	3
2009	8,865	13,294	5,730	65	397	3
2010	8,707	14,370	5,555	64	406	3
2011	8,475	14,366	5,508	65	343	2
2012	8,499	14,837	6,029	71	360	2
2013	9,494	16,167	6,865	72	370	2
2014	9,424	15,546	7,076	75	439	3
2015	9,596	15,820	7,380	77	579	4

following conditions: 1. Because of the bribery, the state or social interests suffer serious losses; 2. Purposefully impeding the work of or threatening of related organs or individuals, causing a pernicious influence; 3. Forceful extortion of property or funds.

EMBEZZLEMENT (贪污)

This crime is defined as the misuse of privileges of state office to embezzle, steal, obtain by fraud or the use of any other method to illegally obtain public property. Suspects of the following conduct should have a case established: (1) Individual corruption of 5,000 Yuan or more. (2) Individual corruption of less than 5,000 Yuan but involves the embezzlement of disaster relief, emergency, flood control, disease prevention, disabled care, poverty alleviation, or emergency funds or donations, stolen or confiscated goods; when the means used are heinous, evidence is destroyed, or stolen goods are transferred.

MISUSE OF PUBLIC FUNDS (挪用公款)

Misuse of public funds is the misuse of privileges of state office to use public funds for individual use, or the misuse of large amounts of public funds to engage in for-profit activity, or the misuse of large amounts of public funds without returning them within three months. Those suspected of the following should have a case established: (1) Misuse of public funds amounting to between 5,000 and 10,000 Yuan (or more) for individual use or use in illegal activities. (2) Misuse of public funds of 10,000 Yuan to 30,000 Yuan (or more) for individual use in profit-seeking activities. (3) Misuses of public funds for individual use between 10,000 and 30,000 Yuan (or more), that has not been returned within three months; the People's Procuratorate of each province can specify specific levels for these amounts within the scope above to accord with local conditions, and report this to the Supreme People's Procuratorate for its records.

APPENDIX: CHAPTER 4

Coding of Chinese Public Compensation

This section reports my method for coding actual compensation rates from the Shandong county line-item budgets, as analyzed in Chapter 4. Existing studies employ government budgets that are published in statistical yearbooks and government websites, which only list budgets by broad spending categories (e.g., education, health, construction). The category of "administration costs" reported in these budgets in fact only partially captures total administrative costs. The line-item budget data that I use has the unique advantage of listing government spending by items for each county in Shandong province. Table A4.1 shows a sample of the data structure (unit = 10,000 Yuan). From the line-item budgets, we can tell how much each county spent on formal salaries, bonuses, allowances, travel, etc.

This data source provides a valuable opportunity to estimate actual compensation levels, including both formal salary and fringe benefits and pay. Measuring formal salary (*jiben gongzi*) is straightforward, as there is a single, clearly defined column for this item. There isn't a single column, however, for "fringe compensation," as it is spread out over multiple line items within the reported budgets. To accurately code fringe compensation, I drew on technical budget manuals that explained the composition of each line item and interviews with more than 40 budgetary officials.

To construct fringe compensation, I included two main line items in the budgets: "personnel spending" and "administrative spending." Personnel spending refers to government spending on financial remuneration for government employees beyond formal salary, such as bonuses, subsidies, and allowances. Administrative spending, on the other hand, captures the provision of in-kind (or non-monetized) staff benefits. For example, a wealthy tax bureau can build a lavish office or disburse gift baskets to

TABLE A4.1 *Deconstruction of budgets*

	Formal salary	Bonuses	Allowances	Travel	Entertainment	Others
County A	8,748	151	7,735	454	569	966
County B	13,339	1,160	11,033	886	1,114	1,783

TABLE A4.2 *Breakdown of compensation and associated line items*

Formal salary	Fringe allowances and benefits	
	Monetary payments	In-kind benefits
Basic wages	Subsidies	Administrative costs
	Bonuses	Operational costs
	Social security payments	Transportation
	Welfare payments	Travel
	Labor fees	Conferences and meetings
	Scholarships	Training
	Other payments	Entertainment and reception
		Rental and maintenance
		Office furnishing
		Vehicles
		Others

TABLE A4.3 *Descriptive statistics of independent and dependent variables*

Variable	Unit	Mean	Standard deviation
Total compensation per employee	Yuan	23,226	13,018
Formal wages per employee	Yuan	5,029	1,658
Fringe compensation per employee	Yuan	18,197	12,036
Tax revenue per capita	Yuan	335	334
Agency collections per capita	Yuan	283	170
Fiscal transfer per capita	Yuan	268	236
Change in tax revenue per capita	Yuan	44	115
Change in agency collections per capita	Yuan	33	76
Change in fiscal transfer per capita	Yuan	42	108
Population	10,000 people	65	28
Share of urban population	%	32	24
Number of public employees	Person	16,366	6,908
GDP per capita	1000 Yuan	12	11

staff members. Other well-documented perks include "entertainment," "training," and "conferences and meetings," which commonly translate into free wining and dining and subsidized vacations for government employees. For a conservative estimate, I excluded administrative spending items that are not likely to contribute to staff welfare (e.g., purchase of specialized equipment and materials). Table A4.2 lists the budgetary line items I included to estimate fringe compensation in the Shandong county governments. Descriptive statistics are presented in Table A4.3.

Four Varieties of Officials

Bo and Ji exemplify Chinese officials who are both corrupt and competent. But not all are like them, of course. We should also be aware of three other varieties of officials: competent but not corrupt, incompetent and corrupt, incompetent and not corrupt (see Table A5.1). It is also useful to know that there are officials who were purged during Xi's anti-corruption drive who did not take bribes but had failed at their jobs, which the Party considers to be a form of corruption,[1] known technically as dereliction of duty.

ENTERTAINER-IN-CHIEF

First, consider the category of incompetent and corrupt, illustrated by Guo Yongchang, Party secretary of Gushi, a rural county in Henan province that is officially designated poor and receives financial assistance from higher-level governments to get by. We can learn a lot about Guo because he is the star of *The Transition Period*, a documentary that filmed the party secretary's daily activities. To classify Guo as incompetent may be unfair because, even though he failed to make his county rich, the documentary shows Guo hard at work all day. He is absorbed in endless meetings, hijacked by ad-hoc crises, intervenes to help workers get their owed wages, and above all, tries hard to promote growth. The most consuming aspect of his work was attracting investors, with whom he negotiated, drank, sang karaoke, and entertained constantly. In a darkly comic scene, an intoxicated Guo smeared a birthday cake on an American investor. Then, the next day, hung over but reflective,

---

[1] Cai (2015).

TABLE A5.1 *Corrupt, competent, both, or neither?*

Competent and corrupt	Competent and not corrupt
Examples: Bo Xilai (provincial Party secretary of Chongqing), Ji Jianye (mayor of Nanjing)	Example: Geng Yanbo (mayor of Datong)
Incompetent and corrupt	Incompetent and not corrupt
Example: Guo Yongchang (county Party secretary of Gushi)	Example: Tong Mingqian (city Party secretary of Hengyang)

he expressed an earnest desire to make a difference to Gushi. "Failing to develop is the worst kind of corruption," he said.[2]

In the final minutes of the film, Guo was hauled away on charges of corruption. Subsequent investigation revealed that he paid a higher-level official 100,000 Yuan for his promotion to county Party secretary.[3] Unlike Bo or Ji, Guo did not turn around the fortunes of his jurisdiction. Despite an increase in foreign investment during Guo's tenure from 800 million Yuan in 2004 to 3.8 billion Yuan in 2009, Gushi remained poor. Worse, the county government incurred a large deficit of 700 million Yuan, as Guo squandered public funds on white elephant projects, including a new government compound costing 200 million Yuan that local media described as "extravagant like a four-star hotel."[4]

NICE GUYS DON'T GET AHEAD

Then we turn to a second variety of officials, incompetent and not corrupt, but who nonetheless are punished by the Party. Under China's cadre evaluation system, officials can be held responsible for scandals and protests that occur during their tenure, even though they are not directly involved and did not cause them.[5] Tong Mingqian, party secretary of Hengyang city in Hunan Province, is a case in point. (Tong is one of 54 city Party secretaries whose downfall during Xi's anti-corruption crackdown I analyze in Chapter 6.)

---

[2] Also quoted in "China Bets Future on Inland Cities," *Reuters*, 3 August 2010.
[3] "国家贫困县河南固始：顶风建"豪衙" 伸手要救济 [The Poverty County Gushi of Henan]," *Jingji Cankaobao*, 29 October 2007. He was not alone, as studies find the sale of public offices rampant in poor regions of China (Zhu 2008).
[4] *Ibid.*   [5] Whiting (2004); Edin (2005); Cai (2015); Ang (2016).

In 2013, Tong was apprehended in association with a massive vote-buying scandal that broke out in his city when he was party secretary. In this case, 518 members of Hengyang's people's congress, the city legislative body, took a total of 110 million Yuan in bribes from 56 candidates in exchange for voting them into the provincial legislature.[6] Although Tong did not instigate the scheme, nor did he take bribes, he was punished for "dereliction of duty," stripped of party membership and removed from office.[7]

Unlike Bo, Ji, and Guo, Tong was famously clean, even morally stiff and uptight. He refused extravagant dinners, preferring to pack dinner home from the staff canteen and pay for his own meals. "He doesn't smoke and doesn't drink. His only hobby is to take a stroll in the Party secretary's compound after work, with an old security guard at his side," a local newspaper reported. One day, three businessmen who failed to get elected after bribing the city's legislators barged into Tong's office, demanding justice; instead of throwing the rascals behind bars, the Party secretary offered to get their money back.

In the Chinese political system, Tong's "nice guy" (*laohaoren*) qualities are perceived as spinelessness, despised by bureaucratic superiors and even the media, which wrote dismissively, "Lacking audacity and authority, even county Party secretaries didn't take him seriously."[8] Throughout his career, Tong never made a splash, but he hoped that by toeing party lines and avoid making enemies, he could peacefully retire. Tragically, even this modest wish was dashed, as the Party punished him for inaction on the vote-buying scandal. Nice guys, apparently, don't get ahead in Chinese politics.

SLEEPLESS IN DATONG

Lastly, a fourth, ideal variety: competent and not corrupt. A good example is Geng Yanbo, Mayor of Datong, featured in the documentary, *The Chinese*

---

[6] "Hunan City's Top Cadres Hit with Massive Vote-Buying Case," *South China Morning Post*, 30 December 2013.

[7] "童名谦被免去湖南省政协副主席职务 [Tong Mingqian Removed from Office in Connection with Vote-Buying Scandal in Hengyang]," *People's Daily*, 27 January 2014.

[8] "Mediocre official Tong Mingqian" (起底庸官样本童名谦) [Chinese], *Southern Weekend* (*Nanfang Zhoumo*), reposted in *Sohu*, 26 June 2014.

Mayor.[9] Bearing clear resemblance to Ji Jianye, Geng is an insomniac bent on rejuvenating the smog-filled city of Datong through massive urban renewal projects. One review of the documentary aptly describes Geng as "a sort of human bulldozer."[10] At the time the film was made, Geng was abruptly transferred from Datong to Taiyuan, where he still serves as Party secretary. Given that no charges of corruption have been made against Geng, we may assume, for now, that he isn't corrupt. But even officials in this ideal group are controversial because, in China's growth-obsessed autocracy, the use of state power is almost always disruptive.

Providing a count of how many officials fall into each of the four categories is not the task of this analysis. In practice, this is extremely difficult to do, as we will see in Chapter 6 (even when certain officials are exposed for corruption, we cannot know whether the remaining ones are innocent). Nevertheless, by identifying these four varieties of officials, we will see that portrayal of the entire Chinese bureaucracy as "predatory" (grab and give nothing in return) is too simplistic. Even the corrupt leader Guo Yongchang doesn't entirely fit the caricature of "looting, debauchery, and utter lawlessness."[11] Even he was dedicated to growth promotion and had defused social conflicts and raised investment.

---

[9] The filmmaker Zhou Hao also produced the earlier mentioned documentary, *The Transition Period*.

[10] Dennis Harvey, "Sundance Film Review: The Chinese Mayor," *Variety*, 30 January 2015.

[11] Pei (2016, 183).

APPENDIX: CHAPTER 6

TABLE A6.1 *Definition and sources of variables*

Variable	Unit	Definition	Source
Dependent variable: fall	1 or 0	City Party secretary is investigated within this year	Media reports, procuratorate and CCDI websites
Patron fall	1 or 0	Patron falls within the same year and/or has previously fallen	Media reports, procuratorate and CCDI websites
Growth in share of provincial GDP	%	Growth in city's share of provincial GDP in 2012 over 2011	Provincial Statistical Yearbooks
Media mentions	Number	Number of times a Party secretary's name appears in a cluster of 164 central papers and 469 local papers in 2011, normalized by number of local papers in that province	China Core Newspapers Full-Text Database
GDP per capita 2011	%	GDP per capita in 2011	Provincial Statistical Yearbooks
NERI state–market relations	0–10	Province's score on state-market relations	NERI Report 2016
NERI rule of law	0–10	Province's score on rule of law	NERI Report 2016

TABLE A6.2 *Descriptive statistics*

Variable	Mean	Standard deviation	Count = 0	Count = 1
Growth in share of provincial GDP (2012)	0.01	0.04	–	–
Media mentions (2011)	10.86	9.17	–	–
Prefecture GDP per capita (2011) (Yuan)	37,242	25,817	–	–
NERI government-market relations (2012)	5.13	2.67	–	–
NERI rule of law (2012)	4.17	2.16	–	–
Client of 18th Politburo member	–	–	1,194	678
Client of 18th PSC member	–	–	1,812	60
Client of Sun Zhengcai	–	–	1,830	42
Patron fall	–	–	1,739	133

APPENDIX: CHAPTER 7

Construction of Comparative Corruption Indices

Building on Glaeser and Goldin (2006), Ramirez (2014) conducts an innovative historical comparison of Chinese and American corruption at equivalent stages of economic development. He uses media reports in a bundle of American newspapers to approximate the level of corruption in each of the two cases. The comparable periods he uses are China from 1990 to 2011 and United States from 1870 to 1930. He concludes that corruption in China is not as alarming as it appears, compared with the US historical experience. Furthermore, as America grew richer, corruption declined, reaching a similar level to China.

While Ramirez's approach is commendable, there is a serious flaw in his method: he uses American newspapers to measure corruption in the United States and China. Using this source, it is no surprise that reported levels of corruption in China will be considerably lower than in the United States. In other words, he undercounts Chinese corruption.

For my analysis, therefore, I modify Ramirez's analysis in two key respects. First, I measure reported corruption using indigenous news outlets in each case: the same bundle of American papers for the United States and the *People's Daily* in China. I apply the same media measure to the *People's Daily* in Chinese. Corruption (*fubai*) and China (*zhongguo*) are searched together, then deflated by the word "government" (*zhengfu*). The 1990–2011 data is from the People's Daily Electronic Edition; for the 2012–2016 data I took averages of index values for the *People's Daily* from the China National Knowledge Database (CNKI) and the Apabi Digital Newspaper Collection.

Second, I modify Ramirez's selection of comparable years, using income data from the Penn World Table, which is the same source the author used. Upon closer examination of his methodology, I find that his selection of comparable years was open to interpretation and could be improved. I selected a different set of years during which the income per capita of China and that of the United States were, in my judgment, closer than in Ramirez's study. The comparable periods selected for my analysis are listed in Table 7.1.

References

Acemoglu, Daron, and James A. Robinson. 2008. "The Role of Institutions in Growth and Development." Working Paper No. 10. Washington, DC: Commission for Growth and Development.

2012. *Why Nations Fail: The Origins of Power, Prosperity and Poverty.* New York, NY: Crown Publishers.

Ades, Alberto, and Rafael Di Tella. 1999. "Rents, Competition, and Corruption." *The American Economic Review* 89(4): 982–93.

Amsden, Alice. 1989. *Asia's Next Giant: South Korea and Late Industrialization.* New York, NY: Oxford University Press.

Andrews, Matt, Lant Pritchett, and Michael Woolcock. 2013. "Escaping Capability Traps through Problem Driven Iterative Adaptation (PDIA)." *World Development* 51(C): 234–44.

Andrews, Matt, Michael Woolcock, and Lant Pritchett. 2017. *Building State Capability: Evidence, Analysis, Action.* Oxford: Oxford University Press.

Ang, Yuen Yuen. 2012. "Counting Cadres: A Comparative View of the Size of China's Public Employment." *The China Quarterly* 211: 676–96.

2014. "Authoritarian Restraints on Online Activism Revisited: Why 'I-Paid-a-Bribe' Worked in India but Failed in China." *Comparative Politics* 47(1): 21–40.

2016. *How China Escaped the Poverty Trap.* Ithaca, NY: Cornell University Press.

2017. "Beyond Weber: Conceptualizing an Alternative Ideal-Type of Bureaucracy in Developing Contexts." *Regulation and Governance* 11(3): 282–98.

2018a. "Autocracy with Chinese Characteristics: Beijing's Behind-the-Scenes Reforms." *Foreign Affairs* 97(3): 39–46.

2018b. "Domestic Flying Geese: Industrial Transfer and Delayed Policy Diffusion in China." *The China Quarterly* 234: 420–43.

2018c. "The Real China Model: It's Not What You Think It Is." *Foreign Affairs* (29 June).

2018d. "Going Local 2.0: How to Reform Aid Agencies to Make Development Agencies More Than Talk." *Stanford Social Innovation Review,* https://ssir.org/articles/entry/going_local_2.0_how_to_reform_development_agencies_localized_aid# (accessed 11 November 2019).

Ang, Yuen Yuen, and Nan Jia. 2014. "Perverse Complementarity: Political Connections and the Use of Courts among Private Firms in China." *The Journal of Politics* 76(2): 318–32.

Åslund, Anders. 2013. *How Capitalism Was Built: The Transformation of Central and Eastern Europe, Russia, the Caucasus, and Central Asia*, 2nd edn. Cambridge: Cambridge University Press.

Bachman, David. 2017. "China Is Corrupt, but There Is More to the Story." *Asia Policy* 23: 158–62.

Baker, Andrew. 2010. "Restraining Regulatory Capture? Anglo-America, Crisis Politics and Trajectories of Change in Global Financial Governance." *International Affairs* 86(3): 647–63.

Banerjee, Abhijit V., and Rohini Pande. 2007. "Parochial Politics: Ethnic Preferences and Politician Corruption." KSG Working Paper No. RWP07-031, http://dx.doi.org/10.2139/ssrn.976548 (accessed 11 November 2019).

Bardhan, Pranab. 1997. "Corruption and Development: A Review of Issues." *Journal of Economic Literature* 35(3): 1320–46.

2010. *Awakening Giants, Feet of Clay: Assessing the Economic Rise of China and India*. Princeton, NJ: Princeton University Press.

Baum, Richard, and Alexei Shevchenko. 1999. "The 'State of the State,'" in Merle Goldman and Roderick MacFarquhar (eds.), *The Paradox of China's Post-Mao Reforms*. Cambridge, MA:Harvard University Press, pp. 333–60.

Baydar, Nazli, Michael White, Charles Simkins, and Ozer Babakol. 1990. "Effects of Agricultural Development Policies on Migration in Peninsular Malaysia." *Demography* 27(1): 97–109.

Beck, Ulrich, and Christoph Lau. 2005. "Second Modernity as a Research Agenda." *The British Journal of Sociology* 56(4): 525–57.

Becker, Gary, and George J. Stigler. 1974. "Law Enforcement, Malfeasance, and Compensation of Enforcers." *The Journal of Legal Studies* 3(1): 1–18.

Bell, Daniel. 2016. *The China Model: Political Meritocracy and the Limits of Democracy*. Princeton, NJ: Princeton University Press.

Benedict, Ruth. 1974. *The Chrysanthemum and the Sword: Patterns of Japanese Culture*. Scarborough, Ont.; New York, NY: New American Library.

Bernstein, Thomas, and Xiaobo Lü. 2003. *Taxation without Representation in Rural China*. Cambridge: Cambridge University Press.

Besley, Timothy, and John McLaren. 1993. "Taxes and Bribery: The Role of Wage Incentives." *Economic Journal* 103(416): 119–41.

Bhagwati, Jagdish N. 1982. "Directly Unproductive, Profit-Seeking Activities." *The Journal of Political Economy* 90(5): 988–1002.

Bhargava, Vinay. 2005. "The Cancer of Corruption." Paper presented at the World Bank Global Issues Seminar Series, October 2005.

Blanchard, Olivier, and Andrei Shleifer. 2001. "Federalism with and without Political Centralization: China versus Russia." *IMF Staff Papers* 48(S1): 171–79.

Blecher, Marc. 1991. "Developmental State, Entrepreneurial State: The Political Economy of Socialist Reform in Xinju Municipality and Guanghan County," in Gordon White (ed.), *The Chinese State in the Era of Economic Reform: The Road to Crisis*. London: Macmillan, pp. 265–91.

Blecher, Marc, and Vivienne Shue. 2001. "Into Leather: State-Led Development and the Private Sector in Xinji." *The China Quarterly* 166: 368–93.

Bose, Niloy, Salvatore Capasso, and Antu Panini Murshid. 2008. "Threshold Effects of Corruption: Theory and Evidence." *World Development* 36(7): 1173–91.

Brands, H. W. 2010. *American Colossus: The Triumph of Capitalism, 1865–1900.* New York, NY: Doubleday.

Brewer, John. 1988. *The Sinews of Power: War, Money, and the English State, 1688–1783.* London; Boston, MA: Harvard University Press.

Brown, J. David, John S. Earle, and Scott Gehlbach. 2009. "Helping Hand or Grabbing Hand? State Bureaucracy and Privatization Effectiveness." *American Political Science Review* 103(2): 264–83.

Burns, John P. 2007. "Civil Service Reform in China." *OECD Journal on Budgeting* 7 (1): 1–25.

Bussell, Jennifer. 2012. *Corruption and Reform in India: Public Services in the Digital Age.* Cambridge; New York, NY: Cambridge University Press.

   2015. "Typologies of Corruption: A Pragmatic Approach," in Susan Rose-Ackerman and Paul Lagunes (eds.), *Greed, Corruption, and the Modern State.* Cheltenham: Edward Elgar, pp. 21–45.

Cai, Meina. 2014. "Flying Land: Institutional Innovation in Land Management in Contemporary China," in Jessica C. Teets and William Hurst (eds.), *Local Governance Innovation in China: Experimentation, Diffusion, and Defiance.* New York, NY: Routledge, pp. 63–87.

Cai, Yongshun. 2015. *State and Agents in China: Disciplining Government Officials.* Stanford, CA: Stanford University Press.

Carter, David, and Curtis Signorino. 2010. "Back to the Future: Modeling Time Dependence in Binary Data." *Political Analysis* 18(3): 271–92.

Centeno, Miguel. 2002. *Blood and Debt: War and the Nation-State in Latin America.* University Park, PA: Pennsylvania State University Press.

Chan, Hon S., and Jun Ma. 2011. "How Are They Paid? A Study of Civil Service Pay in China." *International Review of Administrative Sciences* 77(2): 294–321.

Chang, Gordon. 2001. *The Coming Collapse of China.* New York, NY: Random House.

Chang, Ha-Joon. 2002. *Kicking Away the Ladder: Development Strategy in Historical Perspective.* London: Anthem.

Chen, Hui, David Parsley, and Ya-Wen Yang. 2015. "Corporate Lobbying and Firm Performance." *Journal of Business Finance & Accounting* 42(3–4): 444–81.

Chen, Ling. 2014. "Varieties of Global Capital and the Paradox of Local Upgrading in China." *Politics and Society* 42(2): 223–52.

Chen, Nan, and Zemin Zhong. 2017. "The Economic Impact of China's Anti-corruption Campaign." *SSRN Electronic Journal* (16 September), http://dx .doi.org/10.2139/ssrn.2996009 (accessed 12 November 2019).

Chen, Yunling, Ming Liu, and Jun Su. 2013. "Greasing the Wheels of Bank Lending: Evidence from Private Firms in China." *Journal of Banking and Finance* 37(7): 2533–45.

Coase, Ronald, and Ning Wang. 2012. *How China Became Capitalist.* New York, NY: Palgrave Macmillan.

Colclough, Christopher. 1997. *Public Sector Pay and Adjustment: Lessons from Five Countries.* New York, NY: Routledge.

Cole, Matthew, Robert Elliott, and Jing Zhang. 2009. "Corruption, Governance and FDI Location in China: A Province-Level Analysis." *The Journal of Development Studies* 45(9): 1494–512.

Collier, David, and Robert Adcock. 1999. "Democracy and Dichotomies: A Pragmatic Approach to Choices about Concepts." *Annual Review of Political Science* 2: 537–65.

Collier, David, Jason Seawright, and Henry E. Brady. 2003. "Qualitative versus Quantitative: What Might This Distinction Mean?" *Qualitative Methods* 1(1): 1–8.

Coyne, Christopher. 2013. *Doing Bad by Doing Good: Why Humanitarian Action Fails.* Stanford, CA: Stanford University Press.

Crowley, Joceleyn, and Theda Skocpol. 2001. "The Rush to Organize: Explaining Associational Formation in the United States, 1860s–1920s." *American Journal of Political Science* 45(4): 813–29.

Davis, James, and John Ruhe. 2003. "Perceptions of Country Corruption: Antecedents and Outcomes." *Journal of Business Ethics* 43(4): 275–88.

De Boef, Suzanna, and Luke Keele. 2008. "Taking Time Seriously." *American Journal of Political Science* 52(1): 184–200.

Di Tella, Rafael, and Raymond Fisman. 2004. "Are Politicians Really Paid Like Bureaucrats?" *The Journal of Law and Economics* 47(2): 477–513.

Di Tella, Rafael, and Ernesto Schargrodsky. 2003. "The Role of Wages and Auditing during a Crackdown on Corruption in the City of Buenos Aires." *The Journal of Law, Economics and Organization* 46(1): 269–92.

Dickson, Bruce J. 2008. *Wealth into Power: The Communist Party's Embrace of China's Private Sector.* Cambridge: Cambridge University Press.

2016. *The Dictator's Dilemma: The Chinese Communist Party's Strategy for Survival.* New York, NY: Oxford University Press.

Ding, Xueliang. 2000. "The Illicit Asset Stripping of Chinese State Firms." *The China Journal* 43: 1–28.

Dubrow, Joshua. 2015. *Political Inequality in the Age of Democracy: Cross-National Perspectives.* London; New York, NY: Routledge.

Duckett, Jane. 1998. *The Entrepreneurial State in China: Real Estate and Commerce Departments in Reform Era Tianjin.* London; New York, NY: Routledge.

Economy, Elizabeth. 2018. *The Third Revolution: Xi Jinping and the New Chinese State.* New York, NY: Oxford University Press.

Edin, Maria. 2003. "State Capacity and Local Agent Control in China: CCP Cadre Management from a Township Perspective." *The China Quarterly* 173: 35–52.

2005. "Remaking the Communist Party-State: The Cadre Responsibility System at the Local Level in China." *China: An International Journal* 1(1): 1–15.

Ehlers, Torsten, Steven Kong, and Feng Zhu. 2018. "Mapping Shadow Banking in China: Structure and Dynamics." Bank for International Settlements Working Paper 701.

Ehrlich, Isaac, and Francis Lui. 1999. "Bureaucratic Corruption and Endogenous Economic Growth." *Journal of Political Economy* 107(S6): 270–93.

Evans, Peter. 1989. "Predatory, Developmental, and Other Apparatuses: A Comparative Political Economy Perspective on the Third World State." *Sociological Forum* 4(4): 561–87.

    1995. *Embedded Autonomy: States and Industrial Transformation.* Princeton, NJ: Princeton University Press.

Evans, Peter, and Peter Heller. 2013. "Human Development, State Transformation and the Politics of the Developmental State," in Stephan Leibfried, Frank Nullmeier, Evelyne Huber, Matthew Lange, Jonah Levy, and John D. Stephens (eds.), *The Oxford Handbook of Transformations of the State.* Oxford: Oxford University Press.

Evans, Peter, and James Rauch. 1999. "Bureaucracy and Growth: A Cross-National Analysis of the Effects of 'Weberian' State Structures on Economic Growth." *American Sociological Review* 64(5): 748–65.

Faccio, Mara. 2006. "Politically Connected Firms." *American Economic Review* 96 (1): 369–86.

Fan, Chengze Simon, Chen Lin, and Daniel Treisman. 2010. "Embezzlement versus Bribery." NBER Working Paper 16542.

Fan, Gang, and Xiaolu Wang. 2000. *NERI Index of Marketization of China's Provinces.* Beijing: Economic Science Press.

Fenno, Richard. 1978. *Home Style: House Members in Their Districts.* Boston, MA: Little, Brown.

Fisman, Raymond, and Miriam Golden. 2017. *Corruption: What Everyone Needs to Know.* New York, NY: Oxford University Press.

Fisman, Raymond, and Jakob Svensson. 2007. "Are Corruption and Taxation Really Harmful to Growth? Firm Level Evidence." *Journal of Development Economics* 83(1): 63–75.

Fisman, Raymond, and Yongxiang Wang. 2014. "Corruption in Chinese Privatizations." NBER Working Paper No. 20090.

Frye, Timothy, and Andrei Shleifer. 1997. "The Invisible Hand and the Grabbing Hand." *The American Economic Review* 87(2): 354–58.

Geddes, Barbara. 1994. *Politician's Dilemma: Building State Capacity in Latin America.* Berkeley, CA: University of California Press.

George, Alexander, and Andrew Bennett. 2005. *Case Studies and Theory Development in the Social Sciences.* Cambridge, MA: MIT Press.

Gerring, John, and Strom C. Thacker. 2004. "Political Institutions and Corruption: The Role of Unitarism and Parliamentarism." *British Journal of Political Science* 34(2): 295–330.

Gilens, Martin. 2012. *Affluence and Influence: Economic Inequality and Political Power in America.* Princeton, NJ: Princeton University Press.

Glaeser, Edward, and Claudia Goldin. 2006. *Corruption and Reform: Lessons from America's Economic History.* Chicago, IL: University of Chicago Press.

Gong, Ting. 2002. "Dangerous Collusion: Corruption as a Collective Venture in Contemporary China." *Communist and Post-communist Studies* 35(1): 85–103.

Gould, David, and Jose Amaro-Reyes. 1983. "The Effects of Corruption on Administrative Performance: Illustrations from Developing Countries." World Bank Working Papers No. 580.

Gray, Cheryl W., and Kaufman, Daniel. 1998. *Corruption and Development.* PREM Notes No. 4. Washington, DC: World Bank.

Grimmer, Justin, Sean Westwood, and Solomon Messing. 2014. *The Impression of Influence.* Princeton, NJ: Princeton University Press.

Gunter, Frank. 2017. "Corruption, Costs, and Family: Chinese Capital Flight, 1984–2014." *China Economic Review* 43(C): 105–17.

Guo, Gang. 2009. "China's Local Political Budget Cycles." *American Journal of Political Science* 53(3): 621–32.

Guo, Yong. 2008. "Corruption in Transitional China: An Empirical Analysis." *The China Quarterly* 194: 349–64.

Haggard, Stephan. 2018. *Developmental States.* New York, NY: Cambridge University Press.

Han, Sang-Jin, and Young-Hee Shim. 2010. "Redefining Second Modernity for East Asia: A Critical Assessment." *The British Journal of Sociology* 61(3): 465–88.

Hao, Yufan, and Michael Johnston. 1995. "China's Surge of Corruption." *Journal of Democracy* 6(4): 80–94.

He, Zengke. 2000. "Corruption and Anti-corruption in Reform China." *Communist and Post-communist Studies* 33(2): 243–70.

Heilmann, Sebastian, and Elizabeth Perry. 2011. *Mao's Invisible Hand: The Political Foundations of Adaptive Governance in China.* Cambridge, MA: Harvard University Press.

Heinrich, Carolyn. 2004. "Measuring Public Sector Performance and Effectiveness," in Guy Peters and Jon Pierre (eds.), *Handbook of Public Administration.* London: Sage Publications, pp. 25–37.

Hicken, Allen. 2011. "Clientelism." *Annual Review of Political Science* 14: 289–310.

Hillman, Ben. 2014. *Patronage and Power: Local State Networks and Party-State Resilience in Rural China.* Stanford, CA: Stanford University Press.

Hilton, Root. 1996. "Corruption in China: Has It Become Systemic?" *Asian Survey* 36(8): 741–57.

Hoffman, David. 2002. *The Oligarchs: Wealth and Power in the New Russia.* New York, NY: Public Affairs.

Houston, Joel, Liangliang Jiang, Chen Lin, and Yue Ma. 2014. "Political Connections and the Cost of Bank Loans." *Journal of Accounting Research* 52 (1): 193–243.

Howson, Nicholas. 2017. "A Partial View of China's Governance Trajectory." *Asia Policy* 23: 162–66.

Hsueh, Roselyn 2011. *China's Regulatory State: A New Strategy for Globalization.* New York, NY: Cornell University Press.

Huang, Philip C. C. 2011. "Chongqing: Equitable Development Driven by a 'Third Hand'?" *Modern China* 37(6): 569–622.

Huang, Yukon. 2017. *Cracking the China Conundrum: Why Conventional Economic Wisdom Is Wrong.* New York, NY: Oxford University Press.

Hui, Eddie Chi-Man, Cong Liang, Ziyou Wang, Bo-Tong Song, and Qi Gu. 2012. "Real Estate Bubbles in China: A Tale of Two Cities." *Construction Management and Economics* 30(11): 951–61.

Hui, Victoria Tin-bor. 2005. *War and State Formation in Ancient China and Early Modern Europe.* New York, NY: Cambridge University Press.

Huntington, Samuel P. 1968. *Political Order in Changing Societies.* New Haven, CT: Yale University Press.

Igan, Deniz, Prachi Mishra, and Thierry Tressel. 2011. "A Fistful of Dollars: Lobbying and the Financial Crisis." NBER Working Paper No. 17076.

International Monetary Fund. 2016. "IMF and Good Governance," www.imf.org/external/np/exr/facts/gov.htm (accessed 26 August 2019).

Issacharoff, Samuel. 2010. "On Political Corruption." *Harvard Law Review* 124(1): 118–42.

Jain, Arvind. 2001. "Corruption: A Review." *Journal of Economic Surveys* 15(1): 71–121.

Jia, Nan. 2014. "Are Collective Political Actions and Private Political Actions Substitutes or Complements? Empirical Evidence from China's Private Sector." *Strategic Management Journal* 35(2): 292–315.

2016. "Political Strategy and Market Capabilities: Evidence from the Chinese Private Sector." *Management and Organization Review* 12(1): 75–102.

Jia, Nan, Jing Shi, and Yongxiang Wang (Forthcoming). "The Interdependence of Public and Private Stakeholder Influence: A Study of Political Patronage and Corporate Philanthropy in China." *Advances in Strategic Management.*

Jia, Ruixue, Masayuki Kudamatsu, and David Seim. 2015. "Political Selection in China: The Complementary Roles of Connections and Performance." *Journal of the European Economic Association* 13(4): 631–68.

Johnson, Chalmers. 1995. *Japan: Who Governs? The Rise of the Developmental State.* New York, NY: Norton.

Johnston, Michael. 2008. "Japan, Korea, the Philippines, China: Four Syndromes of Corruption." *Crime, Law and Social Change* 49(3): 205–23.

Joseph, Richard A. 1987. *Democracy and Prebendal Politics in Nigeria: The Rise and Fall of the Second Republic.* Cambridge: Cambridge University Press.

Kalathil, Shanthi. 2018. "China in Xi's 'New Era': Redefining Development." *Journal of Democracy* 29(2): 52–58.

Kang, David C. 2002a. "Bad Loans to Good Friends: Money Politics and the Developmental State in South Korea." *International Organization* 56(1): 177–207.

2002b. *Crony Capitalism: Corruption and Development in South Korea and the Philippines.* Cambridge; New York, NY: Cambridge University Press.

Kaufman, Herbert. 1960. *The Forest Ranger: A Study in Administrative Behavior.* Baltimore, MA: Johns Hopkins Press.

Kaufmann, Daniel, Aart Kraay, and Pablo Zoido-Lobatón. 1999. "Governance Matters." Policy Research Working Paper no. WPS 2196. Washington, DC: World Bank.

Kaufmann, Daniel, and Shang-Jin Wei. 2000. "Does 'Grease Money' Speed up the Wheels of Commerce?" IMF Working Paper.

Kenny, Charles. 2017. *Results Not Receipts: Counting the Right Things in Aid and Corruption.* Washington, DC:Center for Global Development.

Khan, Mushtaq. 2010. "Political Settlements and the Governance of Growth-Enhancing Institutions." Working Paper. School of Oriental and African Studies, University of London.

2012. "Governance and Growth Challenges for Africa," in Akbar Noman, Kwesi Botchwey, Howard Stein, and Joseph Stiglitz (eds.), *Good Growth and*

Governance in Africa: Rethinking Development Strategies. Oxford: Oxford University Press, pp. 114–39.

Kim, Jin-Hyuk. 2008. "Corporate Lobbying Revisited." *Business and Politics* 10(2): 3–23.

King, Gary, and Jonathan Wand. 2007. "Comparing Incomparable Survey Responses: Evaluating and Selecting Anchoring Vignettes." *Political Analysis* 15(1): 46–66.

King, Gary, Robert Keohane, and Sidney Verba. 1994. *Designing Social Inquiry: Scientific Inference in Qualitative Research.* Princeton, NJ: Princeton University Press.

King, Gary, Christopher J. L. Murray, Joshua A. Salomon, and Ajay Tandon. 2004. "Enhancing the Validity and Cross-cultural Comparability of Measurement in Survey Research." *American Political Science Review* 98: 191–207.

King, Gary, Michael Tomz, and Jason Wittenberg. 2000. "Making the Most of Statistical Analyses: Improving Interpretation and Presentation." *American Journal of Political Science* 44(2): 347–61.

Klitgaard, Robert E. 1988. *Controlling Corruption.* Berkeley, CA: University of California Press.

Ko, Kilkon, and Cuifen Weng. 2012. "Structural Changes in Chinese Corruption." *The China Quarterly* 211: 718–40.

Kohli, Atul. 2004. *State-Directed Development: Political Power and Industrialization in the Global Periphery.* New York, NY: Cambridge University Press.

Kostka, Genia, and Xiaofan Yu. 2014. "Career Backgrounds of Municipal Party Secretaries: Why Do So Few Municipal Party Secretaries Rise from the County Level?" *Modern China* 41(5): 467–505.

Krueger, Anne. 1974. "The Political Economy of the Rent-Seeking Society." *American Economic Review* 64(3): 291–303.

Kung, James Kai-Sing, and Shuo Chen. 2011. "The Tragedy of the Nomenklatura: Career Incentives and Political Radicalism during China's Great Leap Famine." *American Political Science Review* 105(1): 27–45.

La Porta, Rafael, Florencio Lopez de Silanes, Andrei Shleifer, and Robert W. Vishny. 1999. "The Quality of Government." *Journal of Law, Economics and Organization* 15(1): 222–79.

Lah, Tae Joon, and James L. Perry. 2008. "The Diffusion of the Civil Service Reform Act of 1978 in OECD Countries: A Tale of Two Paths to Reform." *Review of Public Personnel Administration* 28(3): 282–99.

Landry, Pierre. 2008. *Decentralized Authoritarianism in China: The Communist Party's Control of Local Elites in the Post-Mao Era.* Cambridge; New York, NY: Cambridge University Press.

Lane, Jan-Erik. 2000. *New Public Management.* London: Routledge.

Lardy, Nicholas. 2014. *Markets over Mao: The Rise of Private Business in China.* Washington, DC: Peterson Institute for International Economics.

2019. *The State Strikes Back: The End of Economic Reform in China?* Washington, DC: Peterson Institute for International Economics.

Larsson, Tomas. 2006. "Reform, Corruption, and Growth: Why Corruption Is More Devastating in Russia Than in China." *Communist and Post-communist Studies* 39(2): 265–81.

Lau, Lawrence J., Yingyi Qian, and Gérard Roland. 2000. "Reform without Losers: An Interpretation of China's Dual-Track Approach to Transition." *Journal of Political Economy* 108(1): 120–43.

Lazear, Edward P. 1995. *Personnel Economics.* Cambridge, MA: MIT Press.

Leahy, Nathan. 2010. "The Panic of 1893 and 'The £1,000,000 Bank-Note.'" *The Mark Twain Annual* no. 8: 76–85.

Lee, Charlotte. 2015. *Training the Party: Party Adaptation and Elite Training in Reform-Era China.* Cambridge; New York, NY: Cambridge University Press.

Leff, Nathaniel H. 1964. "Economic Development through Bureaucratic Corruption." *American Behavioral Scientist* 8(3): 8–14.

Lessig, Lawrence. 2018. *America, Compromised.* Chicago, IL: University of Chicago Press.

Li, Bobai, and Andrew G. Walder. 2001. "Career Advancement as Party Patronage: Sponsored Mobility into the Chinese Administrative Elite, 1949–1996." *The American Journal of Sociology* 106(5): 1371–408.

Li, Hongbin, and Li-An Zhou. 2005. "Political Turnover and Economic Performance: The Incentive Role of Personnel Control in China." *Journal of Public Economics* 89(9–10): 1743–62.

Li, Hongbin, Lingsheng Meng, Qian Wang, and Li-An Zhou. 2008. "Political Connections, Financing and Firm Performance: Evidence from Chinese Private Firms." *Journal of Development Economics* 87(2): 283–99.

Li, Hongbin, Lingsheng Meng, and Junsen Zhang. 2006. "Why Do Entrepreneurs Enter Politics? Evidence from China." *Economic Inquiry* 44(3): 559–78.

Lieberthal, Kenneth. 1995. *Governing China: From Revolution through Reform.* New York, NY: W. W. Norton.

Lin, Chen, Randall Morck, Bernard Yeung, and Xiaofeng Zhao. 2016. "Anti-corruption Reforms and Shareholder Valuations: Event Study Evidence from China." NBER Working Paper 2201.

Lin, Karen Jingrong, Jinsong Tan, Liming Zhao, and Khondkar Karim. 2015. "In the Name of Charity: Political Connections and Strategic Corporate Social Responsibility in a Transition Economy." *Journal of Corporate Finance* 32(C): 327–46.

Lindauer, David, and Barbara Nunberg. 1994. *Rehabilitating Government: Pay and Employment Reform in Africa.* Washington, DC: World Bank.

Lipsky, Michael. 1980. *Street-Level Bureaucracy: Dilemmas of the Individual in Public Services.* New York, NY: Russell Sage Foundation.

Lu, Fengming, and Xiao Ma. 2018. "Is Any Publicity Good Publicity? Media Coverage, Party Institutions, and Authoritarian Power-Sharing." *Political Communication* 36(1): 64–82.

Lu, Xiaobo. 2000. "Booty Socialism, Bureau-preneurs, and the State in Transition: Organizational Corruption in China." *Comparative Politics* 32(3): 273–94.

Lü, Xiaobo. 2000. *Cadres and Corruption: The Organizational Involution of the Chinese Communist Party.* Stanford, CA: Stanford University Press.

Lü, Xiaobo, and Pierre F. Landry. 2014. "Show Me the Money: Interjurisdiction Political Competition and Fiscal Extraction in China." *American Political Science Review* 108(3): 706–22.

Lu, Xi, and Peter Lorentzen. 2016. "Rescuing Autocracy from Itself: China's Anti-corruption Campaign." *SSRN Electronic Journal*, 6 November, http://dx.doi.org/10.2139/ssrn.2835841 (accessed 9 November 2018).

Mahoney, James. 2009. "After KKV: The New Methodology of Qualitative Research." *World Politics* 62(1): 120–47.

Malesky, Edmund J., and Markus David Taussig. 2008. "Where Is Credit Due? Legal Institutions, Connections, and the Efficiency of Bank Lending in Vietnam." *The Journal of Law, Economics, and Organization* 25(2): 535–78.

Manion, Melanie. 1996. "Corruption by Design: Bribery in Chinese Enterprise Licensing." *Journal of Law, Economics, and Organization* 12(1): 167–95.

2004. *Corruption by Design: Building Clean Government in Mainland China and Hong Kong.* Cambridge, MA: Harvard University Press

2016. "Taking China's Anticorruption Campaign Seriously." *Economic and Political Studies* 4(1): 3–18.

Mauro, Paolo. 1995. "Corruption and Growth." *Quarterly Journal of Economics* 110(3): 681–712.

1996. "The Effects of Corruption on Growth, Investment, and Government Expenditure." IMF Working Paper WP/96/98. Washington, DC: International Monetary Fund.

McDonnell, Erin Metz. 2017. "Patchwork Leviathan: How Pockets of Bureaucratic Governance Flourish within Institutionally Diverse Developing States." *American Sociological Review* 82(3): 476–510.

McFaul, Michael. 1995. "State Power, Institutional Change, and the Politics of Privatization in Russia." *World Politics* 47(2): 210–43.

McMillan John, and Pablo Zoido. 2004. "How to Subvert Democracy: Montesinos in Peru." *Journal of Economic Perspective* 18(4): 69–92.

Mehta, Pratap Bhanu, and Michael Walton, 2014. "Ideas, Interests, and the Politics of Development Change in India." Global Development Institute Working Paper Series, ESID-036–14, University of Manchester.

Menes, Rebecca. 2006. "Limiting the Reach of the Grabbing Hand: Graft and Growth in American Cities," in Edward Glaeser and Claudia Goldin (eds.), *Corruption and Reform: Lessons from America's Economic History.* Chicago, IL: University of Chicago Press, pp. 63–94.

Méon, Pierre-Guillaume, and Khalid Sekkat. 2005. "Does Corruption Grease or Sand the Wheels of Growth?" *Public Choice* 122(1): 69–97.

Minzner, Carl. 2015. "China after the Reform Era." *Journal of Democracy* 26(3): 129–43.

Mo, Pak-Hung. 2001. "Corruption and Economic Growth." *Journal of Comparative Economics* 29(1): 66–79.

Moe, Terry. 1984. "The New Economics of Organization." *American Journal of Political Science* 28(4): 739–77.

Montinola, Gabriella, and Robert Jackman. 2002. "Sources of Corruption: A Cross-country Study." *British Journal of Political Science* 32(1): 147–70.

Montinola, Gabriella, Yingyi Qian, and Barry R. Weingast. 1995. "Federalism, Chinese Style: The Political Basis for Economic Success in China." *World Politics* 48(1): 50–81.

Mookherjee, Dilip. 1997. "Incentive Reforms in Developing Country Bureaucracies: Lessons from Tax Administration." Paper presented at the

Annual World Bank Conference in Development Economics, Washington, DC.

Mulvad, Andreas. 2015. "Competing Hegemonic Projects within China's Variegated Capitalism: 'Liberal' Guangdong vs. 'Statist' Chongqing." *New Political Economy* 20(2): 199–227.

Mungiu-Pippidi, Alina. 2015. *The Quest for Good Governance: How Societies Develop Control of Corruption.* Cambridge: Cambridge University Press.

Nathan, Andrew J. 1973. "A Factionalism Model for CCP Politics." *The China Quarterly* 53: 34–66.

2003. "Authoritarian resilience." *Journal of Democracy* 14(1): 6–17.

Naughton, Barry. 1995. *Growing out of the Plan: Chinese Economic Reform, 1978–1993.* New York, NY: Cambridge University Press

2018. *The Chinese Economy: Adaptation and Growth.* Cambridge, MA: MIT Press.

Nee, Victor. 1989. "A Theory of Market Transition: From Redistribution to Markets in State Socialism." *American Sociological Review* 54(5): 663–81.

Nichols, Philip M. 2017. "What Is Organizational Corruption?," in Michael S. Aßländer and Sarah Hudson (eds.), *The Handbook of Business and Corruption: Cross-sectoral Experiences.* Bingley: Emerald Publishing, pp. 3–23.

Nichols, Philip M., and Diana C. Robertson (eds.). 2017. *Thinking about Bribery: Neuroscience, Moral Cognition and the Psychology of Bribery.* Cambridge: Cambridge University Press.

Niehaus, Paul, and Sandip Sukhtankar. 2013. "Corruption Dynamics: The Golden Goose Effect." *American Economic Journal: Economic Policy* 5(4): 230–69.

North, Douglass C., John Wallis, and Barry R. Weingast. 2009. *Violence and Social Orders: A Conceptual Framework for Interpreting Recorded Human History.* Cambridge; New York, NY: Cambridge University Press.

Nye, Joseph S. 1967. "Corruption and Political Development: A Cost–Benefit Analysis." *The American Political Science Review* 61(2): 417–27.

O'Brien, Kevin J. 2006. "Discovery, Research (Re)Design, and Theory Building," in Maria Heimer and Stig Thøgersen (eds.), *Doing Fieldwork in China.* Hawaii, HI: University of Hawaii Press, pp. 27–41.

Oded, Galor. 1996. "Convergence? Inferences from Theoretical Models." *The Economic Journal* 106(437): 1056–69.

OECD. 2006. *Challenges for China's Public Spending: Toward Greater Effectiveness and Equity.* Paris: OECD Publishing.

2008. *Corruption: A Glossary of International Standards in Criminal Law.* Paris: OECD Publishing.

2016. "Putting an End to Corruption," www.oecd.org/corruption/putting-an-end-to-corruption.pdf (accessed 26 November 2019).

2018. "OECD Strategic Approach to Combating Corruption and Promoting Integrity," www.oecd.org/corruption/oecd-strategic-approach-to-combating-corruption-and-promoting-integrity.htm (accessed 11 November 2019).

Oi, Jean C. 1985. "Communism and Clientelism: Rural Politics in China." *World Politics* 37(2): 238–66.

1992. "Fiscal Reform and the Economic Foundations of Local State Corporatism in China." *World Politics* 45(1): 99–126.

1999. *Rural China Takes Off: Institutional Foundations of Economic Reform.* Berkeley, CA: University of California Press.

Oi, Jean C., and Steve Goldstein (eds.). 2018. *Zouping Revisited: Adaptive Governance in a Chinese County.* Stanford, CA: Stanford University Press.

Olken, Benjamin. 2009. "Corruption Perceptions vs. Corruption Reality." *Journal of Public Economics* 93(7–8): 950–64.

Olowu, Bamidele. 1999. "Redesigning African Civil Service Reforms." *The Journal of Modern African Studies* 37(1): 1–23.

2010. "Civil Service Pay Reforms in Africa." *International Review of Administrative Sciences* 76(4): 632–52.

Olson, Mancur. 2000. *Power and Prosperity: Outgrowing Communist and Capitalist Dictatorships.* New York, NY: Basic Books.

Osburg, John. 2013. *Anxious Wealth: Money and Morality among China's New Rich.* Redwood City, CA: Stanford University Press.

Overholt, William. 1986. "The Rise and Fall of Ferdinand Marcos." *Asian Survey* 26(11): 1137–63.

Parrillo, Nicholas. 2013. *Against the Profit Motive: The Salary Revolution in American Government, 1780–1940.* New Haven, CT: Yale University Press.

Pastor, Robert, and Qingshan Tan. 2000. "The Meaning of China's Village Elections." *The China Quarterly* 162: 490–512.

Pei, Minxin. 1999. "Will China Become Another Indonesia?" *Foreign Policy*, 116: 94–109.

2006. *China's Trapped Transition: The Limits of Developmental Autocracy.* Cambridge, MA: Harvard University Press.

2016. *China's Crony Capitalism: The Dynamics of Regime Decay.* Cambridge, MA: Harvard University Press.

Perry, Elizabeth. 2011. "From Mass Campaigns to Managed Campaigns: 'Constructing a New Socialist Countryside,'" in Elizabeth Perry and Sebastian Heilmann (eds.), *Mao's Invisible Hand: The Political Foundations of Adaptive Governance in China.* Cambridge, MA: Harvard University Press, pp. 30–61.

Perry, James L. 1996. "Measuring Public Service Motivation: An Assessment of Construct Reliability and Validity." *Journal of Public Administration Research and Theory* 6(1): 5–22.

Perry, James L., and Lois Recascino Wise. 1990. "The Motivational Bases of Public Service." *Public Administration Review* 50(3): 367–73.

Piketty, Thomas. 2018. *Capital in the Twenty-First Century.* Cambridge, MA: Harvard University Press.

Pitcher, Anne. *Party Politics and Economic Reform in Africa's Democracies.* New York, NY: Cambridge University Press, 2012.

Pomeranz, Kenneth. 2000. *The Great Divergence: China, Europe, and the Making of the Modern World Economy.* Princeton, NJ: Princeton University Press.

Pritchett, Lant, Kunal Sen, and Eric Werker (eds.). 2018. *Deals and Development: The Political Dynamics of Growth Episodes.* Oxford: Oxford University Press.

Pritchett, Lant, and Michael Woolcock. 2004. "Solutions When the Solution Is the Problem: Arraying the Disarray in Development." *World Development* 32(2): 191–212.

Pritchett, Lant, Michael Woolcock, and Matt Andrews. 2013. "Looking Like a State: Techniques of Persistent Failure in State Capability for Implementation." *Journal of Development Studies* 49(1): 1–18.

Qian, Yingyi. 2003. "How Reform Worked in China," in Dani Rodrik (ed.), *In Search of Prosperity: Analytic Narratives on Economic Growth*. Princeton, NJ: Princeton University Press, pp. 297–333.

Quade, Elizabeth A. 2007. "The Logic of Anticorruption Enforcement Campaigns in Contemporary China." *Journal of Contemporary China* 16(50): 65–77.

Rainey, Hal G. 1997. *Understanding and Managing Public Organizations*, 2nd edn. New York, NY: Wiley.

Ramirez, Carlos D. 2014. "Is Corruption in China 'out of Control'? A Comparison with the US in Historical Perspective." *Journal of Comparative Economics* 42(1): 76–91.

Rasul, Imran, and Daniel Rogger. 2018. "Management of Bureaucrats and Public Service Delivery: Evidence from the Nigerian Civil Service." *The Economic Journal* 128(608): 413–46.

Rasul, Imran, Daniel Rogger, and Martin Williams. 2017. "Management and Bureaucratic Effectiveness: A Scientific Replication in Ghana and Nigeria." International Growth Centre Policy Brief 33301.

Rawski, Tom. 2017. "Growth, Upgrading and Excess Cost in China's Electric Power Industry." Unpublished manuscript.

Razafindrakoto, Mireille, and François Roubaud. 2010. "Are International Databases on Corruption Reliable? A Comparison of Expert Opinion Surveys and Household Surveys in Sub-Saharan Africa." *World Development* 38(8): 1057–69.

Reed, Bradly Ward. 2000. *Talons and Teeth: County Clerks and Runners in the Qing Dynasty*. Stanford, CA: Stanford University Press.

Reinikka, Ritva, and Jakob Svensson. 2004. "Local Capture: Evidence from a Central Government Transfer Program in Uganda." *The Quarterly Journal of Economics* 119(2): 679–705.

Richard, Walker. 2013. "Strategic Management and Performance in Public Organizations: Findings from the Miles and Snow Framework." *Public Administration Review* 73(5): 675–85.

Riggs, Fred Warren. 1964. *Administration in Developing Countries: The Theory of Prismatic Society*. Boston, MA: Houghton Mifflin.

Rock, Michael T., and Heidi Bonnett. 2004. "The Comparative Politics of Corruption: Accounting for the East Asian Paradox in Empirical Studies of Corruption, Growth and Investment." *World Development* 32(6): 999–1017.

Rodrik, Dani. 2007. *One Economics, Many Recipes: Globalization, Institutions, and Economic Growth*. Princeton, NJ:Princeton University Press.

Rose-Ackerman, Susan. 1978. *Corruption: A Study in Political Economy*. New York, NY: Academic Press.

1997. "The Role of the World Bank in Controlling Corruption." *Law and Policy in International Business* 29: 93–114.

1999. *Corruption and Government: Causes, Consequences, and Reform*. New York, NY: Cambridge University Press.

2002. "When Is Corruption Harmful?," in Arnold J. Heidenheimer and Michael Johnston (eds.), *Political Corruption: Concepts & Contexts*, 3rd edn. New Brunswick, NJ: Transaction Publishers.

Saich, Anthony. 2002. "The Blind Man and the Elephant: Analysing the Local State in China," in Luigi Tomba (ed.), *East Asian Capitalism: Conflicts and the Roots of Growth and Crisis.* Milan: Fondazione Giangiacomo Feltrinelli, pp. 75–99.

Scott, James. 1972. *Comparative Political Corruption.* Englewood Cliffs, NJ: Prentice-Hall.

Seligson, Mitchell A. 2006. "The Measurement and Impact of Corruption Victimization: Survey Evidence from Latin America." *World Development* 34 (2): 381–404.

Sen, Amartya. 1999. *Development as Freedom.* New York, NY: Oxford University Press.

Sen, Kunal, Badru Bukenya, and Sam Hickey. 2014. *The Politics of Inclusive Development: Interrogating the Evidence.* Oxford: Oxford University Press.

Shih, Victor. 2008. *Factions and Finance in China: Elite Conflict and Inflation.* Cambridge; New York, NY: Cambridge University Press.

Shih, Victor, Christopher Adolph, and Mingxing Liu. 2012. "Getting Ahead in the Communist Party: Explaining the Advancement of Central Committee Members in China." *The American Political Science Review* 106 (1): 166–87.

Shirk, Susan L. 1993. *The Political Logic of Economic Reform in China.* Berkeley, CA: University of California Press.

Shleifer, Andrei, and Daniel Treisman. 2000. *Without a Map: Political Tactics and Economic Reform in Russia.* Cambridge, MA: MIT Press.

Shleifer, Andrei, and Robert W. Vishny. 1993. "Corruption." *The Quarterly Journal of Economics* 108(3): 599–617.

1998. *The Grabbing Hand: Government Pathologies and Their Cures.* Cambridge, MA: Harvard University Press.

Singh, Prena. 2013. "Subnationalism and Social Development: A Comparative Analysis of Indian States." Paper presented at the Princeton–Oxford Conference on State Capacity in the Developing World.

Solinger, Dorothy J. 2018. "A Challenge to the Dominant Portrait of Xi Jinping." *China Perspectives* no. 1/2: 3–6.

Solnick, Steven Lee. 1996. "The Breakdown of Hierarchies in the Soviet Union and China: A Neoinstitutional Perspective." *World Politics* 48(2): 209–38.

Stephenson, Matthew C. 2015. "Corruption and Democratic Institutions: A Review and Synthesis," in Susan Rose-Ackerman and Paul Lagunes (eds.), *Greed, Corruption and the Modern State.* London: Edward Elgar, pp. 92–133.

Stockman, David. 2013. *The Great Deformation: The Corruption of Capitalism in America.* New York, NY: Public Affairs.

Stromseth, Jonathan, Edmund Malesky, Dimitar D. Gueorguiev, Hairong Lai, Xixin Wang, and Carl Brinton. 2017. *China's Governance Puzzle: Enabling Transparency and Participation in a Single-Party State.* Cambridge: Cambridge University Press.

Sun, Yan. 1999. "Is Corruption Less Destructive in China Than in Russia?" *Comparative Politics* 32(1): 1–20.

2004. *Corruption and Market in Contemporary China.* Ithaca, NY: Cornell University Press.

Sun, Yan, and Michael Johnston. 2010. "Does Democracy Check Corruption? Insights from China and India." *Comparative Politics* 42(2): 1–19.

Svensson, Jakob. 2003. "Who Must Pay Bribes and How Much? Evidence from a Cross Section of Firms." *The Quarterly Journal of Economics* 118(1): 207–30.

2005. "Eight Questions about Corruption." *The Journal of Economic Perspectives* 19(3): 19–42.

Teachout, Zephyr. 2014. *Corruption in America: From Benjamin Franklin's Snuff Box to Citizens United.* Cambridge, MA: Harvard University Press.

Theobald, Robin. 1990. *Corruption, Development, and Underdevelopment.* London: Macmillan.

Transparency International. 2016. "What Is Corruption?," www.transparency.org/what-is-corruption/ (accessed 28 August 2019).

Treisman, Daniel. 2000. "The Causes of Corruption: A Cross-national Study." *Journal of Public Economics* 76(3): 399–457.

2007. "What Have We Learned about the Causes of Corruption from Ten Years of Cross-national Empirical Research?" *Annual Review of Political Science* 10: 211–44.

Tsai, Kellee. 2004. "Off Balance: The Unintended Consequences of Fiscal Federalism in China." *Journal of Chinese Political Science* 9(2): 1–27.

2007a. *Capitalism without Democracy: The Private Sector in Contemporary China.* Ithaca, NY: Cornell University Press.

Tsai, Lily. 2007b. *Accountability without Democracy: Solidary Groups and Public Goods Provision in Rural China.* New York, NY: Cambridge University Press.

Tsui, Kai-yuen, and Youqiang Wang. 2004. "Between Separate Stoves and a Single Menu: Fiscal Decentralization in China." *The China Quarterly* 177: 71–90.

Van Rijckeghem, Caroline, and Beatrice Weder di Mauro. 2001. "Bureaucratic Corruption and the Rate of Temptation: Do Wages in the Civil Service Affect Corruption, and by How Much?" *Journal of Development Economics* 65(2): 307–31.

Vogel, Ezra. 2011. *Deng Xiaoping and the Transformation of China.* Cambridge, MA: Belknap Press.

Wade, Robert. 1990. *Governing the Market: Economic Theory and the Role of Government in East Asian Industrialization.* Princeton, NJ: Princeton University Press.

Walder, Andrew G. 1995a. "China's Transitional Economy: Interpreting Its Significance." *The China Quarterly* 144: 963–79.

1995b. "Local Governments as Industrial Firms: An Organizational Analysis of China's Transitional Economy." *American Journal of Sociology* 101(2): 263–301.

1996a. *China's Transitional Economy.* Oxford; New York, NY: Oxford University Press.

1996b. "Markets and Inequality in Transitional Economies: Toward Testable Theories." *American Journal of Sociology* 101(4): 1060–73.

2002. "Markets and Income Inequality in Rural China: Political Advantage in an Expanding Economy." *American Sociological Review* 67(2): 231–53.

2003. "Elite Opportunity in Transitional Economies." *American Sociological Review* 68(6): 899–916.

2004. "The Party Elite and China's Trajectory of Change." *China: An International Journal* 2(2): 189–209.

2018. "Back to the Future? Xi Jinping as an Anti-bureaucratic Crusader." *China: An International Journal* 16(3): 18–34.

Walder, Andrew G., and Songhua Hu. 2009. "Revolution, Reform, and Status Inheritance: Urban China, 1949–1996." *American Journal of Sociology* 114(5): 1395–427.

Wallis, John Joseph. 2001. "What Caused the Crisis of 1839?" NBER Historical Working Paper 133.

2005. "Constitutions, Corporations, and Corruption: American States and Constitutional Change, 1842 to 1852." *The Journal of Economic History* 65(1): 211–56.

Walton, Michael. (Forthcoming). "An Indian Gilded Age? Continuity and Change in the Political Economy of India's Development," in Liz Chatterjee and Matthew McCartney (eds.), *The Political Economy of Development in India Revisited*. Oxford: Oxford University Press.

Wang, Yuhua. 2013. "Connected Autocracy." Working Paper, University of Pennsylvania.

2015. *Tying the Autocrat's Hands: The Rise of the Rule of Law in China*. New York, NY: Cambridge University Press.

Weber, Max. 1968. *Economy and Society: An Outline of Interpretive Sociology*. New York, NY: Bedminster Press.

Wedeman, Andrew. 1997. "Looters, Rent-Scrapers, and Dividend-Collectors: Corruption and Growth in Zaire, South Korea, and the Philippines." *The Journal of Developing Areas* 31(4): 457–78.

2000. "Budgets, Extra-Budgets, and Small Treasuries: Illegal Monies and Local Autonomy in China." *Journal of Contemporary China* 9(25): 489–511.

2004. "The Intensification of Corruption in China." *The China Quarterly* 180: 895–921.

2005a. "Anticorruption Campaigns and the Intensification of Corruption in China." *Journal of Contemporary China* 14(42): 93–116.

2005b. "Review of *Corruption and Market in Contemporary China*." *The China Quarterly* 181: 177–79.

2012. *Double Paradox: Rapid Growth and Rising Corruption in China*. Ithaca, NY: Cornell University Press.

Wei, Shang-Jin. 2000. "How Taxing Is Corruption on International Investors?" *Review of Economics and Statistics* 82(1): 1–11.

Wei, Yifan, Nan Jia, and Milo Wang. 2019. "Beware of Strange Bed-Fellows: An Analysis of Public–Private Partnerships in Managing Government Guiding Funds in China." Working Paper.

White, Richard. 2011. *Railroaded: The Transcontinentals and the Making of Modern America*. New York, NY: W. W. Norton.

Whiting, Susan. 2001. *Power and Wealth in Rural China: The Political Economy of Institutional Change*. New York, NY: Cambridge University Press.

2004. "The Cadre Evaluation System at the Grass Roots: The Paradox of Party Rule," in Barry Naughton and Dali L. Yang (eds.), *Holding China Together: Diversity and National Integration in the Post-Deng Era*. New York, NY: Cambridge University Press.

Whyte, David. 2015. *How Corrupt Is Britain?* London: Pluto Press.

Wilson, James. 1989. *Bureaucracy: What Government Agencies Do and Why They Do It.* New York, NY: Basic Books.

Wong, Roy Bin. 1997. *China Transformed: Historical Change and the Limits of European Experience.* Ithaca, NY: Cornell University Press.

Woolcock, Michael, and Narayan Deepa. 2000. "Social Capital: Implications for Development Theory, Research, and Policy." *The World Bank Research Observer* 15: 225–49.

World Bank. 1997a. *World Development Report 1997: The State in a Changing World.* Washington, DC: World Bank.

  1997b. *Helping Countries Combat Corruption: The Role of the World Bank.* Washington, DC: World Bank.

  2004. "Human Resource Management," in *Zambia: Public Expenditure Management and Financial Accountability Review.* Washington, DC: World Bank.

World Bank and DRC of State Council. 2013. *China 2030: Building a Modern, Harmonious, and Creative Society.* Washington, DC: World Bank.

  2014. *Urban China: Toward Efficient, Inclusive, and Sustainable Urbanization.* Washington, DC: World Bank Publications.

Xu, Songtao. 2007. *Huimou zhongguo renshi zhidu gaige 28 nian* [*Looking Back at 28 Years of Personnel Reform*]. Beijing: Zhongguo Renshi Press.

Yang, Dali. 2004. *Remaking the Chinese Leviathan: Market Transition and the Politics of Governance in China.* Stanford, CA: Stanford University Press.

Yang, Jisheng. 2012. *Tombstone: The Great Chinese Famine, 1958–1962,* 1st American edn. New York, NY: Farrar, Straus and Giroux.

Yang, Rui. 2015. "Corruption in China's Higher Education System: A Malignant Tumor." *International Higher Education* 39 (Spring): 18–20.

Zeng, Qingjie, and Yujeong Yang. 2017. "Informal Networks as Safety Nets: The Role of Personal Ties in China's Anti-corruption Campaign." *China: An International Journal* 15(3): 26–57.

Zhang, Xuehua. 2017. "Implementation of Pollution Control Targets: Has a Centralized Enforcement Approach Worked?" *The China Quarterly* 231: 749–74.

Zhao, Shukai. 2013. "Rural China: Poor Governance in Strong Development." Conference paper presented at Stanford University's Center on Democracy, Development and the Rule of Law.

Zhao, Tan. 2018. "Vote Buying and Land Takings in China's Village Elections." *Journal of Contemporary China* 27(110): 277–94.

Zhu, Jiangnan. 2008. "Why Are Offices for Sale in China? A Case Study of the Office-Selling Chain in Heilongjiang Province." *Asian Survey* 48(4): 558–79.

  2018. "Corruption in Reform Era: A Multidisciplinary Review," in Weiping Wu and Mark W. Frazier (eds.), *The SAGE Handbook of Contemporary China.* Newbury Park, CA: SAGE Publications.

Zhu, Lin. 2015. "Punishing Corrupt Officials in China." *The China Quarterly* 223: 595–617.

Zuo, Cai. 2015. "Promoting City Leaders: The Structure of Political Incentives in China." *The China Quarterly* 224: 955–84.

Index

Page numbers in italics denote figures and tables.

Abramoff, Jack, 191
access money, 14, 20, 24–25, 37, 49, 51, 120, 181, 182, 190–93
  analogous to drugs, *12*
  from businessperson's point of view, 12
  China vs. India's, 41, *42*, 43
  China vs. Russia's, 39
  China vs. United States', 44–45, *45*
  combating, 209
  concept of, 204
  definition, 10
  fertile soil for, 203
  illegal forms of, 10, 11
  institutionalized and legal, 191–92
  measurement in UCI, 29
  side effects for economy, 13
  steroids of capitalism, 12–13
  wealthier countries, 46, *48*
access money, indirect harm of, 146–48, 151
  distorting allocation of resources, 147–48
  inequality within society and firms, 147
  real estate, 146–47
administration costs, 222
administrative reform, transitional
    strategies of, 115. *See also* transitional
    administrative institutions
agency collection, 101
  and tax revenue impact on
    compensation, 102–7
  vs. tax revenue on, long-term effects of,
    106, 107
  vs. tax revenue on, short-term effects of,
    105–7
agency-level corruption, 109
aggregate corruption scores

China vs. United States, 44
  wealthy countries, 50
"Alleviate the Burden of Grassroots
    Cadres Year," 177
American crony capitalism, 181
America's and China's Gilded Ages,
    parallels between, 211
  access money, 190–93
  comparative-historical data, 184–86
  corruption trends, 186–88
  modifying earlier, 189–90
  Progressive Era, 186–88
anti-corruption campaign, 1, 6, 19, 21, 65,
    69, 119
  backlash of, 176–77
  city-level Party secretaries, 153
  falls of national and local officials, 173,
    174
  impact on China's growth, 174–77
  officials disciplined in, 153, 156, 209
  patronage and, 154
  straightening bureaucratic norms, 157
  "tigers" and "flies" purged in, 76–77,
    156–57
  tool for tightening political control,
    175–76, 202, 209
  wide-ranging and penetrative, 157
anti-corruption exhibition, *155*
arbitraries, 56
Asian financial crisis of, 1997, 61

bank loans, 13
Bell, Daniel, 197
Belt and Road Initiative, 203
Benedict, Ruth, 210

bottom-up initiatives, 210
Bo Xilai, 1, 21, 30, 119–20, 125
 connections to Xu, 142–43
 family during Cultural Revolution, 125
 grave violations of party discipline,
  134–36, 154
 milestones in career path, 125–26, *126*
 political stand-off with leadership, 121
 second-generation aristocrat, 125
 strategies for growth promotion,
  148–49
 stripped of his position, 134
Bo Xilai, Chinese media coverage of, *122*
 accomplishments, 121
 prior to being investigated for
  corruption, 123
 top 10 words describing, 121–23, *122*
Bo Xilai, Chongqing under, 127–33
 "celebrate red and smash black"
  campaign, 132
 economic downturn of, 132–33
 economic growth of, 127, *128*
 government revenue and FDI, 127
 infrastructure projects in, 128–29
 investment in, *131*
 as land of laptops, 129
 rising debt-to-GDP ratio of, 131, *132*
 social welfare initiatives, *130*
 urban residential income, 127
Bo Yibo, 125
BRI, *see* Belt and Road Initiative
bribery, 8, 16, 21, 72
 decline of, 190
 definition, 219–21
 and embezzlement by rank of officials,
  75, 76
 and embezzlement trend by monetary
  size, 73–74, *74*
 large-sum cases, 77
 by low- vs. high-rank cases, *220*
 rise in, *73*, 73, *74*
 by small vs. large cases, *220*
British corruption, 191
budgets by spending categories, 222
bureaucratic compensation, 86, 92
 capitulation wages, 88, 93
 dual-track, 115, 209
 and financial outcomes, systematic links
  between, 86
 fringe benefit and allowances, *see* fringe
  compensation
 higher "efficiency" wages, 88

independent and dependent variables,
 223
institutional arrangement, 95
long-term effects of agency collections vs.
 tax revenue on, 106, 107
low rates of, 92–93
promotion incentives, 95
"shared expectations" about structure of,
 96
short-term effects of agency collections
 vs. tax revenue on, 105–7
standard regressions of, 102–5
topped with allowances and perks, 93–94
total compensation, *223*
bureaucratic extortion, media mentions of,
 81

campaign finance restrictions, 191
campaign-style policy implementation, 162
capability traps, 113
capacity-building measures, 16–17, 183, 209
capital flight, 175
capitalism
 access money as steroids of, 12–13
 corruption and, *see* corruption
 rise of, 211
capitulation wages, 88
CCP, *see* Chinese Communist Party
centrally appointed officials, fall of, 173
Central Party Secretariat, 177
Chen Chuanping, 165
Chengdu, 91
Cheng Li, 133
Chen Liangyu, 75, 111
China
 2012 CPI ranking of, 2
 as gigantic outlier, 2–5, *4*
 nineteenth-century America and,
  comparison of, 18–19
 single-party autocracy, 19
 UCI and CPI rank comparison, 34
 and United States at equivalent levels of
  income, *185*
China's Crony Capitalism (book), 119
China's economic expansion, 2, 21
China's economy, 83
 boomed after, 1993, 61
 driven by private sector, 67
 Western media portrayal of, 67
China vs. India's corruption
 CPI scores, 40
 petty bribery, 41–42

political regimes and, 40, 43
speed money and access money, 41, *42*, 43, 50
structure of, 40
UCI scores, *41*
China vs. Russia's corruption
access money, 39
anecdotal comparisons, 38
grand theft, 39
reasons for difference in, 37–38
speed money, 39, *40*
structure of, 40
UCI scores, 38–40, *39*
China vs. United States' corruption
access money, 44–45, *45*
aggregate corruption scores, 44
UCI scores, *44*
Chinese bureaucracy, 89
attracting and serving investors, 91
bureaucratic compensation, *see* bureaucratic compensation
focus on monetary incentives, 114
layers of, 76, *89*
99 percent of public employees, 90–91
predatory states vs., 21
profit-sharing mechanism, *see* profit-sharing mechanism
street-level bureaucrats, *see* Chinese street-level bureaucrats
Chinese Communist Party, 202
anti-corruption campaigns, 6
concentration of power, 199
discipline inspection committees, *see* discipline inspection committees
list of eight regulations, 157, 159
new roles post-1993 reforms, 61
Organization Department, 198
political scandal, 1
Chinese corruption, 5, 53, 180
access money, *see* access money
autocracy and capitalism shaping, 199–200
Bo Xilai's arrest, 1
CCL definition, 68–69
Chinese infrastructure expansion and, *see* Chinese infrastructure expansion
competing characterizations of, 47
cyclical pattern, 69
decline in, 52
Deng Xiaoping and, *see* Deng Xiaoping
economically destructive corruption and, 49

forces driving present pattern of, 52–53
during "growing out of the plan," 54–57
intensification of, 69–70
involving larger sums over time, *70*
during Maoist era, 54
post-1993 reforms, 61–62
regime collapse risk with, 200–2
sources of, 67–68
structure of, 24–25, 52
studies on, 5
temporal patterns, 82, 83
Chinese corruption and economic growth, paradox of, 5–7, 51
access money, 14, 182
capacity-building reforms, 16–17, 183
challenging belief of, 151
data to shed light on, 19–20
explanation for, 17–18
penalizing speed money payments, 17
profit-sharing arrangements, 14–16, 182–83
regional competition, 17, 183
Chinese Criminal Law (CCL), corruption definition of, 68–69
Chinese crony capitalism, 148–51
competition, 150
cronyism, 149–50
economic development and social welfare, 148–49
provision of preferential policies, 150–51
system of elite profit-sharing, 149
Chinese highways, construction of, 62
Chinese infrastructure expansion
government debts financing, 62–63
land-related proceeds financing, 62
shadow financing, 64
train station, 62
Chinese leadership, 19
Chinese officials, varieties of, 225, *226*, 228
competent and not corrupt, 227–28
incompetent and corrupt, 225–26
incompetent and not corrupt, 226–27
Chinese paradox, *see* Chinese corruption and economic growth, paradox of
Chinese Party-state apparatus
civil servants, 90
non-civil service public employees, 90
political elites, 89–90
ranks of officials in, 76
Chinese political elites, *see* political elites

Chinese political system
  bureaucracy, *see* Chinese bureaucracy
  Confucian-style meritocracy, 197–98
  patronage, 198–99
Chinese street-level bureaucrats
  common knowledge among, 118
  curbing extractive behavior, 96–97
  income source of, 96
Chongqing, 127
city Party secretaries, 197
  performance measures, 163–64
  roles of, 163
city Party secretaries, anti-corruption
    campaign outcome for, 163
  event history analysis, *see* event history
    analysis
  geographic patterns of fall, 167–68, *168*
  hazard rate of fall, *166*, 166–67
  high turnover rate, *167*
  individual characteristics, 168–69
  inverted V-shape pattern of political fall,
    166
  patronage effects and, 164–65
  variables for studying, 163, 165–66,
    229
Civil Service Law, 60
civil service pay, 86
compensation practices, *see* bureaucratic
    compensation
competition between superpowers, 210
comprehensive administrative reforms of,
    1998, 53, 109–12
  cashless payments, 111
  controlling financial transactions, 109
  creation of TSA, 110
  establishment of TDC, 110–11
  local measures, 112–13
Confucian-style meritocracy, 197–98
corruption, *9*, 50
  access money, *see* access money
  analogous to drugs, 11, *12*
  bundled scores for, 7
  capitalism and, relationship between, 7
  citizens' ability to monitor, 210
  classic models of, 8
  comparative patterns, 50–51
  crises linked to, 13
  definition, 7, 203–5
  exchange-based, *see* exchange-based
    corruption
  fighting, 208–10
  GDP per capita and, *3*, 3

grand theft, *see* grand theft
  impact on economic growth, 1–2, 206–7,
    215–16
  inequality caused by, 207–8
  involving elites vs. non-elites, 8–9
  involving two-way exchanges, 8
  measurement, 205–6, *see also* corruption
    indices
  petty theft, *see* petty theft
  poverty and, correlation between, 1
  problems with national classification in,
    49
  speed money, *see* speed money
  structure of, 50
  systematic qualitative comparisons,
    47–49
  unbundling, 24
  wealthy economies, 14
corruption categories, *9*
  and countries, 28–29
  unbundled into sub-categories, *28*, 208
corruption indices
  CPI, *see* Corruption Perception Index
  measuring effectiveness of, 24
  perception-based survey, 24
  problems with, 25–26
Corruption Perception Index, 23
  authoritative gauge of corruption, 25
  China's 2012 score, 2
  China's 2014 score, 25
  first-world bias, 25–26, 35
  flaws in, 25–26
  masking structural variances, 50
  UCI advantages over, 31
  UCI rank comparison with, 33–35
corruption scandals, 119
  Bo Xilai, *see* Bo Xilai
  Ji Jianye, *see* Ji Jianye
corruption schemes among Chinese
    political elites, 11
corruption with exchange, trends of, 71, *72*
corruption with theft
  central authorities permitting, 82
  mitigating, 209
  trends of, 71, *72*
county Party secretaries, 76
CPI, *see* Corruption Perception Index
CPI scores
  China vs. India's, 40
  plotted against average growth rates, 215
Crisis of 1893, 18
crony capitalism

American, 181
Chinese, *see* Chinese crony capitalism
structural risks linked to, 201
Cui Manli, 139

deal-making corruption, 21
Dehao Corporation, 146
democracy and corruption, 50
Deng Xiaoping, 181
banner, 57
control over officials, 54–55
corruption forms under, 55–57
decision to open markets, 15
economic growth under, 57
market liberalization, 54, 55, 57
norm of collective leadership, 161
Southern Tour, 57
descriptive statistics, *229*
developing countries, study of, 118
development challenges to China, 65
development outcomes and bureaucratic
efforts, 96
discipline inspection committees, 68
disciplinary actions by, 68
drugs, corruption analogous to, 11, *12*
dyadic patron–client relations, 159

East Asian economies, 133
economic growth, 18
Chinese corruption and, paradox of, *see*
Chinese corruption and economic
growth, paradox of
corruption impact on, 1–2, 206–7,
215–16
UCI scores and, correlations between,
46–47, *47*
Economist Intelligence Unit, 25
efficiency wage, 15
Egypt, predatory corruption in, 201
elite exchanges, 51
elites vs. non-elites, corruption involving,
8–9, *28*
embezzlement, 16, 72
and bribery by rank of officials, *75*, 76
and bribery trend by monetary size, *74*, 75
decline in, *73*, 73
definition, 221
large-sum cases, 77
by low- vs. high-rank cases, *220*
by small vs. large cases, *220*
tolerating small-scale, 82
"Embezzlement vs. Bribery" (article), 82

event history analysis, 169–73
definition, 169
discrete-time hazard model, 170
hazard rate for city leaders, 171–73
patron downfall determinants, 170–71,
171
results of, 173
splines for hazard interpretation, 170
exchange-based corruption, 12–13
expert surveys in UCI, 27
extra-budgetary revenue, 55

federal lobbying expenses, 192
fee collection from businesses, blanket
order to prohibit, 112
First Amendment of US Constitution, 193
fiscal transfers, 101
fly, definition of, 76
formal public salaries, *see* bureaucratic
compensation
fragmented democracies, 199
fringe compensation, 15, 88, 118
difficulty in measuring, 97–98
fringe benefit and allowances, 88, 93
income source for, 94
Tanzania, 97
fringe compensation in Shandong
dataset for estimating, 98–99, 222–24
formal public wages and, 100, 102, *103*
forms of, 100
growth of, 102, *103*
regional variance in, 100, *101*
share in total compensation, *100*

GCB, *see* Global Corruption Barometer
GDP growth and corruption, 215–16
GDP per capita, corruption plotted against,
3, 3
Geng Yanbo, 227–28
GGF, *see* government guiding funds
Global Corruption Barometer, 41–42
golden goose maxim, 86
Golden Mantis, 143
government procurement projects
awarded to, 143–44
IPO on stock market, 144
government debts, 62–63
government guiding funds
for industrial and innovation promotion,
202–3
susceptibility to corruption, 203
government spending by items, 222, *223*

grand theft, 9
  analogous to drugs, *12*
  China vs. Russia's, 39
  definition, 10
  in Nigeria, 37
Guo Boxiong, 156
GuoYongchang, 225–26

HDI, *see* Human Development Index
higher "efficiency" wages, 88
high-income countries, 28
Hubei province, 112
  leadership's slogan in, 17
Hu Jintao, 121
Human Development Index, 207
"Humble Dwellings" (drama series),
  147
Hunan province, 112

India and China's corruption, *see* China vs.
  India's corruption
inequality within society and firms, 147,
  181, 207–8
institutional corruption, 29, 193
investors, attracting and serving, 91

Jiang Zemin, 57
Jiang–Zhu leadership, 60
Ji Jianye, 21, 64, 136
  contributions to Yangzhou, 139
  demolition schemes, 138
  development works in Kunshan, 137
  government procurement projects to
    Golden Mantis, 143–44
  indicted on corruption, 140–41
  industrial policy for Yangzhou, 139
  massive infrastructural overhaul of
    Nanjing, 140
  milestones in career path, 136–37,
    137
  "Operation Iron Wrist," 64, 140
  strategies for growth promotion,
    148–49
  transferred to Yangzhou, 137
Ji Jianye, Chinese media coverage of, *124*
  after announcement of investigation, 123
  prior to being investigated for
    corruption, 123
  top 10 words describing, *124*

Lai Xiaomin, 157
Lambsdorff, Johann, 25

land-based public finance
  land-related proceeds, 62
  public infrastructure construction with,
    62
"large-sum" corruption cases, 68
"leave businesses alone days," 112
legal-rational bureaucracy, 176
liberal market economies, 176
Ling Jihua, 156
lobbying
  corruption and, 204–5
  expenses, federal, 192
local governments, revenue sources for, 101
local leaders
  competing to offer preferential policies,
    17
  motivated to curb "grabbing hands," 17,
    18
  profit-sharing among, 21
  promotion tied to economic growth, 15
low-income countries, 28

Manion, 77
mass protests, 57
media coverage, word cloud analysis of, 121
media mentions of corruption, *see also* Bo
    Xilai, Chinese media coverage of; Ji
    Jianye, Chinese media coverage of
  "bribery" and "bribe-giving," 79
  "elegant bribery," 80
  limitations of, 78
  money laundering, 79–80
  "naked official," 80
  non-transactional forms of corruption,
    81
  official statistics vs., 78
  "rent-seeking" and "hidden rules," 80
  terms falling under, 78
  vote-buying, 79–80, 81
  Wen Qiang, 80
middle-income countries, 28
Minxin Pei, 5–6, 197
misappropriation of public funds, 16, 69,
    72
  decline in, *73*, 73
  media mentions of, 81
misuse of public funds, 221
mixed methods research, 116
money politics, 192
monitoring agencies for local businesses,
    112
monopoly privileges, 145

Murong Xuecun, 160
mutual prosperity, 144

Nanjing, 64
National Development Reform
    Commission, 175
National Supervisory Commission, 157
NDRC, *see* National Development Reform
    Commission
NERI (National Economic Research
    Institute) Marketization Index, 165
Nigeria's corruption
    grand theft, 37, 52
    UCI and CPI rank comparison, 34–35

Office for Enhancing Business
    Environment, 112
official statistics on corruption
    investigations
    corruption categories captured by, 70, *71*
    embezzlement, misuse of public funds,
        and bribery, 72–75
    limitations of, 68–69
    low- and high-rank officials, 75–76
    trends of corruption with exchange, 71,
        72
    trends of corruption with theft, 71, *72*
"Operation Iron Wrist," 64, 140
organizational corruption, 56, 86
    media mentions of, 81

patronage, 154, 164–65, 198–99
pay-for-performance models, 113, 114
petty bribery
    China vs. India's, 41–42
    mitigating, 209
petty theft, 9, 56
    analogous to drugs, *12*
    definition, 10
    Thailand, 37
Politburo Standing Committee
    members of, 161
    top post within, 161
political elites, 89–90, 118
    above *chu* rank, 77
    corruption schemes among, 11
    profit-sharing mechanism among, 14–16
political regimes and corruption, link
    between, 40, 43, 50
Political Risk Services Guide, 25, 26
political survival, predictor of
    economic performance, 159

patronage, 159–62
    timing, 162
prebendalism, 114
    in pre-modern times, 87
    replacement with fixed salaries, 87
predatory corruption
    Egypt, 201
    regional competition checking, 17
predatory states, 200
private farming, 55
private investment, decline in, 66
private sector
    contributions in China's economy, 67
    embracing, 59
    on illegal state seizures of private assets,
        66–67
procuratorate, 68, 76
profit-sharing mechanism, 14–16, 21, 56,
    118, 182–83
    allowances and perks, 93–94
    among leaders, 21
    bureaucratic compensation, *see*
        bureaucratic compensation
    "carrot and stick" approach, 107–9
    consequence of, 95
    wage linked with tax and non-tax income,
        94
profit-sharing model, 86
Progressive Era, 186–88, 192
promotion incentives among elites, 91
prosperity and corruption, paradox of, *see*
    Chinese corruption and economic
    growth, paradox of
provincially appointed officials, fall of,
    174
PSC, *see* Politburo Standing Committee
public administration
    practices of first world, 85–86
    standard theories of, 87
    transformation to state-funded, 87
    Western centeredness, 115
public agents, 85
public compensation, *see* bureaucratic
    compensation
public esteem, 120
public sector incentives, problem of,
    114
public sector reforms, 209
    China's experience, 114–15
    objectives of, 113
    raising formal wages, 113
    reasons for failure of, 113–14

public sector wage incentives, classical
theories of, 88
in developing countries, 88
higher "efficiency" wages, 88
limitations of, 88
"public service motivation," literature on,
115

qualitative and quantitative research,
116–17

rank-and-file bureaucrats, profit-sharing
among, 15
refund, 95
regional competition, 17, 183
resource allocation risk with access money,
13
revenue sources
link with compensation, 102–7
local governments, 101
Rudd, Kevin, 160
Russia and China's corruption, *see* China vs.
Russia's corruption

self-finance, 112
shadow financing, 64
Shide Private Limited, 142
single bundled perception and UCI scores,
comparison of, 35–36
small treasuries, 56
socialist market economy
administrative modernization campaign,
59–61
CCP's decision to establish, 57
integration into global economy, 59
meaning of, 57–58
private sector, 59
role of communist officials in, 52–53
state enterprise downsizing and reform,
58–59
social norms, triggering change in, 86
SOEs, *see* state-owned enterprises
Soviet Union, 16
speed money, 10, 37, 52
analogous to drugs, *12*
analogy of "greasing the wheels," 11
China, 49
China vs. India's, 41, *42*, 43
China vs. Russia's, 39, *40*
definition, 10
enhancing efficiency, 12
imposing cost on citizens, 12

as painkillers, 12
wealthier countries, 46, *48*
spending categories, budgets by, 222
Stanford, Leland, 180
state dominance in economy, resurgence
of, 66
state-owned enterprises, 55, 58
stimulus package, 63
subways, construction of, 62
Sun Zhengcai, 156, 160, 165
"super-clientelism," 65

Tanzania, fringe compensation in, 97
tax revenue, 101
and agency collection impact on
compensation, 102–7
TDC, *see* Treasury Disbursement Centers
Thailand, petty theft in, 37
TI, *see* Transparency International
Tiananmen crisis, 60
Tong Mingqian, 226–27
total compensation, *100, 223*
train station, 62
transactional corruption, 24
transitional administrative institutions, 115,
209
Transition Period, The (documentary), 225
Transparency International
anti-corruption efforts, 26
third-party surveys for CPI, 25–26
Treasury Disbursement Centers, 110–11
Treasury Single Account, 110
TSA, *see* Treasury Single Account
two-way exchanges, corruption involving, 8

UCI, *see* Unbundled Corruption Index
UCI scores
China vs. India's, *41*
China vs. Russia's, 38–40, *39*
China vs. United States', *44*
and economic growth, correlations
between, 46–47, *47*
and ranks by country, 32, *33*
in typological clusters, 32
Unbundled Corruption Index, 20, 27–32,
50, 208
advantages over standard measurements,
31, 36–37
comparing overall perception scores and,
35–36, *36*
corruption categories and countries,
28–29, *218*

CPI rank comparison with, 33–35, *34*
  expert surveys in, 27
  methodological innovations, 29–31
  survey methodology, 217–18
  total and unbundled scores, 32–33, *33*
undue influence, 204
United States, 50
  battle against graft in Progressive Era, 19
  China as "gigantic outlier" *vis-à-vis*, *4*, 4
  and China at equivalent levels of income, *185*
  and China, comparison of Gilded Ages of, 181
  vs. Chinese corruption, *see* China vs. United States' corruption
  contemporary China and, comparison of, 18–19
  Gilded Age in, 67–68
  resilience despite corruption crises, 201–2
  taxless (public) financing in, 63–64
  UCI and CPI rank comparison, 35
United States Financial Crisis Inquiry Commission, 192
urban housing, 147
  soaring prices, 147
  speculative bubbles and over-construction, 146–47

validity problem, 30
vignette-focused survey, evaluating corruption using, 29–31
  access money, 29
  based on real events, 30
  conflict of interest among influential actors, 30
  perceptions of corruption, 29
vote-buying scandal, 227

Wang Lijun, 133
Wang Qishan, 65
wealthy countries

corruption, 14
  low aggregate corruption scores, 50
  speed money and access money in, 46, *48*
Wen Jiabao, 121, 134
Wen Qiang, 80
Wolf, Martin, 199
word cloud analysis of media coverage, 121
World Bank's Control of Corruption Index, 26
World Competitiveness Yearbook, 26

Xi Jinping, 152, 154
  anti-corruption campaign, *see* anti-corruption campaign
  bottom-up initiatives, 210
  centralization of power, 193
  coming to power in 2012, 65
  first speech before the Politburo, 154
  recentralizing personal power, 161
  social and political freedoms, 176
  speech to the CCDI in 2019, 175–76
  stance on state's role in economy, 66
  top-down disciplinary apparatus, 192
Xinhai Square, 143
Xu Dongming, 141, 143
Xu Ming, 142–43, 145
Xu Songtao, 92

Yangzhou, 137
  canal tourism, 138–39
  city-wide greening campaign, 138
  demolition schemes, 138
  industrial policy for, 139
  Ji's contributions to, 139
Yuan Chunqing, 165

Zambia, fringe benefit and allowances of, 88
Zhou Yongkang, 30, 42, 156
Zhu Rongji, 17, 57, *60*, 109
Zhu Tianxiao, 141, 146
Zhu Xinliang, 143

CPSIA information can be obtained
at www.ICGtesting.com
Printed in the USA
LVHW041756250721
693625LV00007B/1028

9 781108 745956